GREAT EXPECTATIONS

New Directions in Anthropology

General Editor: **Jacqueline Waldren**, *Institute of Social Anthropology, University of Oxford*

GREAT EXPECTATIONS

Imagination and Anticipation in Tourism

Edited by
Jonathan Skinner
Dimitrios Theodossopoulos

Berghahn Books
New York • Oxford

First published in 2011 by

Berghahn Books

www.berghahnbooks.com

Library of Congress Cataloging-in-Publication Data

Skinner, Jonathan, Ph. D. Great expectations: imagination and anticipation in tourism /
Jonathan Skinner, Dimitrios Theodossopoulos.
    p. cm. Includes bibliographical references and index.
    ISBN 978-0-85745-277-1 (hardback : alk. paper) -- ISBN 978-0-85745-278-8 (ebook :
alk. paper) 1. Tourism--Psychological aspects. 2. Travelers--Psychology. I. Theodossopoulos,
Dimitrios. II. Title.
    G155.A1S5615 2011 306.4'819--dc23
    2011029397

British Library Cataloguing in Publication Data

A catalogue record for this book is available from the British Library

Printed in the United States on acid-free paper

ISBN: 978-0-85745-277-1 (hardback)
ISBN: 978-0-85745-278-8 (ebook)

Contents

Chapter 1
INTRODUCTION: THE PLAY OF EXPECTATION IN TOURISM

Jonathan Skinner and Dimitrios Theodossopoulos

> As I had grown accustomed to my expectations, I had insensibly begun to
> notice their effect upon myself and those around me. Their influence on my
> own character, I disguised from my recognition as much as possible, but I
> knew very well that it was not all good. I lived in a state of chronic uneasiness …
> (*Great Expectations* by Charles Dickens)

Great Expectations is one of those classic English texts set for reading on school
syllabi, watched on television or on stage as a period drama, or heard on the radio.
It is the tale of Pip, his adventures and, critically for us, how Pip's expectations
guide him through life.[1] Dickens presents Pip's journey as a secular pilgrimage,
one dependent upon the imagination and consumption of desire – for
acceptance, love, wealth, status and, eventually, happiness. Each time Pip's
expectations are dashed new ones rise up, as though Dickens were offering us a
tale of the human condition: we think therefore we desire. This disappointment
is bred from a deep-seated capitalist-driven reproduction of expectation and
desire which we believe to be intrinsic in society; both real and apparent, it runs
from colonialism and Orientalism through to tourism, operating upon desire, a
play of the imagination and, ultimately, conquest – visual and/or embodied (cf.
Young 1995; Campbell 1987).

The principles of Dickens's fiction are akin to those of travel writing, the
creation of an 'imaginative geography' that works off anticipation, expectation
and 'the pleasures of curiosity' (Chard 1999: 32–33). As Colin Campbell (1987)
puts it, the imagination of desire is deliberately implicated in consumption

practices, using the reproduction of expectation as a motivating but constantly evolving process. The realization of an expectation often leads to an anti-climax, since reality rarely meets the anticipated desire, idealized through day-dreaming and the hedonism of the imagination.[2] The disillusionment of this fulfilled expectation is thus replaced by the anticipation of a new desire. What remains constant in this cyclical articulation of desire and imagination is the longing generated by expectation itself (Campbell 1987: 89–90). This is tied with tourism as Campbell's tourist is very much 'an artist of the imagination' (Campbell 1987: 78), one who peddles in the anticipation of an experience. It is in this respect that expectation can be regarded as a powerful motivating force.

In this volume we are concerned with the dialectic of expectation and imagination in the interaction between tourists, their object of desire, and the people who prepare or embody the object of the tourist desire. We approach the negotiation of expectations in social life, and in tourism more specifically, as a dynamic process, always fluid, always in the making. This process, we argue, affects in fundamental ways the lives of both the tourists and their hosts (tourism professionals or local communities), and plays an important role in the success or failure of the overall tourism experience. Expectations, we argue, can help us to uncover the secret charm of the tourism encounter, the logic that makes tourism a quintessential experience of modern life.

So, here, and in the rest of this volume, we explore processes such as the following: the anticipation of destinations unknown, prescribed and familiar; the interface – and holes in the wall – between expectations held by local communities, tourist professionals, and tourists; and the role of expectations in refuelling the imagination of those involved in the tourist experience. We are also concerned with the asymmetry of expectations between tourists and host communities, and the disjunctures – 'that account for the globalized production of difference' (Appadurai 1996: 199) – emerging out of this asymmetry. We examine how local actors strive to access the knowledge necessary for developing tourism, how they perfect their skill of enchanting the tourist audience, or how, sometimes, they 'miss the mark'. We also look carefully at the tourists' desire to fulfil their own expectations; the tendency among some of them to deny the contradictions between their expectations and local social reality, to compartmentalize their experiences so that they can maintain their expectations unchallenged; or, finally, the discrepancies and congruence between tourist expectation and experience.

Introducing Expectation in Tourism

The act of expecting, or state of being expected, incorporates a range of meanings and understandings that range from eager anticipation of an event, situation or person (whether looked forward to or feared) through to the prospects and gains one might hold or lose (such as financial wealth or social acclaim), and the belief that one should behave in a particular way (social norms and cultural etiquette, for instance). We suggest, here, that expectation is critical and fundamental to tourism, a motivating force that inspires economic activity, movement in space, social change and reorganization in particular local settings. It plays a fundamental role in shaping the tourist experience – in determining its success or failure – in motivating local communities or tourism practitioners to adapt or explore new possibilities across cultural boundaries. This concern is typically implicit in other social scientists' tourism studies.

John Urry (1990) draws our attention to the nature of expectation in tourism in his highly celebrated *The Tourist Gaze*. From a tourist industry perspective, Urry points out that it is important to recognize the fact that tourists will have high expectations 'when away', perhaps even higher than when at home given the significance and specialness they attribute to their tourist activities. Urry draws our attention to consumer services and their efforts to satisfy the tourist during an 'extraordinary' time (Urry 1990: 40) that is expected to be dissimilar from ordinary life. It is, in fact, this very distinction between the everyday world and the tourist world that lies at the heart of Urry's theoretical perspective. This separation presupposes a certain distance that is encapsulated in the emphasis – and, we would say, preoccupation – he attributes to the idea of 'the gaze'.

Twenty years on from the first publication of *The Tourist Gaze*, the boundaries between tourist spaces and ordinary social life, between tourist and non-tourist dimensions of experience and consciousness, seem strained and blurred (Franklin and Crang 2001; Franklin 2003). This is particularly evident in cityscapes that are simultaneously the loci of tourist and mundane activity. But tourism is also blurred with the everyday in peripheral non-urban contexts. To accommodate these blurrings, contemporary tourism theory has expanded beyond the realm of the visual to encompass embodiment, often adopting a position of theoretical plurality. Tourism is not separable but infused into everyday life (Franklin 2003; see also Coleman and Crang 2002, and Gmelch 2009, for overviews).

The notion of the post-tourist, another conceptualization that received serious attention by Urry (1990: 90–92) and was originally developed by Feifer (1985), encourages a perspective that challenges the dichotomy between the domain of tourism and the everyday. The accessibility of the tourist imagery in global media and popular culture, but also – we would like to add – the availability of affordable embodied experiences (cf. Abram and Waldren 1997; Tucker 1997; Crouch 1999; Saldanha 2002), has demystified the pursuit of the authentic. The tourist of the postmodern era is not necessarily expecting to meet an undiscovered social life (Buzard 1993: 336–37); she or he is aware of our interconnected world and knows how to enjoy a staged reproduction, playfully moving in between the extraordinary and the mundane whilst they are at leisure (see Bruner 1994). Thus, post-tourists know, more or less, what to expect; they are, at least, better prepared to anticipate the discrepancies and blurred boundaries of the 'touristy' and the 'non-touristy' (Franklin

2003) and to enjoy this postmodern confusion with a playful disposition (Urry 1990).

The playful post-tourist awareness of an interconnected world can be compared with a less complicated type of tourist expectation that focuses on the pursuit of a singular authenticity defined in essentialist terms. The latter is often expected to be discovered in the exotic and the undiscovered, in those parts of the world that are imagined to be isolated from or at the periphery of modernity (West and Carrier 2004): among 'tribal' indigenous groups, 'simple' rural communities, people who live closer to 'nature' with little access to the benefits or the shortcomings of Western civilization. Pre-modern and pre-commoditized destinations of that type are more easily perceived as 'authentically social' (Selwyn 1996: 21). The quest for such an easily identifiable and self-contained authenticity – understood in contradistinction to modernity – has been theorized by MacCannell in his classic *The Tourist* (1976). To explain the negotiation of the expectation of the authentic, MacCannell distinguished between the front- and back-regions of tourist activity: the former accommodate tourist expectations by staging the objects of tourist desire; the latter represent a refuge from the tourists, a space where the locals carry on with their ordinary lives or reassert their identity boundaries.

The distinction between front- and back-regions in tourism offered opportunities for analysis – especially by anthropologists concerned with the coping mechanisms of host communities burdened by the influx of considerable numbers of guests and protected by directing tourist attention to staged authenticity in the front-regions (see for example, Boissevain 1996a, 1996b, 1996c). It is assumed that as long as tourists' expectations are fulfilled at the front stage (often by tourist-oriented, partially inauthentic products or performances), authentic social life remains intact in the back stage. As a result of this, authenticity, as pursued by the tourist, remains elusive and difficult to grasp (MacCannell 1976) or at best only visually appreciated (Urry 1990). In this respect, authenticity can be compared with the notion of expectation that is equally elusive and self-perpetuating (Campbell 1987) and is more likely to remain unfulfilled than realized.

It is for this reason that we have chosen to move our analysis of tourist expectation beyond the limiting parameters of a singular and consumable notion of authenticity and the contrasting inauthenticity that this implies. The authenticity-inauthenticity opposition is only meaningful, we argue, following Bruner (2005: 5), to the degree that it is recognized or discussed by the social groups that participate in the tourist encounter. Even in these cases, however, inauthenticity rests on an essentialist foundation, denigrating one type of culture or expectation as less authentic than another. Such an exclusive logic does not encourage the conceptualization of plural identities that belong to more than one place or culture (Coleman and Crang 2002: 5). As Bruner (1994, 2005) has clarified, all cultures are in a process of evolving, inventing or reinventing

4

themselves, experimenting with new possibilities; tourism adds to this dynamic unexplored possibilities for the self-conscious negotiation of cultural representation. It is therefore analytically dubious, and in many cases undeserving, to single out inauthentic identities, performances, or cultural products, and inadvisable to attempt a separation between authentic and non-authentic expectations. Inauthenticity is not 'a *thing* that we (in the public or in the academy) should be looking for at all, but rather a process or a characteristic' (Kaul 2007: 713).

Liberated from the constraining pursuit of a singular authenticity, we suggest that the meaning of expectations in tourism is dependent upon the social context of their production, and that they are never static but constantly open to creative reinterpretation and improvisation. Tourists' expectations may develop in response to new cultural syntheses that sometimes involve the combination of old sets of meaning with new narratives, and which may or may not be influenced by tourism itself. Furthermore, we should stress, it is not only the tourists who raise expectations but also tourism professionals and host societies in anticipation of their guests' expectations. In this process, they often find themselves one step ahead or several steps behind. This, we suggest, is a fluid and continuous dynamic between anticipation and expectation.

Expectation as Transformation

The analytical parameters for discussing tourists and host communities have been already set by colleagues who have studied tourism in detail and from a comparative perspective. In a number of edited collections that have made a significant impact in the field, the anthropologists of tourism escaped from earlier dichotomies and constraining oppositions and established a contextual appreciation of the complexity of the tourism exchange (see Graburn 1976; Smith 1989; Boissevain 1996a; Selwyn 1996; Abram et al. 1997; Coleman and Crang 2002; Gmelch 2009). Many of the authors who contributed to these publications encourage a movement beyond typologies that confine tourism and tourists into fixed categories, and redirect our attention to the fluidity and the diverse sets of practices that make up the tourism phenomenon (Abram and Waldren 1997; Stronza 2001; Bruner 2005).

'Movement is, after all, life' explains Kirby (2009: 15), articulating our inhabitation of a postmodern postcolonial world where tourism has taken over as 'the colonisation of pleasure and desire' (Kaur and Hutnyk 1999: 3). Passing through this 'boundless world' (Kirby 2009) does not necessarily lead to the uprooting of society and the disembeddedness/disembodiedness of identity as Giddens (1991) proposes. In a hyper-real world, it is possible to 'restory the self' (Holstein and Gubrium 2000: 3), to play as 'post-tourists' at ease in a simulacrum of authenticity (Urry 1990: 100), to live at home in a world of movement

(Rapport and Dawson 1998: 30). In her study of migrants' privileged movements, namely British citizens moving to Spain, Caroline Oliver (2007: 134) suggests that even the movement process acts as a trigger to strong individualism, self-sufficiency and independence. Tourist movements, likewise, act as a driver for personal change, whether expected or unexpected: 'tourism as a personal transition' for Nash (1996: 39), 'the transformation of self in tourism' for Bruner (1991; see also Choy 2004). That transformation may be desired by the tourist but it is not always enacted.

In 2001, on a conference break in Poland, academic anthropologist Nigel Rapport (2008) 'walks Auschwitz' to try to understand the place, the people and the experience he had read about: 'I acted the tourist' (Rapport 2008: 36), so he puts it. For Rapport, the visit failed: outside of the camp life is too normal to be set up against the Holocaust; inside, Rapport feels like he is 'on a film-set', or 'a voyeur at a theme park, being titillated by an obscene event' (37). Key to his reactions, Rapport writes, 'I cannot imagine it, any more than I can live in the 1940s tout court' (37). He adds, 'The emotions that I conjure up and to which I lay claim are, at least, partly, secondhand' (38), coming from writers' texts at a remove from the reality of the horrors which ended history.

In a comparable example, Hazel Tucker describes tourists attracted to Göreme, Turkey, the troglodytic village built underground or carved out of the rock face. 'Many tourists go to Göreme with expectations of experiencing something of the "real" pre-modern lives of the contemporary cave-people of Göreme, in order, as a Canadian tourist expressed it, to "experience the simpler, pure life that we've lost"' (Tucker 2002: 149). The tourists are attracted to the site where they can enact their fantasies and pursue their quests. As such, these troglodyte tourists turn the venue into a playground for 'the Western imaginary' (Bruner 1989: 440, cited in Tucker 1997: 109).

Tucker and Rapport are anthropologists engaging with tourism as researcher and participant. Both encounter failed expectations: Rapport as the experience fails to live up to his readings, and Tucker as tourists become disenchanted by Göreme's 'cavey identity', primitive, primordial, stone-hewn and real in what they consider to be a plastic postmodern age: 'Flintstones-land', a 'Disneyesque fairy chimney land' (Tucker 2002: 158). Whereas Tucker adopts the role of tourism researcher in her studies, Rapport embodies tourism as he tries to come to reconcile what he has read, seen on television and in the movies, and what he has heard from relatives about the horrors of Auschwitz. But it is not a history that man can easily come to terms with, let alone experience as a tourist on a conference break. Although in the real place, Rapport finds the approach to the camp too everyday, too normal and not foreboding enough; he is more disturbed by his reactions and distance from the tour than by the contents of the camp exhibits themselves.[3] For Rapport the tour was too scripted. It did not touch him but only reminded him of films about the camp and the atrocities committed there in the past, or academic materials and studies of the camp that he had read and and which felt more substantial to him than his tourist visit. Rapport's reaction to walking Auschwitz was unexpected and not what he had been anticipating.

Göreme and Auschwitz are very different tourist destinations providing very different tourist experiences, and yet in these cases above the tourists have similar reactions. Their expectations are not realized as either the burden and mantle of suffering is not taken on or the connection between the place and the person is not felt, despite the want in the tourist. Israeli anthropologist Jackie Feldman (2005) discusses similar failed tourist expectations in his study of educational visits to Poland for Israeli schoolchildren. These part-pilgrimage tours often fail because of a 'cognitive dissonance' (Feldman 2005: 228) between the tourists' expectations and their experiences. If the site does not look authentic, or the sensory envelope of the site is not all convincing and embracing, then the tourist experience does not succeed: a fragment of the Warsaw Ghetto Wall should look untouched since 1945, for example. If the students have expectations as to how the destination will look or how they will react to it that are not met by the experience, then they will potentially feel let down, deflated or even an emptiness or void:

> During the first evening discussion on one of the voyages, a student complained: 'We were in Treblinka and they tell me that people died here. And I see myself staring at the grass and trying to understand what happened here. They shot people and here there are fences and candles and flowers and I can't understand. And I find myself trying, by force, to imagine, but I don't want to do it by force. If it doesn't speak to me it doesn't; maybe it will come with time. But I'm unable and it's very frustrating'. (Feldman 2005: 230)

Feldman makes an important point following this extract when he notes that the students generally came to change and modify their expectations according to their ongoing experiences. Furthermore, Feldman (2005) also draws our attention to the fact that the tour organizers, teachers, guides and educators all had expectations not just for the trip but also for the behaviour of the schoolchildren tourists themselves. Occasionally, even these expectations were challenged, such as in the case of student disinterest in the exhibitions or in their rowdy behaviour at night. These too were subject to change.

These examples can help us appreciate that tourists have the potential to change, just as much as their expectations – whether those expectations are met and fulfilled or not. When challenged or confronted or disappointed, the tourists react by amending or revising their expectations, or critiquing and complaining about them. This relationship between expectation and satisfaction will be explored in more detail in the next section.

Expectation Dissonance

'Travel and expectation go hand in hand. Whether it is a rumour heard, a book read, brochure borrowed or package bought, we all travel hopefully' (Pocock 1992: 242). Without expectation there is no tourist for it is expectation that motivates the tourist to plan, book and execute their vacation experience. It is that special time – sacred (Graburn 1989), ludic (Lett 1983), a counterpoint to the everyday (Leite and Graburn 2009: 37) – that they live for and look forward to. As such, expectations are linked with pre-visit knowledge, with consumer-driven images, thoughts and desires. This is true for both the structured package tourist and the wandering backpacker – and even, so O'Reilly (2006) notes, the drifter or gap-year tourist, both of whom are now mainstream travel consumers. Expectation is ever present. Tourists visiting South Tyneside do so because it has been promoted as 'Catherine Cookson Country' to readers of her novels. In a 1990 survey of these visitors, Pocock (1992: 241) notes that 63 per cent of pre-visit expectations referred to the work or play of their imagination in the expectation to gain an authentic experience of her and her place. Without taking the tourist expectations and experiences further, Pocock (243) concludes that 'experience must be consistent with expectations'. This is a lesson for the tourist industry, whether in Cookson Country in the north of England or at Robben Island Museum in South Africa (see Phaswana-Mafuya and Haydam 2005). And yet, surveys are not the only recourse social scientists have for measuring tourist expectations and their importance.

As anthropologists, our preference is by way of extended case study gleaned through long-term participant observation, of working with those involved in the tourist experience, of living with them and trying to understand the full and rich, complex and nuanced context and meaning for their positions, beliefs, attitudes and actions. A museum survey of visitor expectations and motivations might tell us about a connection between perception, expectation and satisfaction, and the relationship between heritage and expectation: the closer the site to the tourist's own heritage, the greater their expectations (Poria et al. 2006: 173). Performance and expectation can be turned into ratios and formulas by regression manipulation of pre- and post-purchase data (Oliver 1980). But these types of study cannot make up for the researcher tracking the tourists through the duration of their tour (see Bruner 2005; Skinner, this volume chapter 7), living through their expectations, experiences and memories.

Mike Crang and Adrian Franklin (2001) open the first volume of their tourism journal *Tourist Studies* by examining 'The trouble with tourism and travel theory'. In this post-Fordist economy, Crang and Franklin suggest, there has been an increased touristic sensibility, a routinization of the extraordinary in the everyday such that not only has tourism become an expectation and right, but we also inhabit a 'touristic culture' (Picard 1996). This 'tourism of everyday life' incorporates 'the preparation of people to see other places as objects of tourism, and the preparation of those people and places to be seen' (Franklin and Crang 2001: 10). As such, 'the touristic gaze and imaginary shape and mediate our knowledge of and desires about the rest of the planet' (ibid.; see also Salazar 2010).

It is, so Franklin and Crang (2001) critique Urry, more than just a gaze in that it is all-embracing: from embodied to psychological/psychogenic (self-actualization and self-satisfaction of the ego [MacCannell 2002]) and sociopsychological (where motivation, satisfaction and self-actualization are key [Cohen 1984: 377]). The tourist encounter is imaginative, performative, based upon an embodied semiotics and prompted by expectation. In the same journal edition, Crouch et al. reflect upon this 'uneven encounter' (2001: 265), using the work of Johan Asplund (1992) to link expectation to tourism as a value quotient: 'expectation value', the opportunity and possibility for encounters that, in the context of tourism, give on to new networks and occasions. No doubt the expectation quotient for tourism is high as the experiences are generally new, refreshing and beyond the ordinary.

So, expectation is key to the study of tourism, whether semiotic, embodied, person-centred, or whether a psychoanalytical approach is taken. It impels the tourist by co-opting their imagination. It is a constituent part of the tourist imaginary; and, as with the tourist imaginary, expectation – to paraphrase Salazar (2010: 6) – 'produces the reality that simultaneously produces it'. Without tourist expectations, there would be no tourist bookings! Nor, as we intend to show in this section, would there be tourist satisfaction or dissatisfaction. Ironically, expectations may be wanted and desired as thoughtful breaks disrupting daydreams and fantasy escapism from the habitual performance of our everyday but, in reality, the expectation is frequently lost in the adventure, chaos and disruptions of travel and tourism – this is particularly so for the allocentric 'venturer' (Plog 1973).

This point is especially not lost on the marketers whose job is to build tourist expectations and deal with expectation fulfilment (Seabra et al. 2007). They are fully cognisant of the fact that 'image moulds expectations' (del Bosque and San Martin 2008: 557). The tools of the trade, here, are generally institutional and commercial brochures, travel agents and the internet. And the language of the trade is hyperbole regarding the destination's characteristics and attributes and the tourist's experiences. Fortunately for these advertisers, the tourists are a part of the expectation fulfilment formula as they seek to fulfil their expectations when visiting the destination.

This is why, from a consumption perspective, there should be 'congruity' between the tourist's self-concept of the tourist experience and the image of the destination (Beerli et al. 2007). This type of self-concept is another expectation component. It also relates to forthcoming tourist satisfaction. Oliver (1980: 460–61) explains clearly how expectations are met or not:

[E]xpectations are thought to create a frame of reference about which one makes a comparative judgement. Thus, outcomes poorer than expected (a negative disconfirmation) are rated below this reference point, whereas those better than expected (a positive disconfirmation) are evaluated above this base.

De Rojas and Camarero (2008: 526) paraphrase Oliver's conceptualization of this function in Oliver's (1997) later work when they write that 'satisfaction is a function of disconfirmation, and disconfirmation is a function of expectations and of fulfilment'. De Rojas and Camarero go one step further to quantify expectations by number-crunching a survey of customers. Whilst this might not be a useful source of substantiation, they do connect, appropriately, expectation as a causal factor for satisfaction. This can apply to post-encounter 'retrospective expectation' in the expectation-disconfirmation paradigm, as backward assimilation takes place with the tourist 'syncing' back their experiences to a new version of their expectations (see Oliver and Burke 1999: 198). 'I want to break bread with the Inuit' the London investment banker declares as his sole reason for visiting Alaska. And once he has taken an organized tour into a Native community, and met some of Alaska's indigenous people in their own homes, he is happy to return to his own home (Nuttall 1997: 228–29).

Del Bosque and San Martin (2008) make explicit this link between satisfaction and tourism in their recent article 'Tourist Satisfaction: A Cognitive-Affective Model' which is key to the debate. Life/leisure satisfaction, well-being and happiness are all conditional upon an individual's cognitive-affective state, the congruence between 'predictive expectation' (Del Bosque and Martin 2008: 553) and tourist experience/tourism reality. Thus, if a tourist experience meets or surpasses expectation, the result is a happy and satisfied tourist, one who has had a positive disconfirmation in the words of Oliver (happy emotions of the pleased, enchanted, impressed, surprised tourist [Del Bosque and Martin 2008: 560]). Conversely, Rapport's tourist experience, and some of Tucker's examples (see previous section) are cases of dissatisfaction, frustration and unsated want: negative disconfirmation (the bored, displeased, disappointed and angry tourist [Del Bosque and Martin 2008: 560]). In these scenarios, expectations are defined as 'the individual's beliefs about how a product is likely to perform in the future' (Del Bosque and Martin 2008: 554, adapted from Oliver 1987). Moreover, in negative disconfirmation, there is a conflict or discrepancy between tourism experience and tourist prior beliefs.

In these situations, consumers – read 'tourists' on occasion – adjust perception of their expectations to reduce or eradicate that tension (Del Bosque and San Martin 2008: 554). Expectation, then, this 'comparison standard' (ibid. 2008: 553), is a flexible and negotiable determiner – 'the benchmark of tourist satisfaction' in the eyes of Xia et al. (2009: 404) who take a structural modelling approach. For the latter, the expectation-disconfirmation paradigm is useful for highlighting concerns such as the problem that if tourist expectations are not matched by the tourist reality, tourists will in fact magnify the discrepancy, thereby extending their dissatisfaction. In practice, this means that tourist dissatisfaction is frequently magnified if expectations are not met. Interestingly, a second irony connected with dissatisfaction is the fact that it might be hyperbolized in the '*extra*ordinary' tourist context in the same manner of the hyperbole attached to the initial sale of the tourist encounter.

'[E]xpectations are tentative (mental or neural) representations of future events or unfinished learning processes', writes Juergen Gnoth (1997: 298). Gnoth comments upon the nature of expectation in his attempt at modelling the motivation-expectation process according to 'felt needs' in the tourist self. This is a particularly dynamic and person-centred approach. Gnoth (1997: 287) attends to the difference between the tourist's real self and their ideal self, and the behaviours they undertake to narrow the perceived gap between the two. As a tourist, there is a 'felt need to self-actualize' through the envisaged holiday which 'raises expectations (or expectational attitudes) of future satisfaction, both cognitively and emotionally' (Gnoth 1997: 287). In this respect, Gnoth is referring to cognitive representations such as knowledge and beliefs, and emotions such as drive, feeling and instinct. A person who feels deprived has a 'felt need' to indulge, luxuriate and enjoy a hedonistic vacation. Or a person who thinks of him/her-self in a particular class will feel that the holiday experience should suit their social status – a European skiing holiday in winter and a Caribbean resort vacation for the affluent, but a holiday camp for the less well-off, for instance. This approach, for all its Pavlovian emphases, does not undermine tourism as a performance stance – the tourist as role-playing actor – first proposed by Judith Adler (1989), then developed by Franklin and Crang (2001), and now illustrated by Rapport above.

Great Expectations – Chapters in Review

Asymmetry, Exoticization and Respect

Against this background we are now well equipped to explore the positive and negative disconfirmation of tourist expectations through detailed examples. We start with 'a revelatory incident' – a charged moment 'in human relationships … pregnant with meaning' (Fernandez 1986: xi). One of us ventures into Western Panama, this time as a tourist on a visit to a Ngäbe community where he has an unexpected encounter:

> A little Ngäbe boy appeared suddenly in our path asking for dollars. So did his younger brother who arrived running behind him. Both stood for a few seconds, catching their breath, looking at us. My wife and I were Westerners, 'gringos', visitors to their

community, tourists – of the variety that wanders off the main track and, to the amusement of the locals, get lost!

So, we looked back at them, measuring up their expectations. Then, drawing from my anthropological experience with the Emberá (another indigenous group in Panama, who confidently present aspects of their culture to tourists) I said: 'If you want money, you'll have to do something ... for example, something that you know well'.

Now it was the two boys who hesitated, measuring up our expectations. For a second I thought they would run away, hide in the luscious vegetation from which they had suddenly emerged. Maybe I expected too much. Or maybe not. ... Then, swiftly, with a sudden burst of energy, they improvised. They climbed on the nearby trees and the metal columns of the primary school, they hung from branches and metal poles, they unleashed an impressive repertoire of acrobatic moves.

Within a couple of minutes a dozen or so boys joined the unstructured but artful frenzy of acrobatics. They accompanied us to the village port and, like professional performers, laughing all the while, they entertained us, putting to use all the moves they had readily at hand. All for a few cents, the amount of money we felt was appropriate to give.

Two little girls were waiting next to the boat that brought us there. They wanted 'to do something' as well, but having no idea, they simply smiled and waved their hands goodbye as our boat went away. The same night, writing my diary, I imagined the little boys and girls in the community wondering: Is this what these tourists had wanted? What is it that tourists want? How can we make more tourists come?

DT fieldnotes. Sunday 13 April 2008. Isla Popa, Bocas del Toro, Panama.[4]

In the context of unpredictable and irregular tourist encounters, localized actors – young and old, men and women, even children – will not hesitate to grasp the opportunity of an occasional and transient tourist visit and offer what they imagine might be of interest to their visitors, or simply, like in the incident above, what they readily have at hand. In most cases, the local actors who pursue this interaction wish to engage with tourism in a more regular manner, they desire to control the tourist economy, the flow of tourists, the knowledge about the tourists' expectations and desires. But, lacking the necessary experience or infrastructure, they experiment by trial and error, exploring possibilities, experimenting with what they can offer to those visitors that pass by. Sometimes, they discover even simple things that they can do: the smile of a child, a taste of a local recipe, or the sale of locally produced handicrafts.

In a very similar revelatory incident, Hazel Tucker (chapter 2) allows us to obtain an in-depth look at the asymmetry of expectations in precarious tourist exchanges of that type. Tucker describes an encounter of two German tourists with a local woman in Göreme, a village in Central Turkey. The local woman invites the tourists to visit her cave house (and a ruined church) in the hope of selling them handicrafts. Unaware of what might interest her guests, she introduces the handicrafts that she hopes to sell in a rather brusque manner, to the discomfort of the tourists. Eventually, the tourists depart, making suggestions about how the local woman – a divorcee who raises her daughter on her own – could benefit from tourism by promoting those experiences more likely to be appreciated by the tourist audience (her cave house, not the handicrafts).

As Tucker explains, the failure of the women in Göreme to enchant their visitors is related to their relative isolation in the domestic sphere. Deprived of opportunities to engage with tourism in public spaces, or observe how other tourist entrepreneurs charm their customers, they are restricted to limiting their interaction with tourists to within their cave houses, bringing 'the public realm' home. Unlike the local men, who firmly and confidently control the local tourism business, the women of Göreme do not have a clear picture of the tourists' imagination. Failing to read the tourist expectations, they are less able to enchant and entertain; they inevitably draw undue attention to the commoditized dimension of the particular exchange, the sale of handicrafts, which is for them the main incentive for interacting with the tourists in the first place.

The women of Göreme, the Ngäbe children in the incident above, and other local actors who wish to develop tourism but are failing to do so successfully, are trapped in a vicious circle: limited practice and participation in the tourist exchange offers limited opportunities to explore the desires of the tourist audience, leading to limited awareness of the tourist expectations which inevitably restricts the opportunities to practise the necessary skills that could bring success in tourism. Knowledge here – as Foucault (1980) would have argued – is closely associated with power or, more specifically in this case, with the ability to benefit from tourist expectations. Failure to understand the desires of the tourist audience accentuates the existing asymmetry of expectations between host communities and their guests, often encouraging the local protagonists to feel that their culture is 'taken away' or appropriated (cf. Kirtsoglou and Theodossopoulos 2004).

Yet, at the same time, the resulting disjuncture of expectations does not always remain immutable, maybe because expectations themselves, and the tourist encounter, are not static. We would thus like to believe that the Ngäbe children or the Turkish women in the incidents described above will slowly succeed in bridging the gap that separates their imagined worlds (Appadurai 1996) from those of the tourists. With time, and by trial and error, they might eventually become better equipped to read and anticipate the desires of their visitors; they might even succeed in breaking the vicious circle that perpetuates the asymmetry of expectations. As we shall see in the following examples, some indigenous minorities have realized a more confident engagement with tourism. In fact, through tourism they have achieved a certain representational visibility, which – in comparison to their previous disenfranchisement – represents a change of significant proportions.

A small number of Emberá communities in Panama have recently succeeded in developing indigenous tourism. They now spend more time 'working with their culture' and become, through daily practice, knowledgeable in most matters

Emberá: they collect information about their history, reconstitute the narratives of their tradition, construct artefacts for the tourist market in a greater variety of designs than ever before, and generate new choreographic variations of traditional dances. Theodossopoulos (chapter 3) examines how the Emberá handle the contradictory nature of the tourist expectations that oscillate between an admiration of uncontaminated Indian purity (Ramos 1998) and Western civilization priorities. Undoubtedly, the expectations of foreign visitors add an additional level of complexity to the challenges set by the contemporary world, and invite new adaptation strategies. At the same time, however, the interest and attention of the tourist audience reminds the Emberá that their unique way of life is now more widely accepted, that their cultural difference is not anymore an embarrassment but an asset providing a better future – one of recognition and respect. So the Emberá learn how to anticipate the expectations of their visitors, and in this process they embark on a fascinating exploration of their own culture.

Other indigenous groups have practised indigenous tourism for longer and claim an even more dynamic control over the representation of their culture: to confront the exoticizing expectations of the tourists they do not hesitate to employ self-irony, or confidently underline that they too, like the tourists, exist in the modern world. In Alaska the indigenous tourism professionals of the Tlingit tribe have marked out their own niche in the local tourist industry, making available a native perspective for the tourist audience (Bunten, in chapter 4). In Sitka, a town with a Russian and Tlingit heritage, the indigenous tourist agency 'Tribal Tours' – a non-profitmaking subsidiary of the tribal government – is successfully competing with non-indigenous tourist businesses. Far from being passive recipients of exoticized expectations, the guides of Tribal Tours interact face to face with their tourist audience, and politely confront hegemonic stereotypes. Sometimes they prefer to reply with wit or sarcasm to those 'white' tourists who claim that 'they too' share a remote Indian ancestry, or to the souvenir dealers who sell native art by appropriating a distant tribal connection.

Breaking away from the stereotype of 'tribal wisdom', the Tlingit tourist guides will not hesitate to admit that they learnt about the ecology of the indigenous wildlife on the Discovery Channel. This is how the projection of a much less exoticized identity paves the way for presenting oneself as a citizen of the contemporary world. In Bunten's account (chapter 4), the interaction with the tourists inspires the Tlingit to tackle the misplaced expectations of the non-Tlingit world and, simultaneously, to articulate new narrative-portraits of Tlingit identity and history. In this respect, the negotiation of expectations in the tourist encounter provides the Tlingit – and other indigenous groups such as the Emberá – with opportunities to re-evaluate their own expectations and adapt their cultural and political representations accordingly. The resulting awareness of the ways (or the stereotypes) of others can inspire pride in the cultural distinctiveness of one's host culture, and encourage the indigenous tourist entrepreneurs to guide the visitors into their own local worlds with confidence and self-respect.

Compartmentalized Expectations

Aware of the commoditized nature of mass tourism, an increasing number of tourists aspire to spend their vacation participating in projects with certain significance, to forge a meaningful relationship with particular localities. In many cases, however, the relationships they eventually establish do not fully communicate with the reality of local social life. A very good example of this is provided by Jacqueline Waldren (chapter 5) who examines the perspectives of volunteers participating in an archaeological excavation in Majorca. The volunteers arrive in Majorca with the expectation of immersing themselves in a journey of discovery into the island's culture and history. They soon learn how to put their archaeological imagination to use to recreate the past, uncovering in this process the different temporal landscapes of Majorca. Through their participation in the excavation, their familiarization with the landscapes of the past, and the aesthetic appreciation of the physical environment in the present, they construct in their minds a highly idealized understanding of the island. This differs from the perceptions of other people they meet on the island: tourists, who unlike the volunteers allow themselves to enjoy the pleasure of holiday activities, or the local Majorquin, who share a long-term and socially informed relationship with the land (see also Waldren 1996).

For the duration of their participation in the excavation, the volunteers' privileged connection with the archaeological landscapes of Majorca remains divorced from the pragmatic consideration of everyday life on the island, compartmentalized in the separate layers of a personalized reality, protected from contradiction. As Waldren (this volume, chapter 5) explains, the volunteers eventually depart, thrilled by their acquaintance with a different and unique Majorca and before they are confronted by the contradictions between the island's social and temporal landscapes. Unlike professional archaeologists who use their imagination as an epistemological tool, or the local Majorquin who inhabit landscapes of dense social relationships, the volunteers indulge themselves in the imagination of an idealized connection with the island and often crave to come back, to relive this overwhelming experience again and again.

We can see a similar compartmentalization of expectations in another telling example. George Paul Meiu (chapter 6) examines the impact of a novel, *The White Masai* by Corinne Hofmann, in which the novelist immortalizes her love affair with a Samburu man in Kenya. The popularity of the novel, Meiu demonstrates, can help us appreciate the tourist fascination with the unexpected: the encounter with cultural difference opens new possibilities for both Western women and local men. In fact, the novel has become emblematic of Kenyan cultural-*cum*-sexual tourism, fuelling the expectations of Western women (desiring to consume exotic sensations) and Samburu or Maasai men (hoping to benefit economically from their Western lovers). For the past thirty years, unmarried Samburu men, taking advantage of their cultural relatedness with their famous neighbours the Maasai, have been migrating to coastal tourist resorts to work in cultural tourism and pursue, when possible, affairs with Western women.

In the post-colonial global market of desire, argues Meiu, the bodies of exotic men can be transformed into value-laden objects of desire that incorporate Western stereotypes about beauty and cruelty, pleasure and danger in a transgressive space ostensibly far removed from civilization and modernity. But while some Samburu men gradually realize that their 'exoticized' identity as *moran* (warriors) carries value, their Western lovers – 'the white Maasai' – come to realize that the pursuit of difference remains elusive: unable to reconcile the discrepancies in cultural values, they end up essentializing a difference between European and African worlds. As Meiu explains 'beyond every difference there is more difference': such is the political economy of the expectations of the unexpected.

Discord and Discrepant Expectations

The mismatch between anticipation and actual experience in tourism can sometimes generate a pleasant surprise or a spontaneously genuine *cum*-authentic adventure. It can also produce tensions or contradictions that may be decisive in shaping the tourism experience. In order to shed some light on the resulting incongruities, we take, once more, inspiration from Appadurai's (1996) notion of disjuncture. This involves, in the cases we examine in this volume, the discrepancies between the global circulation of images and information and the expectations they generate. In tourism, an increasingly globalized domain of expectations is put to the test during the tourist encounter, making visible previously unforeseen disjunctures between tourist anticipation and local social realities.

We have seen these discrepancies unravelling themselves as part of otherwise promising tourist projects that carry the potential to enchant by offering unique cultural experiences but failing to deliver. The most extreme case of this in *Great Expectations* comes from Jonathan Skinner's tracking of a jive dance holiday – a package tour to Cuba that was being piloted but never took off after it failed to meet the expectations of tour operators and tourists. Acting as a dance tourist and anthropologist researcher, Skinner was in the fortunate position of being able to follow from start to finish an organized holiday from London (U.K.) to Havana (Cuba) for dancers who were buying into a specific form of jive (*ceroc*) and a specific type of dance destination – hot, spicy, sexy, 'exotic' Cuba. Whilst the travel company operates a successful (popular in demand and financially lucrative) salsa dance package holiday to Cuba, they sought to extend this option with a jive holiday. The holiday promises fell through in this case as tourist jive dancers failed to mix with local salsa and rumba dancers, and night club dance floors had to be rented by the hour for the imported jive music to be played.

Furthermore, the tourists all came with different expectations for the vacation on 'pleasure island', ranging from socialism in the sun to sex tourism, and from dance tourism through to 'that quick getaway'. But after arriving with many different expectations, the tourists all returned home with a host of uncertainties and complaints. This is an example of negative disconfirmation in the tourist experience.

In chapter 8 of this volume, Kelli Ann Malone considers the relationship with, and activities undertaken for, visiting tourists by 'coach fellas'. Here, we have an exploration of the coach tour around parts of Ireland with the author writing as the anthropologist and tour guide about this 'cinematic' experience from the coach window. From her research position, Malone is able to carefully assess the match or mis-match between the tourists' expectations and their delivery by their coach driver and tour organizer. In this tourism role, the 'coach fella' tries to meet and exceed the tourists' expectations, particularly as to what constitutes 'genuine Irishness': his is a struggle to accommodate the discrepancy between the idyllic Ireland the tourists' imagined and the contemporary reality of the dynamic modern nation. With each tour, the driver develops a deeper insight into the tourist experience and becomes aware of the divergence in the tourist expectations. From the driver's point of view, the tourists 'see' but do not really experience: they go to Ireland without actually being there.

The coach driver also has to try to offset the tourism expectations and qualities coming from sitting and seeing sites through the window, a consumption of Ireland which – although not entirely a tourist bubble (cf. Oliver 2000, 2003) – always delivers differently to one's expectations. The tour company has to engage with the tourists and their suspicions or sense of 'inauthenticity' about their experiences that stem from their desire for a long and deep connection with their destination. Malone cleverly elucidates the tourists' wants and needs, and the often irreconcilable differences between 'going to Ireland' and 'being in Ireland'; between tourist dreams and realities; between the compulsion to consume Ireland and the reality of 'sleeping through Ireland' from the back of the coach. The reality of the tourist experience is beyond expectation, Malone argues, making a point integral to this volume. It is a case, then, of pleasing and placating the tourist. Malone suggests this whilst also looking at how tourists connect with the past, 'commune with ancestral spaces'.

This task is also undertaken by Jennifer Iles (chapter 9) who examines veteran holiday explorers and those visiting the First World War battlefields of the old Western Front. Iles presents a case of dark tourism as a pilgrimage and performance for the visitors to the former war zone. Her example is about how senses (multi-) and feelings (such as empathy) instil a sense of ownership over the trenches in France and Belgium, and the remaining mass cemeteries – 'the silent cities'. Visiting these battlefields, touring them and paying homage to the sacrifices made there, British visitors find themselves in a landscape of collective and family memory: their expected reactions – especially for the repeat visitor –

of pride, heritage, nostalgia for an imagined past, and sentimentality are all pulled up out of the earth.

The battle scars pitting the French and Belgian landscape are seen to have a morbid authenticity about them. They attract war tourists and descendents of those who fought or fell during the Great War. In this dark attraction, there is a resulting tension in that the past is preserved, often at the expense of development in the present, as whole swathes of the countryside are kept as a tomb to unknown soldiers, preserved for posterity, preserved for pilgrimage ('lest we forget'), and sometimes preserved from new roads and 'new build' – much to the frustrations of those living in, around and on the battlefields. As Iles points out, the expectations of the living are contested here between tourist and resident, both deeply affected by the shattered expectations of those doomed youths.

As another example of touring the dead, Jane Desmond (chapter 10) makes the point that the imagination is engaged by the tourism organizers who plan and purchase the right look, hype the tourist event, and build the tourists' expectations. The destination images in her chapter are dead, plastinated bodies – posed, advertised and used to create 'scopic enchantment' in the visitor. Desmond's chapter presents the interesting phenomenon of the tourist attraction coming to the tourist. It is an example of a touring exhibition of human bodies set on display for part education and part entertainment ('edu-tainment') purposes – a living anatomy. A 'blockbuster exhibit' like the Gunther von Hagens *Body Worlds* requires considerable investment, and so the organizers carefully survey the potential destinations and people who might attend. When in London, the exhibit was billed as 'fascination beneath the surface'; brochures and exhibition books stress the dignity of the individual – on display and as viewer. It is all set as an 'arty' large-scale display in an old industrial building.

In California, the exhibition was set in the California Science Center, and what was stressed more than in other destinations was the 'donated-for-science' bodies (many former criminals) status of the exhibits, and their state-sanctioned approval. Demographics showed that fewer African American and Asian American visitors attended in relation to their usual exhibition attendance demographic. This is an indication of exhibition expectation and the disjuncture between organizer/promoter and tourist attendee. Furthermore, Desmond shows us how the organizing of the tour encouraged a medico-scientific tourist gaze inculcating awe and respect in a hushed, dimmed expansive art warehouse, industrial installation or museum environment. The global *Body Worlds* tour is as much a tour of the self as it is a tour of the Other. It is raw, real, and as one participant notes, 'beneath the skin'. In touring the dead, we come to see ourselves alive.

The fallout from discrepancies between expectation and experience – negative disconfirmation to the tourism theorist – can lead to a loss in repeat bookings and many complaints as the tour operator, the dance instructor or the 'coach fella' struggles to accommodate or deal with highly demanding tourists seeking value for money and the promise they have made for their brief liminal time away from home. Above, we have introduced the examples from this volume that can be read in more detail in the coming pages. In their various ways, they illustrate how sometimes the planning by the professional holidaymakers underestimates local culture and local social dynamics, not least those tourists on their programmes. It is meeting – providing for, catering to – the tourists' expectations that determines success in tourism. And yet, in dealing with desire, promise, and imagination, it is no surprise that expectations remain unmet and unfulfilled. Perhaps this failure to satisfy expectations is a part of the human condition? Tour operators and drivers might try to resolve tensions imaginatively, deal with innocent tourists patiently, but discrepancies are complex, ever-emergent, sometimes impossible or unrealistic, belonging and obstinately remaining in the realms of the imaginary.

The Great 'Expectationscape'?

Whether from Turkey, Panama, France, Cuba or Kenya, it is through the negotiation of expectations that tourist professionals, tourists and host communities actively imagine, re-imagine and construct or co-construct each other. Their success or failure to meet the expectations of others – the mismatch between anticipation and the actual experience (see Bruner, chapter 11 of this volume) – can teach us valuable lessons about the discrepancies between more or less privileged communities, their perceptions of power and powerlessness, and their participation in the global consumption of culture. We have approached the practice of imagining the expectations of others – which often involves 'entering into the imaginings of others' (Salazar 2010: 5) – as a dynamic process involving members from right across the hierarchical spectrum. In this process, local actors and tourist professionals, but also the tourists themselves, are active participants in the production of the imagination of cultural difference and the making of the tourism experience. In their expectations, they enter 'into the imagining of others' (Salazar 2010: 5).

The proclivity of the Western tourism audience to exoticize – to sensationalize cultural difference (Herzfeld 1987) – to consume indigeneity, or to nostalgically desire a state of humanity forever lost (Rosaldo 1989), has been a constant inspiration for the tourist imagination. More recently, however, this search for authentic cultural difference is mediated by the inquisitive gaze of a new generation of tourists, 'post-tourists' (Urry 1990), some of whom share an increasing awareness of cultural interconnections (Franklin 2003), a playful disposition (Cohen 1985), or a penetrating 'second gaze' that can see beyond the touristically obvious (MacCannell 2001). So tourist expectations are changing, probably faster than ever before; they are becoming more nuanced, creating in turn new expectations, 'disjunctures and conjunctures in the globalized production of difference' (Appadurai 1996: 199).

Some indigenous communities are able to take advantage of the new technologies and interconnections made available by globalization (Strathern and Stewart 2009; Theodossopoulos 2009) while some others respond hesitantly, unable to regulate the flow of tourists (Tucker, in chapter 2) or the very processes that perpetuate their exoticization (Meiu, in chapter 6). We have noticed that the ability to read the expectations of the tourists determines a wide variety of local adaptations that range from apprehension and disempowerment to active engagement and cultural revitalization. The asymmetry of expectations between tourists and hosts sometimes creates cultural rifts that are difficult to overcome, whilst at other times it motivates the local tourist entrepreneurs to openly address their exoticization and emerge out of the resulting negotiation of expectations as indigenous 'cultural producers' who control their own representation within the immediate tourist interaction (Bunten, in chapter 4).

It is apparent that tourism expectations do not necessarily confine indigenous tourism into stagnant, mechanical or commoditized cultural reproduction (see also Cohen 1988; Abram and Waldren 1997; Coleman and Crang 2002; Bruner 2005). In many cases, the tourism exchange adds global visibility to the cultures consumed. It could also facilitate the communication of admiration and respect to the consuming audience towards the indigenous tourist entrepreneurs (Theodossopoulos, this volume; 2010) adding to the global awareness of the latter, or inspiring the creation of narratives that oppose previous stereotyping and exoticization (Bunten, this volume; 2008). Apart from the political or economic benefits of this 'touristy' type of representation, the host communities experience countless opportunities to practise and develop their indigenous traditions, to improvise – to work out the script of their cultural life (Ingold and Hallam 2007) – as they carry on with their daily routines of making their culture available to tourists. It is in this respect that the expectations of the global tourist audience can stimulate creativity and cultural improvization (see Bruner 1993).

So we have seen that in response to tourist expectations, cultural practices with an indigenous history are rediscovered, re-evaluated, brought forth to become part of emerging tourist narratives. Sometimes these processes include the involvement of state authorities that might encourage the cultivation of particular cultural displays or sets of aesthetics. Supported by state apparatuses that promote tourism, 'local populations construct a representation of their culture *simultaneously* based upon their own indigenous system of references and their understanding of the tourists' expectations' (Picard 1990: 44; our emphasis). This is how cultural tourism may become part of the official doctrine and transform a culture from within – as for example Picard (1990, 1997) has shown in his work about Bali. The expectations of the tourists, but also the expectations of the hosts, play an important role in the emerging cultural syntheses: they provoke, inspire or frustrate. They also necessitate compromises.

From the point of view of the tourists, the most striking compromises involve the discontinuity between expectation and reality (MacCannell 1976) or expectation and experience (Bruner, this volume). Those who dare to come closer to other cultures, driven by a desire to experience and embody the local, often have to deal with irreconcilable cultural perspectives that challenge their initial expectations. Such is the motivating power of their expectations that many aficionados of cultural adventure – travellers, summer-project volunteers, adventurous allocentric tourists – prefer to compartmentalize the resulting contradictions to safeguard the memory of the experience (Waldren, Meiu, this volume). The resulting experiences of cultural difference are sanitized, protected from contradiction in separate sets of memories, narratives, and landscapes of imagination.

Thus, expectations are also comparative and evaluative frames of reference and so are anthropological in timbre. Tourist satisfaction is a function of the expectation – a positive experience giving on to positive disconfirmation; a negative experience resulting in negative disconfirmation (Oliver 1980; De Rojas and Camarero 2008; Del Bosque and San Martin 2008). The results of these expectations will always await the basking tourist. Discordant, discrepant, disjunctured, these expectations make or break the tourist experience – beginning, middle and end – whether seductive Cuban jive holidays mis-sold to the lusting tourist (Skinner, this volume) or mis-matched coach tours around parts of Ireland (Malone, this volume). These expectations are wrought by the tourist industry, constructed gazes of preserved battlefields and cemeteries (Iles, this volume) or preserved bodies on global display (Desmond, this volume). The last two examples are particularly morbid and loaded with nostalgia and pride and ownership – a body of land and a human body. They highlight, in particular, the expectations of the living. Expectations are highly temporal, constructed in a present, imagined, and then borne out in the future, and relating to a past from that green fields verge. Expectations are thus dynamic as well as demanding.

The chapters in this volume propel tourism expectations to the fore in the anthropology of tourism and, by 'thinking through tourism' (Scott and Selwyn 2010), to the production of anthropological theory more generally. Hence, we invite the anthropological community to pay careful attention to social expectations and to explore their all-pervasive influence in other domains of human experience. As researchers working in a discipline seeking to establish 'bridgeheads of communication' (Overing 1985: 1), we do so here by presenting, analysing and assisting with the communication and translation of expectations. In the chapters that follow, we explore the dialectic of expectation and imagination in tourism; we pay careful attention to the emerging discrepancies between imagined or anticipated expectations and practice; we witness local communities moving from their tentative early exchanges with tourists to bold engagements with tourism expectations; and we record how tourists deal with failed expectations: how they compartmentalize their expectations in the face of disconfirmation, and how they negotiate their desire and their anticipation. The negotiation of expectation, we argue, is critical, crucial and controversial in all of the journeys we make.

Volume Note

The chapters in this volume originate from a panel organized for the conference 'Thinking through Tourism', the 2007 annual meeting of the Association of Social Anthropologists of the U.K. and Commonwealth. We would like to thank the conference organizers, Tom Selwyn and Julie Scott, for inviting us to participate and providing us with the forum that enabled us to start this work. We also wish to thank and acknowledge the advice and constructive criticism of Michaela Benson, Nigel Rapport and Veronique Altglas in the writing of this Introduction.

Notes

1. These expectations change through the course of Pip's quest for maturity and Dickens's engagement with issues of love, support, status and class through his exploits. His expectations are limited, but also inspired and encouraged by his immediate life experiences outside of his station in life. It is not until the latter phases of the novel that Pip comes to appreciate the realities of social relations, high society characters, and social and economic life. It is then, after leaving and returning to the country – as an exile rather than as a tourist – that he comes to appreciate his condition and that wealth and social climbing are not the measure of every success and so, for Dickens, the story ends with the quest fulfilled and expectations checked, reappraised, and ultimately sated.
2. Here we are thinking of imagination as a human capacity to imagine things other than they are, rather than some Kantian reflection or Aristotelian phantasia/fancy (see Sparshott 1990). This is strongly guided and sold by the tourism industry.
3. Whilst he went on the tour, during a different conference break, I [JS] too visited the camp, but opted out of the tour group, wanting to be able to dwell in and upon the place and its past. My own expectations were surpassed at the time, and my self remains shaken by the witnessing.
4. The acrobatics of the Ngäbe boys in this short tourist encounter was not a 'cultural' performance such as those carried out by many indigenous groups for the entertainment of tourists. The adults of this particular community welcome the possibility of organizing cultural performances and have previously executed traditional dances for visiting groups of tourists in a manner comparable to Panama's other indigenous groups such as the Kuna and the Emberá. Yet the supply of tourists remains unstable and the community has not been able to make a sustainable living out of tourism. This particular community, like other Ngäbe communities (Karkotis n.d.), aspires to benefit from tourism and negotiate its 'articulation with an ever changing world' (Young and Bort 1999: 133).

References

Abram, S. and J. Waldren. 1997. 'Introduction: Identifying with People and Places', in S. Abram, J. Waldren and D.V.L. Macleod (eds), *Tourists and Tourism: Identifying with People and Places.* Oxford: Berg, pp. 1–11.

Abram, S., J. Waldren and D. Macleod (eds). 1997. *Tourists and Tourism: Identifying with People and Places.* Oxford: Berg.

Adler, J. 1989. 'Travel as Performed Art', *American Journal of Sociology* 94(6): 1366–91.

Appadurai, A. 1996. *Modernity at Large: Cultural Dimensions of Globalization.* Minneapolis: University of Minnesota Press.

Asplund, J. 1992. *Storsäderna och det forteanksa livet.* Gothenborg: Bokforlaget Korpen.

Beerli, A., G. Menses and S. Gil. 2007. 'Self-Congruity and Destination Choice', *Annals of Tourism Research* 34(3): 571–87.

Boissevain, J. (ed.). 1996a. *Coping with Tourists: European Reactions to Mass Tourism.* Oxford: Berghahn Books.

Boissevain, J. 1996b. 'Ritual, Tourism and Cultural Commoditization in Malta: Culture by the Pound?', in T. Selwyn (ed.), *The Tourist Image: Myths and Myth Making in Tourism.* Chichester: Willey & Sons, pp. 105–20.

Boissevain, J. 1996c. '"But we live here!" Perspectives on Cultural Tourism in Malta', in L. Briguglio et al. (eds), *Sustainable Tourism in Islands and Small States: Case Studies.* London: Pinter, pp. 220–40.

Bruner, E. 1989. 'Of Cannibals, Tourists and Ethnographers', *Cultural Anthropology* 4(4): 438–45.

Bruner, E. 1991. 'The Transformation of Self in Tourism', *Annals of Tourism Research* 18(2): 238–50.

Bruner, E. 1993. 'Epilogue: Creativity persona and the problem of authenticity', in S. Lavie, K. Narayan and R. Rosaldo (eds), *Creativity/Anthropology.* Ithaca, NY: Cornell University Press, pp. 321–34.

Bruner, E. 1994. 'Abraham Lincoln as Authentic Reproduction: A Critique of Postmodernism'. *American Anthropologist* 96: 397–415.

Bruner, E. 2005. *Culture on Tour: Ethnographies of Travel.* Chicago: University of Chicago Press.

Bunten, A. 2008. 'Sharing Culture or Shelling Out? Developing the Commodified Persona in the Heritage Industry', *American Ethnologist* 35(3): 380–95.

Buzard, J. 1993. *The Beaten Track: European Tourism, Literature, and the Ways to 'Culture' 1800–1918.* Oxford: Clarendon Press.

Campbell, C. 1987. *The Romantic Ethic and the Spirit of Modern Consumerism.* Oxford: Basil Blackwell.

Chard, C. 1999. *Pleasure and Guilt on the Grand Tour: Travel Writing and Imaginative Geography 1600–1830.* Manchester: Manchester University Press.

Choy, N. 2004. 'THIS TRIP REALLY CHANGED ME: Backpackers' Narratives of Self-Change', *Annals of Tourism Research* 31(1): 78–102.

Cohen, E. 1984. 'The Sociology of Tourism: Approaches, Issues, and Findings', *Annual Review of Sociology* 10: 373–92.

Cohen, E. 1985. 'Tourism as Play', *Religion* 15: 291–304.

Cohen, E. 1988. 'Authenticity and Commoditization in Tourism', *Annals of Tourism Research* 15: 371–86.

Coleman, S. and M. Crang (eds). 2002. *Tourism: Between Place and Performance.* Oxford: Berghahn Books.

Crouch, D. 1999. 'Encounters in Leisure and Tourism', in D. Crouch (ed.), *Leisure/Tourism Geographies: Practices and Geographical Knowledge.* London: Routledge, pp. 1–16.

Crouch, D., L. Aronsson and L. Wahlström. 2001. 'Tourist Encounters', *Tourist Studies* 1(1): 253–70.

Del Bosque, I. and H. San Martin. 2008. 'Tourist Satisfaction: A Cognitive-Affective Model', *Annals of Tourism Research* 35(2): 551–73.

De Rojas, C. and C. Camarero. 2008. 'Visitor's Experience, Mood and Satisfaction in a Heritage Context: Evidence from an Interpretation Center', *Tourism Management* 29: 525–37.

Feifer, M. 1985. *Going Places: The Ways of the Tourist from Imperial Rome to the Present Day.* London: MacMillan.

Feldman, J. 2005. 'In Search of the Beautiful Land of Israel: Israeli Youth Voyages to Poland', in C. Noy and E. Cohen (eds), *Israeli Backpackers and their Society.* New York, NY: State University of New York Press, pp. 217–50.

Fernandez, J.W. 1986. *Persuasions and Performances: The Play of Tropes in Culture.* Bloomington: Indiana University Press.

Foucault, M. 1980. *Power/Knowledge: Selected Interviews and Other Writings, 1972–1977*, trans. C. Gordon. New York: Pantheon Books.

Frankin, A. 2003. *Tourism: An Introduction.* London: Sage.

Franklin, A. and M. Crang. 2001. 'The Trouble with Tourism and Travel Theory?', *Tourist Studies* 1(1): 5–22.

Giddens, A. 1991. *Modernity and Self-Identity: Self and Society in the Late Modern Age.* Stanford, CA: Stanford University Press.

Gmelch, S. (ed.). 2009. *Tourists and Tourism.* Long Grove, IL: Waveland Press.

Gnoth, J. 1997. 'Tourism Motivation and Expectation Formation', *Annals of Tourism Research* 24(2): 283–304.

Graburn, N. (ed.). 1976. *Ethnic and Tourist Arts: Cultural Expressions from the Fourth World.* Berkeley: University of California Press.

Graburn, N. 1989. 'Tourism: The Sacred Journey', in V. Smith (ed.), *Hosts and Guests. The Anthropology of Tourism*, 2nd edn. Philadelphia, PA: University of Pennsylvania Press, pp. 21–36.

Herzfeld, M. 1987. *Anthropology through the Looking-Glass: Critical Ethnography in the Margins of Europe.* Cambridge: Cambridge University Press.

Hofmann, C. 2005. *The White Masai.* London: Bliss Books.

Holstein, J. and J. Gubrium. 2000. *The Self We Live By: Narrative Identity in a Postmodern World.* Oxford: Oxford University Press.

Ingold, T. and E. Hallam. 2007. 'Creativity and Cultural Improvisation: An Introduction' in E. Hallam and T. Ingold (eds), *Creativity and Cultural Improvisation.* Oxford: Berg, pp. 1–24.

Karkotis, A. n.d. '"Now we live together": the poetics of everyday life in a spatially concentrated Ngobe community in Panama'. Bristol: University of Bristol.

Kaul, A.R. 2007. 'The Limits of Commodification in Traditional Irish Music Sessions. *JRAI (N.S.)* 13(3): 703–19.

Kaur, R. and J. Hutnyk. 1999. 'Introduction', in R. Kaur and J. Hutnyk (eds), *Travel Worlds: Journeys in Contemporary Cultural Politics.* London: Zed Books, pp. 1–13.

Kirby, P. 2009. 'Lost in "Space": An Anthropological Approach to Movement', in P. Kirby (ed.), *Boundless Worlds: An Anthropological Approach to Movement.* Oxford: Berghahn Books, pp. 1–28.

Kirtsoglou, E. and D. Theodossopoulos. 2004. '"They are Taking our Culture Away": Tourism and Culture Commodification in the Garifuna Community of Roatan', *Critique of Anthropology* 24(2): 135–57.

Leite, N. and N. Graburn. 2009 'Anthropological Interventions in Tourism Studies', in M. Robinson and T. Jamal (eds), *The Sage Handbook of Tourism Studies.* London: Sage, pp. 35–64.

Lett, J. 1983. 'Ludic and Liminoid Aspects of Charter Yacht Tourism in the Caribbean', *Annals of Tourism Research* 10(1): 35–56.

MacCannell, D. 1976. *The Tourist: A New Theory of the Leisure Class.* New York, NY: Schocken Books.

MacCannell, D. 2001. 'Tourist Agency', *Tourist Studies* 1(1): 23–37.

MacCannell, D. 2002. 'The Ego Factor in Tourism', *The Journal of Consumer Research* 29(1): 146–51.

Nash, D. 1996. *The Anthropology of Tourism*. Oxford: Pergamon.

Nuttall, M. 1997. 'Packaging the Wild: Tourism Development in Alaska', in S. Abram, J. Waldren and D. Macleod (eds), *Tourists and Tourism: Identifying with People and Places*. Oxford: Berg, pp. 223–38.

Oliver, C. 2007. 'Imagined Communitas: Older Migrants and Aspirational Mobility', in V. Amit (ed.), *Going First Class: New Approaches to Privileged Travel and Movement*. Oxford: Berghahn Books, pp. 126–43.

Oliver, R. 1980. 'A Cognitive Model of the Antecedents and Consequences of Satisfaction Decisions', *Journal of Marketing Research* 17(4): 460–69.

Oliver, R. 1987. 'An Investigation of the Interrelationship between Consumer (Dis)satisfaction and Complaint Reports', *Advances in Consumer Research* 14: 218–22.

Oliver, R. 1997. *Satisfaction: A Behavioural Perspective on the Consumer*. New York, NY: McGraw-Hill.

Oliver, R. and R. Burke. 1999. 'Expectation Processes in Satisfaction Formation', *Journal of Service Research* 1(3): 196–214.

Oliver, T. 2000. 'Watch This Space: Observing Patters of Tourist Behaviour on a Cultural Tour', in M. Robinson, P. Long, N. Evans, R. Sharpley and J.Swarbrooke (eds), *Motivations, Behaviour and Tourist Types*. Sunderland: Business Education Publishers, pp. 321–30.

Oliver, T. 2003. 'Journeys of the Imagination: The Cultural Tour Route Revealed', in G.I. Crouch, R.R. Perdue, H. Timmermans and M. Uysal (eds), *Consumer Psychology of Tourism, Hospitality and Leisure*. Wallingford: CABI Publishing, pp. 273–84.

O'Reilly, C. 2006. 'From Drifter to Gap Year Tourist Mainstreaming Backpacker Travel', *Annals of Tourism Research* 33(4): 998–1017.

Overing, J. 1985. 'Introduction', in J. Overing (ed.), *Reason and Morality*. London: Tavistock Publications, pp. 1–29.

Phaswana-Mafuya, N. and N. Haydam. 2005. 'Tourists' Expectations and Perceptions of the Robben Island Museum – a World Heritage Site', *Museum Management and Curatorship* 20: 149–69.

Picard, M. 1990. '"Cultural Tourism" in Bali: Cultural Performances as Tourist Attraction', *Indonesia* 49: 37–74.

Picard, M. 1996. *Bali: Cultural Tourism and Touristic Culture*. Singapore: Archipelago.

Picard, M. 1997. 'Cultural Tourism, Nation-Building, and Regional Culture: The Making of a Balinese Identity', in M. Picard and R.E. Wood (eds), *Tourism, Ethnicity, and the State in Asian and Pacific Societies*. Honolulu, HI: University of Hawai'i Press, pp. 181–214.

Plog, S. 1973. 'Why Destination Areas Rise and Fall in Popularity', *Cornell Hotel and Restaurant Administration Quarterly* 14: 13–16.

Pocock, D. 1992. 'Catherine Cookson Country: Tourist Expectation and Experience', *Geography* 77(3): 236–43.

Poria, Y., A. Reichel and A. Biran. 2006. 'Heritage Site Management: Motivations and Expectations', *Annals of Tourism Research* 33(1): 162–78.

Ramos, A.R. 1998. *Indigenism: Ethnic Politics in Brazil*. Madison, WI: University of Wisconsin Press.

Rapport, N. 2008. 'Walking Auschwitz, Walking Without Arriving', *Journeys: The International Journal of Travel and Travel Writing* 9(2): 32–54.

Rapport, N. and A. Dawson. 1998. 'Home and Movement: A Polemic', in N. Rapport and A. Dawson (eds), *Migrants of Identity: Perceptions of Home in a World of Movement*. Oxford: Berghahn Books, pp. 19–38.

Rosaldo, R. 1989. *Culture and Truth: The Remaking of Social Analysis*. London: Routledge.

Salazar, N.B. 2010. *Envisioning Eden: Mobilizing Imaginaries in Tourism and Beyond*. Oxford: Berghahn Books.

Saldanha, A. 2002. 'Music Tourism and Factions of Bodies in Goa', *Tourism Studies* 2(1): 43–63.

Scott, J. and T. Selwyn. 2010. 'Introduction: Thinking through Tourism – Framing the Volume', in J. Scott and T. Selwyn (eds), *Thinking through Tourism*. Oxford: Berg, pp. 1–25.

Seabra, C., J. Abrantes and L. Lages. 2007. 'The Impact of Using Non-media Information Sources on the Future Use of Mass Media Information Sources: The Mediating Role of Expectations Fulfilment', *Tourism Management* 28: 1541–54.

Selwyn, T. (ed.). 1996. *The Tourist Image: Myths and Myth Making in Tourism*. Chichester: Wiley.

Smith, V.L. (ed.). 1989. *Hosts and Guests: The Anthropology of Tourism*. Philadelphia, PA: University of Pennsylvania Press.

Sparshott, F. 1990. 'Imagination: The Very Idea', *The Journal of Aesthetics and Art Criticism* 48(1): 1–8.

Strathern, A. and P.J. Stewart. 2009. 'Shifting Centres, Tense Peripheries: Indigenous Cosmopolitanisms', in D. Theodossopoulos and E. Kirtsoglou (eds), *United in Discontent: Local Responses to Cosmopolitanism and Globalization*. Oxford: Berghahn Books, pp. 20–44.

Stronza, A. 2001. 'Anthropology of Tourism: Forging New Ground for Ecotourism and Other Alternatives', *Annual Review of Anthropology* 30: 261–83.

Theodossopoulos, D. 2009. 'Introduction: United in Discontent', in D. Theodossopoulos and E. Kirtsoglou (eds), *United in Discontent: Local Responses to Cosmopolitanism and Globalization*. Oxford: Berghahn Books, pp. 1–19.

Theodossopoulos, D. 2010. 'Tourism and Indigenous Culture as Resources: Lessons from the Emberá Cultural Tourism in Panama', in J.G. Carrier and D.V.L Macleod (eds), *Tourism, Power and Culture: Anthropological Insights*. Bristol: Channel View, pp. 115–33.

Tucker, H. 1997. 'The Ideal Village: Interactions through Tourism in Central Anatolia', in S. Abram, J. Waldren and D. Macleod (eds), *Tourists and Tourism: Identifying with People and Places*. Oxford: Berghahn Books, pp. 107–28.

Tucker, H. 2002. 'Welcome to Flintstone-Land: Contesting Place and Identity in Goreme, Central Turkey', in S. Coleman and M. Crang (eds), *Tourism: Between Place and Performance*. Oxford: Berghahn Books, pp. 143–59.

Urry, J. 1990. *The Tourist Gaze*. London: Sage.

Waldren, J. 1996. *Insiders and Outsiders: Paradise and Reality in Mallorca*. Oxford: Berghahn Books.

West, P. and J. Carrier. 2004. 'Ecotourism and Authenticity: Getting Away from It All?', *Current Anthropology* 45(4): 483–98.

Xia, W.J. Zhang, C. Cu and F. Zhen. 2009. 'Examining Antecedents and Consequences of Tourist Satisfaction: A Structural Modelling Approach', *Tsinghua Science & Technology* 14(3): 397–406.

Young, P.D. and R. Bort. 1999. 'Ngóbe Adaptive Responses to Globalization in Panama', in W. Loker (ed.), *Globalization and the Rural Poor in Latin America*. Boulder, CO: Lynne Rienner, pp. 111–36.

Young, R. 1995. *Colonial Desire: Hybridity in Theory, Culture and Race*. London: Routledge.

Chapter 2
SUCCESS AND ACCESS TO KNOWLEDGE IN THE TOURIST-LOCAL ENCOUNTER: CONFRONTATIONS WITH THE UNEXPECTED IN A TURKISH COMMUNITY

Hazel Tucker

The tourist encounter has been described as similar to a love affair (Lengkeek 2002), as a flirtatious encounter (Crouch 2005) and as being full of promise (Lippard 1999). Drawing upon Simmel's ([1910] 1971) notion of 'sociability', Harrison (2003: 46) identifies the expectation in tourist encounters 'to either affirm or experience anew some form of human connection across time, space, or cultural difference'. The meeting of tourists and local 'hosts' is therefore, invariably, a highly complex as well as precarious phenomenon, and this raises questions both about what occurs in hosts' attempts to meet tourists' expectations and about how hosts acquire knowledge, or skill, in relation to meeting those desires. If hosts seek to enchant their tourist guests, how do they come to know *how* to enchant them and thereby entrap them in their hosting intentionalities (Gell 1998; Thomas 2001)? Moreover, what enables some hosts to be successful in their attempts to anticipate the desires of their tourist guests whilst others remain unsuccessful?

This chapter addresses these questions by focusing in particular on the gendered differentiation of tourist encounters in the village of Göreme in central Turkey. The discussion draws upon one particular encounter[1] that took place in

Göreme between a village woman, a German couple and me, a female New Zealand-based researcher with previous ethnographic research experience in the village. The description of this encounter allows us to recognize the precarious nature of tourism interactions, as it illustrates awkwardness and discomfort for all involved and thus highlights asymmetry and miscommunication of expectations between hosts and guests. Moreover, analysis of the encounter elucidates important differences between the men and women of Göreme in their ability to successfully negotiate tourist desires and expectations.

As tourism developed in the region surrounding the World Heritage Site of Göreme during the late 1980s and the 1990s, men became the tourism entrepreneurs and gained tourism employment whilst women remained largely excluded from participating in tourism work as it was deemed inappropriate for women to work in the 'public' sphere. In accordance with Islamic codes and practice (Delaney 1991), there is in Göreme society strict segregation of the sexes with a well-defined distribution of economic and social activity according to gender, upheld by principles of shame and honour (Tucker 2003). Women's lack of involvement in tourism work, then, was not so much because of ideology concerning the division of labour but rather because of ideology concerning notions of 'public' and 'private' and corresponding gender spatial separation (Tucker 2007). As this chapter goes on to discuss, this spatial separation is largely responsible for women's limited knowledge of tourists' expectations when they do have the occasion to interact with and 'host' tourists.

The area of Göreme and the wider Cappadocia region has a seemingly magical volcanic landscape of valleys filled with natural columns and cones, known locally as 'fairy chimneys'. For centuries, dwellings, stables and places of worship have been hewn out of the rock cliffs and fairy chimneys, and these, in both their historic and contemporary forms, have been the focus of 'cultural tourism' in recent years. Whilst the Göreme Open-Air Museum, which is an enclosed area of historic Byzantine monastic remains, is the single main attraction in the Göreme valley, within the contemporary Turkish village of Göreme tourists spend time wandering through the back streets to take a look at the 'troglodyte' village life of today. Seeing tourists' fascination with the caves, many villagers have converted their cave-houses into *pansiyon* (hostel or guest house) accommodation, selling tourists the opportunity to become cave-dwellers themselves. Tourist *pansiyon* accommodation is thus scattered throughout the older residential neighbourhoods of the village, and tourists walking to and from their accommodation, or simply wandering to explore the backstreets of the village, may encounter Göreme women going about their daily lives in the domestic space of their neighbourhood.

This chapter focuses on such encounters and discusses the Göreme women's limited skill in negotiating tourists' expectations and desires compared to the skill of the men who operate and 'host' in the *pansiyons* and other tourism businesses in the village. The discussion draws on my long-term research in Göreme. Since 1995, I have undertaken regular periods of ethnographic fieldwork there, of varying durations up to a year, looking at the changes brought about by tourism in the village and how interactions are played out between tourists, tourism businesses and village life. My initial ethnographic work conducted in the late 1990s was published as a whole in Tucker (2003), and since then my work in Göreme has developed into a longitudinal study examining ongoing tourism development and social change. The following 'encounter' took place during a period of five months sabbatical leave I recently spent in Göreme with my family.

The Encounter

Late one morning I was sitting chatting to three women by the rubbish bins in the square beside the mosque. One of the women was our next door neighbour in the cave house that my family and I were renting during my fieldwork. Upon seeing a tourist couple walking by my neighbour called out to them, 'Come, church'. They didn't understand but came over to see what she was saying. I jumped in to help and translated: 'She's asking if you want to see a church'. They said they did, so we all followed my neighbour. I hadn't actually seen this church even though it was situated on the short narrow street where I was living. We went through a doorway of an empty ruined cave house and inside was a dark church dug out of the rock. It was full of rubble and rubbish, and the German couple didn't seem very impressed. Emine, my neighbour, looked a bit disappointed in that. She told me, in Turkish, that some of the tourists she shows in here go 'Ooh, aah' when they see it. The German man asked how old the church was and I translated the question to Emine. I translated the reply that it was around a thousand years old.

Emine then asked the tourist couple if they wanted to see her cave house. They said they did and I went too, at the request of Emine, in order to translate. Through Emine's front door we came out onto the terrace and the German couple marvelled at the view over the village and the Göreme valley. Emine then led us into a sort of make-shift cave kitchen and sat us down and offered us grapes, saying that they had come from her sister's garden. A conversation about family then ensued with me translating. Emine asked the Germans if they had any children and they replied that they had three. Emine explained that she got divorced when her daughter was three years old and her parents said that she could come and live in the family's old cave house. Her parents had died twelve and fifteen years ago. Emine asked the couple if they liked Göreme and they said that they did. Emine said that when she's coming home from town on the bus sometimes there are tourists on the bus and she notices them being taken aback by the view as they come down into the Göreme valley. She said that the Göreme people were used to the views.

As we sat in the cave kitchen eating grapes, the conversation got difficult for a while. Emine started talking at length about the Göreme mayors and how some had done a lot for tourism and some had not. I translated when I got a chance but was aware that our talk was becoming too in-depth and boring for the Germans. The Germans tried to make conversation with me too by telling me where they had travelled in Australia. Emine couldn't understand and she countered this with a long rant about local politics. The German couple began to look very bored. I jumped up and suggested to Emine that we show the tourists some more rooms.

We went into a beautiful arch-roofed room, the room normally used for receiving guests. In there, Emine immediately emptied the contents of a plastic bag onto the floor. She invited the German woman to sit down and have a look at the pile of headscarfs and knitted socks now on the floor. The couple suddenly became quieter, perhaps starting to sense that the whole thing had been about selling. I felt embarrassed. I knew that Emine would bring out some handicrafts at some point in the hope of selling them but she had done so entirely without grace and had not, I felt, yet given the tourist couple an 'experience' to draw them in and to balance the obligation to buy something. The German woman picked slowly through the pile and said to me 'Well, I suppose I have to buy one now'. I felt even more embarrassed: maybe the Germans were disappointed in me as well now and thought that I was colluding with Emine and was going to get a cut for myself. I tried to make a middle ground for myself, between being a bit surprised at what Emine had done, but also showing that I had semi-expected this to happen. I felt compelled to side with the tourists and to try to rescue their experience of Emine and her house. I attempted to make the headscarves more interesting by asking Emine how she had done the different designs of the crocheted and beaded borders and then translating for the Germans. Emine then said that, because the borders had different levels of difficulty, they varied in price, and she listed the rather high prices of the different designs. The German woman, seemingly reluctantly, chose one to buy – a light blue one costing fifteen lira. She took out a twenty lira note and Emine went off to find change. Now that Emine was out of the room the German woman turned to me and said 'Well, I suppose they have to make money somehow'. I agreed and reiterated the fact that Emine was divorced and had had to raise her daughter on her own. The Germans agreed but also laughed as if to show resignation to the fact that they had also been duped by Emine.

Compelled to now take over the situation and try to help the Germans have more of an experience in exchange for their purchase, I suggested that we look at more of the house and particularly the food storage cave as I thought that would be of interest to them. This cave had some large waist-high storage pots inside. The Germans asked what was in the pots and so I showed them and explained that that is how the villagers store their dry products such as bulgur wheat and dried chickpeas throughout the winter. I asked Emine if she had made the bulgur wheat herself and she replied that no, she had bought it. I tried to make it more interesting for the Germans by telling them that many of the village women make many of these food items themselves, growing and processing the bulgur wheat, making their own vinegar and then pickling the vegetable produce from their gardens to use throughout the winter. I told them how women form groups to make huge piles of flatbread which they also store in the caves for use through the winter. The Germans were becoming more interested, and so I tried to engage Emine with their interest by asking her when she would be making her bread this year. She replied that she didn't make bread herself because it makes her back ache. I didn't translate her reply to the tourists.

Moving towards the exit of the house we went back out onto the terrace. The man took some photographs of the view and the house. He wanted a photo with Emine so I took one of them all with his camera. The man's wife then asked him to go back inside and take a picture of the cave-kitchen. He did that and meanwhile Emine showed the German woman how to wear her new headscarf Göreme-style. Just as we were leaving the house, Emine's teenage daughter arrived home. Emine pointed to her and said to the Germans 'This is my child', which I translated. The daughter protested and said 'I'm not a child'. I translated that also. Everyone laughed and for a brief moment there was a sense of mutual understanding, with the German's already having told us that they had three grown-up children themselves.

The German couple and I said goodbye and thank you and walked off down the lane. The man said 'Very interesting, it's not often you get to see inside people's houses'. The woman agreed, 'Yes, that was very interesting'. As we passed the ruined church the man said that maybe Emine should clean the church up a bit and put in some lights and then she could invite lots of tourists and charge them two lira entrance and then she would make much more money than with the headscarves. The man's wife and I laughed in agreement and then, as we reached the square by the mosque, the woman, still wearing the headscarf, looked at her reflection in a car window and gestured to acknowledge how silly she looked. I said 'You look very Turkish', laughing. We exchanged pleasantries and wished each other enjoyable travels while she untied the headscarf to take it off, and then we parted.

Reflecting on the Encounter

Emine frequently invites passing tourists in to look at her cave-house in the hope of selling them handicraft items. During the past few years Göreme women have increasingly engaged in this form of informal entrepreneurial activity, capitalizing on the apparent tourist interest in their cave-dwelling way of life. Indeed, the residential backstreets of the village have come to represent for tourists something akin to a living museum, with tourists wandering through the narrow winding streets looking for what they consider to be the 'traditional' elements of Göreme life; cave-houses, donkeys and carts, and villagers going about their daily lives (Tucker 2003). The desire to interact with 'traditional' locals has been argued to arise out of a tourist search for the 'authentically social' (Selwyn 1996; Tucker 2003). Indeed, in Tucker (2003) I pointed out that: 'There is the idea here that the premodern authentically social lifestyle perceived by tourists to be lived in Göreme will somehow rub off on them, easing them from the tensions, stresses and monotony of their "rat-race" life at home' (ibid.: 65). Furthermore, I also noted in Tucker (2003) the importance of serendipitous events to 'traveller' tourists because, when incorporated into their travel stories, such chance encounters serve to individualize their experience and identity. The fact that the encounter described above was serendipitous for the tourists, therefore, meant that it held much promise right from the start.

The encounter also relates to what Harrison (2003) describes as the tourist desire to experience human connection, sociability and intimacy. Drawing upon Harrison's arguments allows us to see beyond the tourist quest to experience the difference and perceived 'tradition' in Göreme in order to recognize that the

German couple's acceptance of Emine's invitation might also have contained elements of Simmel's ([1910] 1971) 'sociability impulse'; the desire for human connections as 'simply ends in themselves' (Harrison 2003: 46). This recognition, in turn, allows us to see that whilst tourist desire in this type of encounter might on the one hand be 'closely entwined with the imperial project and colonialism' (Pritchard and Morgan 2007: 21), the encounter also displays from the outset a certain 'willingness of both parties to engage in some form of connection' (Harrison 2003: 47).

However, the problematic nature of this encounter exposes the precariousness of the possibility for that connection. The way that the encounter unfolded appeared to throw into question, for the tourists at least, whether Emine also had any desire for a 'human connection', that is beyond a commercial transaction. But the precariousness of the encounter also throws into question the ability of local 'hosts' to understand, and thus to meet, the desires and expectations of the tourist 'other'. Emine did not appear to really know what it was the tourists might be seeking in their acceptance of her invitation, and she therefore seemed unable, on her own at least, to provide a satisfactory experience for them. She brought out grapes for us to share rather than offer tea, since Turkish tea takes a long time to brew and so is usually only offered to 'real' guests and connotes an invitation to stay a long while. It seemed that this encounter was never intended by either party to go on for too long. The hospitality in offering the grapes was received graciously by the tourists, but Emine's inability, or unwillingness, to make conversation more light-hearted than local politics appeared to alienate her guests. So too, clearly, did the way that she approached the handicraft-selling part of the encounter. I felt that Emine had presented the goods too directly, and brashly, and had not yet 'earned' the sale through providing an adequate experience of her cave-house and, indeed, of herself; she had not succeeded in enchanting them yet. That is why I felt compelled to try to smooth over the sale exchange, and then to spend more time showing the tourists some of the aspects of Emine's life that I anticipated were suitably 'different' from the tourists' lives.

At the end of the encounter the tourists did seem to feel that they had achieved something in getting 'backstage' into a villager's house. They certainly had a few photographs around which to form a good story once back in Germany (it is intriguing to consider how they have indeed told of this encounter since their return home). There were also some short moments of mutual understanding, such as the shared laughter regarding parental relationships and also the potential sense of embodied (gendered) togetherness when Emine tied the scarf on the German woman's head. However, the suggestion made by the man as we walked away from Emine's house concerning Emine selling tickets to enter the church implied that the couple had, overall, summarized the encounter as Emine embarking primarily on a commercial transaction. Emine had done little to enchant them into thinking otherwise.

Upon reflection, I am led to wonder how Emine could have been expected to know what it was the tourists were seeking in accepting the invitation to visit her house. Having never travelled herself, how could she know that tourists 'have always sought the unknown, the difference of alterity from which they were able first to observe, then to construe, the lives of others' (Kuhn 2002)? Furthermore, and again because of never having travelled herself, how could she know what aspects of her life are 'different' for tourists? How could she know that she perhaps ought not to let on to the tourists who visit her house that she buys her bulgur wheat and bread in town rather than making such items herself? Then again, how might the encounter have proceeded if I had not objectified and essentialized Emine and her cave-dwelling life in the way that I had in my 'culture brokerage' role? In considering these questions, along with that of why women like Emine are lacking in success and knowledge in their entrepreneurial encounters with tourists, it will be useful to shift our attention to the relative success of the interactions between Göreme men and tourists.

Göreme Men's 'Connection' with Tourists

Göreme men have been interacting with tourists, and each other, in their tourism entrepreneurial activities for over twenty years. My earlier case study research on tourism development in Göreme (Tucker 2003) drew the general conclusion that the pattern of small and micro tourism business development in Göreme had led to positive local (male) entrepreneurship which in turn led to direct economic benefits for the local community, as well as a positive host–guest relationship between tourists and their male 'hosts'. Being small businesses, the *pansiyons*, restaurants, sightseeing and activity agencies are mostly owned and run by one or two local men, with the owner-operators usually employing a 'boy' (often a younger relative of the owner-operator) to conduct the house-keeping and kitchen work. The businesses have therefore not only become 'male spaces', but also places where the local men directly interact with and 'host' their tourist guests.

Through their close and often fairly prolonged interaction with tourists the men have become rich in know-how concerning tourists' imaginings of the place and of themselves. They have consequently become not only highly competent in playing to those imaginings, but they also seem able to play with them, frequently engaging in ironic performances and caricatures of the tourists' images of themselves as cave-dwellers (see discussion of the Flintstones performances for tourists in Tucker 2002; 2003: 169–80). I always observed the men's high level of competence when it came to dealing with tourists, entertaining them and reflexively playing to tourist expectations of them as the Turkish 'other', whilst at the same time emerging from those expectations by somehow altering the power dynamic encoded in them.

Clearly, though, the tourists' imaginings of the Göreme men in the tourism businesses is quite different from their expectations of what they might experience in relation to the Göreme women in their cave-dwelling context. In the tourism businesses such as the *pansiyons* and restaurants, tourists do not so actively seek to experience the 'real' cave-people of Göreme since they do not expect to find the 'real' in the tourism realm (Tucker 2003). Perhaps, then, it is because they are not objectified and essentialized to the same degree as the Göreme women in the first place, that the men have an easier task of negotiating tourists' expectations and meeting their desire for 'human connection'.

However, it is also undoubtedly because the Göreme men who work in tourism have had plentiful opportunity for repeated and prolonged interactions with tourists in the *pansiyons* and other businesses, as well as through their ability to observe each other interacting with tourists and thereby share their tourism know-how, that the men have such understanding and skill. Indeed, the Göreme men evoke Hannerz's (1990: 239) notion of cosmopolitanism, as marked by 'a personal ability to make one's way into other cultures, through listening, looking, intuiting and reflecting' as well as a 'built-up skill of manoeuvring through systems of meanings' (Vertovec and Cohen 2002: 13). This contrasts significantly from the situation of Göreme women in their interactions with tourists, as illustrated in the encounter described above.

Göreme Women's Limited Connection

Tucker (2003) outlined the conservative Islamic ideology of gender separation in Göreme, rendering tourism business and tourism space the male domain, whilst women, on the whole, have been kept separate from tourism activity. Indeed, the gendered demarcation between a 'public' and a 'domestic' sphere discussed in feminist anthropology (e.g., Ardener 1981; Buitelaar 1998; Rosaldo and Lamphere 1974) as well as cultural geography (Blunt and Rose 1994; Massey 1994; Mills 2005) often plays an important part in boundary maintenance related to gender-specific activities. Göreme women have generally only been able to access the tourism economy indirectly through the earnings of their husband or other male family members, as they have remained separated from tourism business and continued to engage in garden-agriculture and other 'household' and reproductive duties.

During the past few years, however, increasing numbers of women, such as Emine, have started to engage in informal entrepreneurial activity by inviting tourists in to view their cave-houses and attempting to sell them handicrafts (Tucker 2007). This process started in the 1990s with a small number of women who were living on the outskirts of the village having arrangements with tour guides to bring their bus groups of international tourists to their houses, and then the tourists being shown a selection of handicrafts in the hope that they would buy some. Now there are many women living in the more central, older neighbourhoods of the village who have also started inviting passing tourists into their cave-houses.

The women engaging in this type of entrepreneurial activity acknowledge that they would not be able to work in tourism without doing this sort of activity because they could not work in the 'public' sphere (Tucker 2007). Having their cave-house as an attraction and selling handicrafts from home therefore provides them with an opportunity to engage with the tourism economy and to earn some money of their own. Moreover, this informal activity allows these women to 'craft new selves', as Cone (1995) has earlier described it in relation to informal female entrepreneurs in Chiapas in Mexico. Cone also adds a spatial reference to this process of crafting new selves in that she describes the women's participation in tourist craft production as 'stepping outside': 'they "step outside" their domestic spheres – out onto public squares and thoroughfares, social settings that had previously been closed to them' (Cone 1995: 315). The Göreme women who engage in these entrepreneurial activities are also 'stepping outside', but rather than going *out* onto public squares and thoroughfares to do so, they are bringing the public realm *in* to their cave-homes. These entrepreneurial activities are thus working to reconfigure 'domestic' space in its use for economic gain, and are also challenging the ways that gender identities are performed within that space (Tucker 2007; 2009b).

However, it is precisely because these women, in contrast to Göreme men, remain relatively isolated in the confinement of their tourism entrepreneurial activities to 'domestic' space, that they are less able to acquire knowledge of tourist imagination and expectation and thus to learn the 'soft things' (Puwar 2004: 110) that would enable them to be successful in their interactions with tourists. Interactions such as the encounter described above not only necessitate these women negotiating the tourist 'Other', but the process of 'crafting the self' also becomes a negotiation between representing a 'traditional' identity for tourists and yet at the same time emerging from that identity. Such complex negotiations surely require the level of repeated and prolonged interactions with tourists that the Göreme men have been able to have, as well as the opportunity to 'be' in tourism spaces and therefore to observe others' skills and successes in tourist encounters. It is only through such exposure to tourism interactions that the men are able to build up that necessary skill of 'manoeuvring through systems of meanings', as Vertovec and Cohen (2002: 13) refer to it.

It is because of Göreme women's restricted access to the public tourism realm and thus tourism knowledge, then, that they remain limited in their ability to have successful interactions with tourists. Consequently, many people in the village consider the tourism activities of these women to be problematic. A Göreme man who owns a cave hotel situated in the street beyond Emine's house has said that he wished Emine and her neighbours would stop approaching 'his' tourist guests in this way because it disturbs them and makes them feel uncomfortable. He frequently hears stories from his guests similar to the one told above, with the tourists pleased about having been into an 'authentic' village cave-house but also feeling duped by the woman who invited them in when she then clearly expected them to buy her handicraft items. I have also reported on tourists' experiences of such encounters in my previous work on tourism in Göreme (Tucker 2003). Moreover, other Göreme women in the same neighbourhoods, women who have enough financial security themselves to not need to try to sell handicrafts to tourists, criticise the women who invite tourists into their homes for giving a bad impression of the neighbourhood.

Hence the continued isolation of women like Emine in their entrepreneurial endeavours. In turn this compounds women's inability to become more skilled and more successful in turning the prosaic space of their homes into enchanted space for their tourist guests. Success in the tourist encounter is in the expectations, experiences and desires being continuously, performatively negotiated (Crouch 2005). However, whilst the Göreme men have long since figured this point out and are now highly capable of charming, hosting and entertaining tourists with just the right blend of 'the traditional' and the touristic, women like Emine are cut off from this knowledge.

Conclusion

By focusing in on one particular tourism encounter in Göreme, this discussion has highlighted the importance of access to tourism knowledge and the associated ability to anticipate tourist desire. The problematic nature of the encounter exposed the limited ability of Göreme women to understand the desires and expectations of the tourist 'other', an understanding that might enable them to more successfully meet the tourists', as well as their own, desires. In contrast, the Göreme men, who in their entrepreneurial tourism activities have been interacting with tourists and each other in the tourism spaces of Göreme for twenty years, are highly competent in playing both to and with tourists' imaginings of the place and of themselves. The built-up skill of the men highlights the necessity of having repeated interactions with tourists in order to develop skill at both reading tourist desire and responding to it. Göreme women, by comparison, have only recently started to enter tourism spaces and engage in activities from which they have previously been excluded, and they are also relatively isolated in the confinement of their tourism entrepreneurial activities to domestic space. The women are therefore less able to acquire knowledge of tourist imagination and expectation, and are also therefore far less able to develop the skill to negotiate these encounters successfully.

In order to enchant their tourist guests, not only must 'hosts' acquire knowledge of tourist imagination and expectation but they must also learn the 'tacit requirements' (Bourdieu 1984) or 'soft things' that are necessary to enable them to entrap tourists in their hosting intentionalities. These 'soft things' are necessarily embodied skills that can only, it seems, develop through participation in repeated and varied interactions with tourists, as well as having the opportunity to observe the varied skills, successes and non-successes of other 'hosts' in their tourist encounters. This is what is required for hosts to develop knowledge and skill in being able to perform 'difference' whilst simultaneously emerging from it in their developing of new forms of human connection and thus new forms of cultural expression.

My discussion here also leads me to reflect on my own role in this encounter. The uncomfortable nature of the encounter for me led to my positioning myself as go-between or 'culture broker' in an effort to ease my own discomfort and also to try to make the interaction a success for all parties. I felt that I had a reasonable grasp of what Emine's needs and desires were from the interaction (she had been overjoyed when we moved into the house next door, expecting her close contact with us to be an opportunity to benefit financially by helping us out with cooking and cleaning). Similarly, I think I had a reasonable idea of the desires and expectations of the tourists after having spent time with and interviewing so many of them in Göreme during my previous fieldwork there (Tucker 2003). Moreover, my own desires and expectations in 'doing ethnography' in Göreme have most likely never been too far removed from 'doing tourism' in Göreme.

This is where I, and other outsiders like me, become potentially major players in this scenario. By having me as her neighbour and forming a friendship with me, Emine was able to use me and my relative knowledge of tourist desire to mediate the tourists' experience on this occasion. There are now also many other 'foreigners', and many of them women, staying long-term in Göreme, having bought and renovated a cave-house for themselves and becoming resident in Göreme either permanently or for part of the year. Just as the Chiapas women described by Cone (1995: 322), via their friendships with Cone, an anthropologist, and other resident expatriates, became expert at 'putting foreigners at ease' and providing 'ethnic tourists with *entré* into Mayan culture', perhaps by forming relationships with resident foreign (tourist/anthropologist) women the Göreme women might be able, through their embodied 'connections' with them, not only to learn something about the 'difference' that tourists are seeking, but also to recognize tourists' simultaneous desire for human connection across cultural boundaries.

Hence, as well as highlighting important issues concerning the politics of success in the tourist–local encounter, this chapter also raises questions concerning the ethnographer's place in this touristic milieu and about what the ethnographer's role might be in the politics of success in tourism. Analyses of tourism encounters in this way are indeed examples of the potentially rich anthropological studies of the contemporary that Holmes and Marcus describe which incorporate 'both communities of often elite discourse and communities of often subaltern subjects' (2005: 1103). Of course, as anthropologists we are often members of the communities of elite discourse. Therefore, this consideration of success and non-success in meeting the expectations of others reveals not only something of the subtleties of what tourism meetings entail but also questions regarding our own anthropological positioning relating to discrepancies between different hosts' abilities in the art of tourist enchantment.

Notes

1. This encounter is described here more or less as it was written in my fieldnotes during fieldwork I conducted in Göreme, in the Cappadocia region of Turkey, in 2005. The same extract from my fieldnotes is also used as the basis for an article published in *Tourism Geographies* (Tucker 2009a). That article draws heavily on the same fieldwork encounter in order to discuss the emotion of shame and its possibilities in both the tourism and ethnographic research encounter.

References

Ardener, S. (ed.). 1981. *Women and Space: Ground Rules and Social Maps*. London: Croom Helm.

Blunt, A. and G. Rose (eds). 1994. *Writing Women and Space: Colonial and Postcolonial Geographies*. New York: Guildford Press.

Bourdieu, P. 1984. *Distinction: A Social Critique of the Judgement of Taste*. London: Routledge and Kegan Paul.

Buitelaar, M. 1998. 'Public Baths as Private Places', in K. Ask and M. Tjomsland (eds), *Women and Islamization: Contemporary Dimensions of Discourse on Gender Relations*. Oxford: Berg, pp. 103–24.

Cone, C.A. 1995. 'Crafting Selves: The Lives of Two Mayan Women', *Annals of Tourism Research* 22(2): 314–27.

Crouch, D. 2005. 'Flirting with Space: Tourism Geographies as Sensuous/Expressive Practice', in C. Cartier and A. Lew (eds), *Seductions of Places: Geographical Perspectives on Globalization and Touristed Landscapes*. London: Routledge, pp. 23–35.

Delaney, C. 1991. *The Seed and the Soil – Gender and Cosmology in Turkish Village Society*. Berkeley: University of California Press.

Gell, A. 1998. *Art and Agency: an Anthropological Theory*. Oxford: Oxford University Press.

Hannerz, U. 1990. 'Cosmopolitans and Locals in World Culture', in M. Featherstone (ed.), *Global Culture: Nationalism, Globalisation and Modernity*. London: Sage, pp. 237–51.

Harrison, J. 2003. *Being a Tourist: Finding Meaning in Pleasure Travel*. Vancouver: UBC Press.

Holmes, D.R. and G.E. Marcus. 2005. 'Refunctioning Ethnography: The Challenge of an Anthropology of the Contemporary', in N. Denzin and Y. Lincoln (eds), *Handbook of Qualitative Research*, 3rd edn. London: Sage, pp. 1099–113.

Kuhn, L. 2002. 'Trusting Tourists: An Investigation into Tourism, Trust and Social Order', in G.M.S. Dann (ed.), *The Tourist as a Metaphor of the Social World*. Wallingford: CABI Publishing, pp. 109–20.

Lengkeek, J. 2002. 'A Love Affair with Elsewhere: Love as a Metaphor and Paradigm for Tourist Longing', in G.M.S. Dann (ed.), *The Tourist as a Metaphor of the Social World*. Wallingford: CABI Publishing, pp. 189–208.

Lippard, L. 1999. *On the Beaten Track: Tourism, Art and Place*. New York: The New Press.

Massey, D. 1994. *Space, Place and Gender*. Cambridge and Oxford: Polity Press.

Mills, S. 2005. *Gender and Colonial Space*. Manchester and New York: Manchester University Press.

Pritchard, A. and N. Morgan. 2007. 'De-centering Tourism's Intellectual Universe, or Traversing the Dialogue between Change and Tradition', in I. Ateljevic, A. Pritchard and N. Morgan (eds), *The Critical Turn in Tourism Studies: Innovative Research Methodologies*. Oxford: Elsevier, pp. 11–28.

Puwar, N. 2004. *Space Invaders: Race, Gender and Bodies Out of Place*. Oxford: Berg.

Rosaldo, M.Z. and L. Lamphere (eds). 1974. *Women, Culture, and Society*. Stanford, CA: Stanford University Press.

Selwyn, T. 1996. 'Atmospheric Notes from the Fields: Reflections on Myth-collecting Tours', in T. Selwyn (ed.), *The Tourist Image: Myths and Myth Making in Tourism*. New York and London: John Wiley and Sons Ltd., pp. 147–61.

Simmel, G. ([1910] 1971). 'Sociability', in D. Levine (ed.), *On Individuality and Social Forms*. Chicago: University of Chicago Press, pp. 127–40.

Thomas, N. 2001. 'Introduction', in C. Pinney and N. Thomas (eds), *Beyond Aesthetics: Art and the Technologies of Enchantment*. Oxford: Berg, pp. 1–12.

Tucker, H. 2002. 'Welcome to Flintstones-Land: Contesting Place and Identity in Göreme, Central Turkey', in S. Coleman and M. Crang (eds), *Tourism: Between Place and Performance*. Oxford: Berghahn Books, pp. 143–59.

Tucker, H. 2003. *Living With Tourism: Negotiating Identities in a Turkish Village*. London: Routledge.

Tucker, H. 2007. 'Undoing Shame: Tourism and Women's Work in Turkey', *Journal of Tourism and Cultural Change* 5(2): 87–105.

Tucker, H. 2009a. 'Recognising Emotion and its Postcolonial Potentialities: Discomfort and Shame in the Tourism Encounter in Turkey', *Tourism Geographies* 11(4): 444–61.

Tucker, H. 2009b. 'The Cave-homes of Göreme: Performing Tourism Hospitality in Gendered Space', in P. Lynch, A. McIntosh and H. Tucker (eds), *Commercial Homes in Tourism: An International Perspective*. London: Routledge, pp. 127–37.

Vertovec, S. and R. Cohen. 2002. 'Introduction: Conceiving Cosmopolitanism', in S. Vertovec and R. Cohen (eds), *Conceiving Cosmopolitanism: Theory, Context and Practice*. Oxford: Oxford University Press, pp. 1–22.

Chapter 3
EMBERÁ INDIGENOUS TOURISM AND THE WORLD OF EXPECTATIONS

Dimitrios Theodossopoulos

Introduction

Parara Puru, an Emberá community in the Chagres National Park in Panama, is a site where tourists from economically powerful nations have an opportunity to experience aspects of an Amerindian culture. The tourists meet the Emberá inhabitants of the community in the context of half-day organized trips, during which the residents of Parara Puru offer a standard 'cultural package' that includes a music-and-dance presentation, a traditional meal, and a display of handmade Emberá artefacts. This cultural package is adaptable, and the Emberá hosts are prepared to provide extras to meet additional expectations at the request of their visitors: a tour in the rainforest, some guidance on Emberá medicinal knowledge or informal instruction on other aspects of indigenous lifestyle. In this respect, the varied and particular types of tourist encounter provide opportunities for the Emberá to investigate the expectations of their guests and, in an effort to satisfy those expectations, explore additional dimensions of their culture and enhance its representation.

In this chapter I am concerned with how the residents of Parara Puru investigate and anticipate the expectations of their tourists. I pay particular attention to questions asked by the tourists during the tourists' encounter – for example, those that indicate 'a quest for the authentic Indian' (Ramos 1998: 84) or an ambivalence about the position of indigenous people in the interface of tradition with modernity – and the attempts of the Emberá hosts to understand

and diplomatically answer those questions or meet the expectations inherent in them. I argue that the questions of the tourists, and the responses of the Emberá, can help us to explore the meeting ground of two interrelated processes: the development of indigenous cultural representation through tourism, and the growing Emberá awareness of the expectations of the outside world. The latter, the Emberá increasingly realize, have significantly changed, from stereotyping in the past, to idealized admiration in the present.

In all respects, the tourist expectations, as they are offered to the Emberá, are diverse and often contradictory. Some tourists take to the cultural distinctiveness of the Emberá and implicitly encourage a strong adherence to tradition at the exclusion of modernity, an attitude that reflects a nostalgia for the idealized 'vanishing savage' and lost worlds unaffected by (Western) civilizing processes (Clifford 1986; Rosaldo 1989; see also Conklin and Graham 1995; Gow 2007). Others are prepared to see the Emberá as inhabitants of the modern globalized world, people who maintain their identity, but share the benefits, predicaments and technologies of the modern era. Finally, a few non-indigenous Panamanian visitors are happy to realize that the Emberá share common tastes and experiences as citizens of the same nation, and are not so different to them after all. Contradictory expectations such as these encourage the Emberá to slightly underplay or accentuate their cultural difference in their attempts to guide their visitors to varied, well-known, or sometimes unexplored dimensions of their culture.

Overall, the engagement of the Emberá with tourism, and their attempts to understand and anticipate the tourist expectations, has inspired a process of self-reevaluation of Emberá culture, providing new opportunities for the Emberá to improvise and experiment with their cultural representation. In this process, the question of what is authentic has become a topic of concern among the residents of Parara Puru, and the tourist encounter an opportunity to rediscover, reflect upon and reconstitute their indigenous traditions (Abram, Waldren and Macleod 1997). As has been attested by an impressive number of anthropological contributions (see among many, Bruner 2005; Coleman and Crang 2002; Abram, Waldren and Macleod 1997; Selwyn 1996; Boissevain 1996), local conceptualizations of authenticity are undoubtedly shaped through the interaction of expectations in the tourist encounter. In fact, some indigenous communities manifest a remarkable adaptability in taking advantage of the desire of Western audiences to consume authentic 'native' culture. They often recombine and reinterpret old elements of their tradition, or introduce new elements, to produce innovative cultural adaptations or enhance their representation. This has evidently been the case with several Panamanian ethnic groups (cf. Pereiro Pérez 2010; Howe 2009; Velásquez Runk 2009; Guerrón-Montero 2006a, 2006b; Young and Bort 1999; Tice 1995; Taussig 1993; Swain 1989; Salvador 1976).

The following sections focus on the interaction of expectations in the tourist encounter as this takes place in Parara Puru.[1] First I describe how the inhabitants of the community became involved with tourism and how they put into use their culturally embodied knowledge to create an ideal setting for fulfilling tourist expectations. Then I examine how the Emberá in Parara Puru are curious to learn more about their guests and how they obtain an understanding of their guests' expectations through the exploratory questions asked by the tourists. I pay special attention to some questions that reflect ambivalence in the resulting expectations – such as questions about the local code of dress or the use of computers – and add an additional level of complexity to contradictions already experienced by the Emberá, independently of tourism (e.g., indigeneity vs. modernity). Finally, I focus on the cultural improvisation encouraged by the growing awareness of the tourist expectations, and resulting cultural adaptations that involve experimentation or spontaneous deviation from established form. As we shall see in the ethnography that follows, the negotiation of expectations during the tourism exchange in Parara Puru is a dynamic and creative process that has inspired creative adaptations to diverse and contradictory tourist expectations.

An Ideal Setting to Fulfil Tourist Expectations

Surrounded by dense rainforest, and approachable only by canoe, Parara Puru looks at first sight like an isolated community forgotten by time and untouched by modernity. From the point of view of the Western visitor the community emerges out of the lavish vegetation of the Chagres National Park as a small island of inhabited space within an ocean of green. This inhabited space, however, gives the impression of having emerged 'naturally' out of the forest. The wooden, thatched roofed houses blend with the overwhelming naturalness of the surrounding environment, and the bird songs mix with the sound of cumbia-Emberá music, performed by the local inhabitants to welcome incoming groups of visitors. In tune with the music, the relaxed but joyful disposition of the residents of Parara Puru – who walk slowly to meet the tourists, dressed in traditional attire – resonates with Rousseau-ian representations of a seemingly true and authentic life away from the tribulations of Western civilization.

The notion of authenticity in Western imagination has been associated, under the formative influence of Rousseau, with expectations of sincerity, primordial integrity, paradisiacal innocence and purity (Bendix 1997; Lindholm 2008). 'Simple' or 'native' cultures – such as the indigenous peoples of the contemporary world – have been and are still perceived as sharing those qualities in plenty. The rise of popular ecology in the latter part of the twentieth century increased the appeal of the earlier Rousseau-ian vision, idealizing indigenous communities as being closer to nature or encapsulating the primordial essence of ecological wisdom (Morris 1981; Ellen 1986; Conklin and Graham 1995; Milton 1996: 109–14; West and Carrier 2004). In Western discourse, romanticized images of life in the tropics often combine with the critique of modernity, the message of environmentalists, and old colonial narratives of voyages of discovery. An idealized perception of tropical Panama in particular, as Frenkel (1996) explains, has developed since the late nineteenth century, fuelling North American imagination with Edenic images of the Panamanian rainforest.[2]

Drawing elements from idyllic representations of life in the tropics, or from the environment-friendly depictions of indigenous communities in popular ecology, the tourist agencies that organize day-excursions to the Emberá communities in Chagres advertise the beauty of the local environment along with the excitement of meeting one of Panama's indigenous 'tribes'. In tourism advertisements, the Emberá are represented as people with knowledge of the rainforest, who live – and have always lived – in harmony with it. And indeed, the Emberá are people who possess a great deal of knowledge about the rainforest, the result of a long history of living in ecosystems similar to that of Chagres National Park. Although their cultural adaptations, like those of all human groups, involve a certain degree of control over the natural environment, their lifestyle and material culture easily fits within the conceptual framework of the tourists' expectations. Independently of their engagement with tourism, the Emberá in Chagres are, undeniably, dwellers of the rainforest, and in this respect, are sincere when they present themselves to the tourists in those terms.

The inhabitants of Parara Puru do not have to go out of their way to present the tourists with an experience of an indigenous culture in the rainforest. Their village is a real inhabited indigenous community, the home of approximately twenty Emberá families. The houses – all built on stilts, according to Emberá custom – and the surrounding environment bear the mark of continuous habitation, as new structures and pathways emerge organically to meet the requirements of the local inhabitants. Old dwellings are continuously repaired or replaced by new ones, while electric appliances are gradually incorporated into the community's family houses alongside the more traditional fire hearths. In the spaces around their houses, the residents of the community have planted trees and flowers with recognizable cultural significance or use, which mark the domestication – the Emberization – of the local environment (cf. Herlihy 1986; Kane 2004).

Parara Puru is a new Emberá community, but all Emberá communities are relatively new. Until forty or fifty years ago the Emberá favoured a dispersed pattern of settlement, according to which clusters of Emberá families, often related by kinship, built their houses alongside the rivers that served, and are still used, as communication arteries through the rainforest. To search for better opportunities, and avoid external threats or internal quarrels, the Emberá often disassembled the wooden components of their houses to rebuild them in new and more favourable locations. Following this general strategy of dispersion and migration (Williams 2005), the Emberá expanded from the region of Choco in Lowland Colombia to the province of Darien in Eastern Panama where they established a strong presence alongside other groups such as the Kuna and the

Afrodarienitas (see Kane 2004). In the last sixty years, a smaller number of Emberá families migrated further westward into the areas surrounding the river Bayano and – closer to the Canal – the river Chagres.

In Chagres, the Emberá originally followed their traditional preference for dispersed settlement. The foundation of spatially concentrated communities was part of a much wider process which began in Darien in the 1950s and was encouraged by the government in the 1970s and 1980s (see Kane 2004; Herlihy 1986, 2003; Velásquez Runk 2009). Most of the new concentrated communities were formed around newly built primary schools that the government established in the newly founded communities. In Chagres, the Emberá took under consideration the idea of setting up concentrated communities after the establishment of a National Park in 1985. The regulations of the Chagres Park prohibited hunting and systematic cultivation, but the proximity of Chagres to the Canal and Panama City made possible the growth of tourism activities. Panamanian NGOs, supported by the Ministry of Tourism, assisted the Emberá with developing the necessary infrastructure to receive tourists, while a number of tourist agencies, also based in the City, undertook the task of advertising and organizing day trips to the Emberá communities in Chagres.

The success of the tourism-experiment was immediate and profitable to both the Emberá and the tourist agents. Parara Puru, one of the three Emberá communities built on the banks of the river Chagres, was founded nine years ago by an initial core-group of Emberá who were born in the vicinity and wanted to work full-time in tourism. They established a small but vibrant and economically successful community, which, despite its orientation towards tourism, should not be viewed as a tourist enclave: the community's spaces and their aesthetics are not completely 'regulated, commodified and privatised' (Edensor 1998: 47); there is an absence of high-end tourist facilities, while the majority of houses within the community are the permanent residences of the local families and subject to unregulated readjustments. The focal points of the tourism activity are two large communal houses, where the greater part of the cultural presentations take place, although the tourists are free to walk around the community but without entering individual family homes. Tourist groups range from as large as ninety to a hundred visitors, to as small as two or three independent travellers.

The great majority of tourists that visit Parara Puru come from inclusive resorts or cruise-ships passing through the Canal area. They reach Chagres by bus, and are accompanied by guides who gently supervise them for the duration of the trip. In Lake Alajuela, which is fed by the river Chagres, they board motorized canoes navigated by Emberá men in traditional attire. This is their first glimpse of the Emberá. Before entering the community, the canoe navigators take those groups that have more time at their disposal to the nearby waterfalls where some tourists have an opportunity to swim and walk in the rainforest. After this sensually overwhelming experience, the tourists reach Parara Puru, and are welcomed by its inhabitants at the disembarkation point. Following a small break to take photographs – the Emberá of Parara Puru do not shy away from the camera – the tourists are accompanied to communal houses where they admire or buy Emberá artefacts (at a good price, in comparison to the markets in the City) and are offered a meal of fish and fried plantains served inside a folded palm leaf.

The standard presentation to tourists in Parara Puru also includes a speech by one of the leaders of the community that provides basic information about the community, the traditional methods of constructing artefacts, and the amount of labour invested in this process. This is followed by a music and dance performance, the most visually compelling part of the cultural presentation. First the women of Parara Puru dance a couple of traditional animal-dances – imitating the movements of different natural species each time – and then, men and women form pairs and dance cumbia-Emberá and rumba-Emberá,[3] inviting the tourists to join in the dance. The dance performance culminates in a spontaneous 'party', as tourist adults and children from diverse cultural backgrounds are united for a short time by the cheerful sound of rumba-Emberá.

Before the beginning of the dance, the tourists have the opportunity to ask the Emberá questions which the guides translate. Through those questions the Emberá gradually accumulate knowledge about the expectations of their audience. As I will describe in the following sections, the residents of Parara Puru are still learning how to decode and accommodate the complexity of those expectations. This process of decoding is for most of them a long-term undertaking. In the short term, however, and during the duration of the tourists' visit, they remain prepared to answer questions or provide assistance. Some tourists, for example, might request a guided walk around the community, or in the forest, or ask for some informal instruction in Emberá indigenous knowledge. The Emberá of Parara Puru will fulfil most requests of that type, and remain attentive to the tourists' needs until they see them off at the embarkation point in the early afternoon. Most tourists depart from Parara Puru worn out from the tropical heat, but exhilarated from the experience.

Investigating Each Other's Expectations

The inhabitants of Parara Puru became involved with the tourism economy approximately twelve years ago, in the period immediately preceding the foundation of their community in its current composition and location. Although they are comparatively new to tourism, they have already accumulated considerable experience, and appear to control the tourism encounter with confidence. The interaction with new groups of tourists, however, remains an open-ended process and often involves small, unexpected challenges. There are always new questions the tourists ask in a sincere desire to learn about the Emberá, or sometimes in a deliberate attempt to uncover alleged inauthentic dimensions of their indigenous life. In this section I will give attention to some of these questions in an attempt to highlight an important stage in the negotiation of expectations during the tourist encounter.

First, I should clarify that the Emberá in Parara Puru, like in most other Emberá communities, do not speak languages other than Spanish and Emberá. Their communication with the overwhelming majority of tourists who do not speak Spanish is made easier by the involvement of the tourist guides, who are employees of the agencies that bring the tourists to Chagres. The guides try to facilitate, when possible, the interaction between the Emberá and their guests, and translate into the tourists' language (English, French and, more rarely, Italian) the speeches delivered by one of the leaders of the community. 'The speech' (referred to by the Emberá as *explicación* or simply *charla*) is a standard part of the cultural package offered to the tourists: it is delivered in Spanish, includes an explanation of the various methods of Emberá artefact manufacture, and a short presentation on the history of the community. It is always followed by a question-and-answer session, during which members of the audience ask the Emberá speaker for further clarifications with the interpretative help of their tourist guides who often add – during translation – descriptive information or short comments that reveal their opinions.

I should stress at this point that although the visiting tourists readily assume the role of the audience, observing for the most part their hosts, the Emberá of Parara Puru have similar opportunities to observe their guests too. Through daily interaction, the Emberá recognize the ethnic categories of tourists that visit their community and some of their respective characteristics. Tourists from different nationalities behave differently, my respondents explain. Some, for example the North Americans, are likely to buy many artefacts; others, such as the French, fewer; and some, the Germans are a case in point, purchase almost none. German tourists, I was told (and this was verified by my own observations) enjoy walking in the back regions of the community, sometimes with their guides, but very often unsupervised – and have a tendency to break away from their group or 'get lost'! The Italian men, a couple of teenage Emberá girls explained, enjoy posing for photos with Emberá women, even though the women themselves sometimes find this attention uncomfortable.

The comments made by the Emberá about different ethnic groups of tourists represent a significant break away from the old Emberá practice of avoiding contact with the outside world, a strategy that protected the integrity of the Emberá culture but resulted in limited knowledge of the wider world. The introduction of tourism has facilitated the growth of a global awareness among the Emberá (Theodossopoulos 2010), and has instigated a curiosity about the ethnic background of the tourists and their respective countries. Very often, while waiting for the arrival of particular tourist groups, or sometimes just after their departure, young and old Emberá men and women would approach me with questions about countries such as England, France or Italy (from which they receive regular visitors). They are often interested in general information, such as demography, climate and language, or ask, in some cases, more particular questions, such as whether there are any indigenous people like themselves in those countries.

Tourists from Latin American countries can interact directly with the Emberá in Spanish, and ask questions, not only of the leaders who are delivering the speech, but also of any other member of the community. Some residents of Parara Puru, mostly men, but also a few women, are very comfortable with this type of interaction, while others are slightly, but always politely, reserved. Non-indigenous Panamanian visitors represent a small but significant category of Spanish-speaking tourists to whom the Emberá devote special care and attention. Most Emberá have been subjected to systematic stereotyping in the past due to their non-mainstream – and seen as 'not-fully-modernized' – identity. It is not surprising, then, that they are now very happy to receive some positive attention and recognition by their fellow-nationals who have started visiting the community as tourists. Apart from individual families of Panamanian tourists, Parara Puru regularly receives visits from Panamanian higher education institutions, which attempt to cultivate among their students a positive attitude towards the indigenous cultures of 'their' country.

The residents of Parara Puru take all questions seriously and attempt to give the best answer possible, no matter the nationality or size of the visiting group. The leaders of the community who deliver 'the speech' receive most of the questions, and are able to answer competently and diplomatically due to their skills they have developed from daily practice. Some questions asked by the tourists come from a curiosity to learn about particular dimensions of Emberá culture, while some others reflect an implicit desire to question the authenticity of Parara Puru as a truly indigenous community. The result of this type of question-and-answer interaction is a two-way negotiation of expectations that provides both parties – the tourists and the Emberá – with new information about each other's perspectives. In the following sections I will offer some detailed examples.

Tourist Questions and Expectations

It took me some time during my fieldwork to realize that the apparently simple questions the tourists ask – questions that some of my Emberá respondents and I treated as way too obvious – reflected complex tourist experiences and subjectivities. A good example is a question I have heard many times in different periods of my fieldwork: many tourists ask, in a short and straightforward manner, if the Emberá do, in real life, live in Parara Puru. The same question is sometimes phrased in a rather clumsy manner, such as 'do you live here in the forest all the time?' From the point of view of the Emberá, Parara Puru is, without any doubt, not part of the forest (which surrounds the community) but a very much inhabited, domesticated space. After the tourists' departure, some of my respondents have commented with apprehension on the possibility that some tourists have failed to realize that they in fact 'live here' (that is, in the community) and 'not in the forest'. In the presence of the tourist audience, however, they politely reply, that 'yes', indeed, they live here all the time, that is, 'in the *community* of Parara Puru'.

Behind this straightforward question, however, there often lies a more complicated tourist experience. Some well-travelled tourists have attended cultural presentations by other ethnic groups that take place in locations outside the indigenous community, such as sites of historic significance (see Bunten, this volume) or settings especially prepared for tourist performances. The well-travelled tourists are often aware that indigenous performers can travel to designated locations, often dressed in traditional costume, for the sole purpose of the tourism exchange (see Kirtsoglou and Theodossopoulos 2004). This comparative dimension in the critical thinking of some tourists is less obvious, but can become apparent during subsequent conversations with the tourists themselves. In many cases, the tourists' view represents a more widespread wariness towards the commoditized nature of pre-arranged cultural presentations.

This wariness is sometimes directly expressed with questions focusing on the Emberá attire. 'Do you wear these clothes all day?' or 'Are you dressed like this every day?' the tourists often ask. Some tourist guides welcome this type of probing question and, before translating into Spanish, they make small remarks like 'I am interested to know the answer to this question as well', or 'let us see how he [the Emberá leader] will answer this question'. On these occasions, the guides find an opportunity to implicitly stress their modern subjectivity – perceived as parallel to that of their clients – by underlining their ability to challenge the full extent of the Emberá adherence to tradition. The implication here is that the Emberá are not expected to maintain daily their traditional code of dressing in the modern world, according to which the upper part of the body is mostly uncovered, decorated only by body painting, necklaces and bracelets.

The Emberá leaders who deliver 'the speech' answer questions of this type with diplomatic honesty: they explain that the government does not allow them to venture outside of their communities in traditional attire. Non-indigenous Panamanians, they add, are also obliged (by law) to wear at least a T-shirt when they appear in public. They also explain that when the tourists depart, the inhabitants of the community take off their necklaces and bracelets to carry out their daily chores in a more comfortable manner. The women, some Emberá further clarify, wear their traditional skirts (*parumas*) all day, and often outside of the community. All these statements are true: as a matter of principle, the Emberá of Parara Puru rarely lie to enhance their self-representation. Yet, they will diplomatically avoid emphasizing the fact that men, women and children do wear T-shirts both within and outside the community, while men also wear shorts.

As I will further explain in the following section, the issue of 'what clothes the Emberá should wear' is a serious topic for debate even within the Emberá community. The questions of the tourists, however, reflect their perception of the Emberá as inhabiting an ambiguous position at the crossroads of tradition and modernity. There are additional types of questions the tourists ask that indirectly address this ambiguous position, such as for example questions about health and education. Most tourists are fascinated to hear about Emberá shamans (*Jaibanas*), their knowledge of the medicinal properties of plants and, more importantly, the degree to which contemporary Emberá rely on their care and advice. With respect to the last issue, they ask relevant questions and receive honest and direct answers. Some Emberá, the tourists are told, still rely on traditional medicine – sometimes, but not at all times; and yet, to solve more serious medical problems, they take conventional medicines and, if this is absolutely necessary, visit a medical centre or a hospital outside the community.

Questions about the education of the Emberá, as these are articulated by visiting tourists, often conceal the inadvertent recommendation that Emberá children living in the rainforest should not be deprived of educational opportunities. In this respect, and as I will further underline in the following section, the tourists' admiration of premodern cultural lifestyles gives way in the face of their modern values about education. The Emberá of Parara Puru share very similar pro-educational values, and answer these types of question without any ambivalence or hesitation, proudly stating that they have a primary school in the community and that they cherish the education of their children. An issue that is not always made directly obvious to the tourists, but that concerns the Emberá, is that the children of the latter receive education only in Spanish, as very few teachers are qualified to teach the Emberá language and there are currently only a few appropriate textbooks that teach Emberá.[4]

Other types of exploratory questions asked by the tourists in Parara Puru are, for the most part, less controversial, reflecting the traveller's ethnographic curiosity. For example, tourists frequently ask: 'Are you monogamous?' (Usual reply: 'yes'); 'Where do you find partners to marry?' (Usual reply: 'in neighbouring Emberá communities, or in Darien, where many Emberá live'); 'At what age do young people marry?' (Usual reply: 'girls at 16, boys a bit older, unless they want to continue their education'); 'How do young people have fun?' (Usual reply: sometimes in social gatherings in neighbouring Emberá and non-Emera communities, sometimes locally). When some of the same questions are asked by non-indigenous Panamanians, such as Panamanian students on an educational trip, the Emberá of Parara Puru might provide additional details to their answers, making more apparent to their interlocutors that they too live in the same nation and are not too different from them after all. For example, it is more openly admitted in these cases that many residents of Parara Puru go for entertainment to neighbouring non-Emberá communities, that apart from their own Emberá music they like to listen and dance to popular Panamanian musical genres (such as *tipico*); and that when they go to the hospital they have to show, like all Panamanian citizens, their national identity card.

Indigeneity with or without Modernity

As we have already seen, several of the questions that the tourists ask in Parara Puru indicate the ambivalence in the minds of the tourists about the position of the Emberá in the intersection of tradition and modernity. This ambivalence is noticeable in the negotiation of the expectations during the tourism encounter, and becomes more apparent in discussions about certain topics such as the issue of the Emberá traditional attire, and the possibility of introducing computers to the community. Both topics concern the Emberá independently of their interaction with tourists; but the tourists' expectations, as these are gradually communicated during the tourism exchange, add an extra level of complexity to such local concerns.

The issue of the Emberá attire – or, the issue of clothes or clothing (*vestidos*) – represents a broader topic of debate in the Emberá world. There are many Emberá women who feel uncomfortable with the old tradition of having their upper body exposed, covered solely by necklaces and body paint. This is, to a great extent, a response to accusations by non-Emberá Panamanians who associate the lack of clothes with inferior morals or values. Many Emberá women in comparatively inaccessible communities in Darien systematically cover their upper bodies with bras, T-shirts, or both, while they still prefer to cover their lower body with the traditional Emberá skirts (*parumas*). In Parara Puru however, where Emberá tradition is presented to groups of outsiders and is more confidently and systematically celebrated, most Emberá women still feel comparatively comfortable with the traditional Emberá attire.

However, a positive evaluation for the traditional Emberá code of dress is not only found in those communities that have developed tourism. Even in inaccessible Emberá communities, which do not receive tourists, there are some men and women who feel comfortable with fewer clothes and are not embarrassed by the topless-ness of the traditional attire. On the whole, the ambivalence of the Emberá about the question of the Emberá code of dress cuts across the tourism or lack-of-tourism divide, while supporters of all possible positions can be found among young and old. The introduction of tourism has added further complexity to the issue that often results in a three-way contradiction: (a) the social expectation to follow the values of the Panamanian nation and modernity, which clashes not only with (b) traditional practices, but also with (c) the expectation of the tourist audience that the Emberá should hold fast to traditional practices such as their code of dress.

This triple contradiction becomes more evident as the Emberá who engage with tourism gradually become, first, more confident about the value of their traditional practices, which are admired by Western visitors and, second, aware that the latter are pleased to see them in traditional attire, and expect from them adherence to this code of dress more generally, and not only in the context of cultural presentations. A Western preference for the traditional-*cum*-exotic code of dress informs similar dilemmas and contradictions faced by other indigenous groups in Latin America (see Conklin 1997; Gow 2007; Ewart 2007; Santos-Granero 2009). Among the tourists in particular, it is easy to distinguish those who pass judgement on the Emberá based on their suspicion that they dress inauthentically (appearing in traditional dress only for the duration of the cultural presentations), and those who are willing to accept the Emberá as people who can wear modern clothes without compromising their indigenous identity.

On one particular occasion, for example, a small group of Japanese visitors were thrilled to discover a 'made in Japan' label on the bottom edge of a *paruma* skirt. After hearing the explanatory comments made by their guide, they realized that, nowadays, this representatively Emberá type of clothing is manufactured in Asia specifically for the Emberá and according to Emberá specifications.[5] The Japanese tourists were even more thrilled to realise that despite its international record of manufacture, a *paruma* is quintessentially an Emberá garment worn by Emberá women within and outside their communities with the implicit intention of underlining their ethnic origin. The Japanese tourists' ability to accept the Emberá as inhabitants of a globalized world, without challenging their indigeneity, is representative of a significant number of tourists. Others maintain less flexible expectations and, like the examples I offered in the previous section, they question the degree to which the Emberá wear traditional clothes in their daily lives.

Similar contradictions emerge with respect to the introduction of computers in the Emberá community. When considering the use of computers, as with education more generally, several tourists are ready to depart from their exoticized expectation of indigenous people living without modern technology, in harmony with nature. More specifically, the image of young children learning how to use computers is associated with the ideal of education for all which appeals to most Western tourists. The idea of adult indigenous people using computers, however, represents an anomaly for some visitors to Parara Puru, who see the inhabited spaces of the community and its thatched-roof dwellings as an extension of the forest. The tourists would have been surprised to know that several inhabitants of Parara Puru are interested in computers and some are learning how to use them.

In 2008 I met a Peace Corps volunteer, Deborah Rockoff, who devoted a considerable amount of time and effort to teaching children and adults in Parara Puru basic computer skills. She used her own laptop for this purpose, while investigating the possibility of acquiring additional computers for the community's school and the community's main office. Some of the adult members of the community had already benefited from her help, learning how to keep the community's accounts in Microsoft Excel. The Emberá who participated in this experiment were enthusiastic and asked me additional questions about the Internet and the possibility of advertising the community through the Internet. They remained, however, somehow unsure about the impact that computer use might have on the profile of the community with respect to their perceived 'authenticitiy'. Their initial hesitation about what the tourists' opinion might be, allowed me to appreciate the degree to which a certain type of tourist expectation – namely the desire to meet an authentic indigenous community disconnected from the rest of the world – has already added a complex turn to the emerging strategies of Emberá cultural representation. In the section that follows, I will describe how problems of this type are often solved with improvisation and spontaneity, as the community of Parara Puru adapts to the challenges posed by the tourism economy.

Anticipation and Improvisation as a Response to Tourist Expectations

In a short period of approximately twelve years, the residents of Parara Puru have entered the economy of tourism dynamically. At first they learned how to carry out successful cultural performances. Then, through frequent practice, they started accumulating additional experience, gaining knowledge as to how to guide their guests, and inviting them to see the world from their point of view. They are now gradually moving away from the initial stage of hesitant experimentation with presenting facets of an Amerindian culture to an audience of Western tourists, and are slowly entering a more confident second stage of articulating the characteristics of their own cultural tradition to the non-Emberá world. This process of transformation does not merely enhance the representation of the Emberá culture, but also encourages and facilitates its enrichment with new cultural elements.

As my respondents in Parara Puru explained to me, tourism has provided them with an opportunity to spend more time practising their culture. They now devote more time to manufacturing Emberá artefacts, in much greater numbers, and in a greater variety of motifs and variations. They dance their traditional dances daily (as opposed to only on special occasions), and have more opportunities to perfect their talent as dancers or musicians in a much wider repertoire of dance and musical theme variations. They have also become skilled at better articulating the particularities of their culture, such as describing or explaining artefacts, buildings, elements of the physical and man-made environment, techniques of manufacture, cultural traditions and performances. Through practice and improvisation they contribute new elements to the wealth of their culture, opening new possibilities for being Emberá in the contemporary world.

To a significant extent this phase of cultural creativity is stimulated by the negotiation of expectations in the interaction with tourists. Day after day, the Emberá of Parara Puru learn how to anticipate some of the most usual questions the tourists ask, and improve their skill in giving precise, and when necessary, diplomatic answers. Foreign tourists and Panamanian non-indigenous visitors have slightly different expectations, and are likely to admire or criticize different aspects of the indigenous life. The Emberá hosts pay very careful attention to these subtle differentiations in the respective expectations of their guests, and adapt their narratives accordingly, stressing slightly different dimensions of their daily lives. For example, they might, to some small extent, underplay their differences with their Panamanian visitors in an attempt to demonstrate that they too are citizens of the same modern nation, or they might accentuate their cultural distinctiveness in front of North American audiences.

At the same time, however, they become aware that the expectations of the non-Emberá world are diverse and complex, and that this complexity can open up a whole new range of possibilities for the representation of the Emberá culture. For example, it is already apparent to most Emberá in Parara Puru that while, until twenty years ago, the non-indigenous Panamanian majority maintained a stereotyping attitude towards the Emberá indigenous identity, the tourists from the nations of the economically developed world appreciate – and some even approach with awe and admiration – the Emberá indigenous traditions. In a similar manner, an increasing number of the Panamanian middle class are interested in learning more about Emberá culture, and willing to abandon or partly reconsider their previous negative stereotypes.

In Parara Puru, the emerging awareness of these changing expectations has inspired a renewed interest in the issue of the authenticity of indigenous culture. This often takes the form of collective introspection, a concern with the history of the Emberá tradition and the 'truthfulness' of its representation. Now that a wider non-Emberá audience is increasingly paying attention to the Emberá, the Emberá feel a growing responsibility to pay more attention to the details of their own culture. They desire to become more informed and more articulate guides of the Emberá world, able to describe a wider variety of cultural particularities that might interest a larger variety of tourists, including those who are more knowledgeable and inquisitive.

During six sequential periods of fieldwork in Parara Puru – in 2005, 2007, 2008, 2009, 2010 and 2011 – I had the opportunity to observe these nuanced changes in perspective. Year after year, new individuals – men and women – step forward and take a progressively more active role in guiding the visitors, narrating the history of the community, or explaining the making of artefacts, the particulars of the dress code, and specific details of the Emberá way of life. With the increase in the number of voices that contribute to the guiding of the visitors, the narrative about Emberá culture becomes enriched with new details and new perspectives. Each individual, old or young, male or female, introduces life experiences that reflect slightly different skills, and slightly different subjectivities. In this respect, the project of educating the tourists into the basics of Emberá culture gradually accommodates a number of parallel journeys of exploration into the deeper aspects Emberá culture undertaken by the Emberá themselves.

Nevertheless, the collective pool of knowledge about Emberá culture in Parara Puru is not sufficient to answer all potential questions the tourists might ask. For this reason, the majority of the inhabitants of the community, like amateur anthropologists, have their ears open for additional pieces of information that could be gathered during conversations with Emberá from other communities. In this respect, knowledge about cultural issues can make a difference in negotiating tourist expectations (see also, Tucker, Bunten, in this volume). In Parara Puru new information about the cultural particularities of Emberá life is shared throughout the community at speed, between family members, and from one family to another, especially when the new information in question can add a new element to the daily presentations for the tourists. On one occasion, for example, I was fortunate to observe a small change in the daily dance presentations that occurred within less than a week! Rumba-Emberá had typically been danced until then in pairs, with the dancers positioned side-by-side, moving in a circular procession, in a manner choreographically similar to Cumbia-Emberá.[6] Then one day in April 2008, the inhabitants of Parara Puru started dancing the rumba-Emberá in a face-to-face position, again in a circular pattern, but in a freestyle manner, not in procession as before.

The change described above was evidently small and involved the choreographic arrangement of the bodies of the dancing couples, while the music of the dance remained the same. However, since I was concerned at the time of fieldwork with the details of the Emberá dance tradition, I was immediately struck by the changes. I started asking my respondents in the community and I was given, in most cases, more or less the same answer: 'This is the correct way to dance rumba-Emberá'. Considering the small size of the community, it was easy to identify the individuals who had introduced this small change in the style of the dance and their rationale for implementing it. In the Chagres area, the numbers of the Emberá are small, and their experience with dancing rumba-Emberá before the introduction of tourism was limited. But it became apparent during my fieldwork that this free-style arrangement of the dancing couples was closer to the way the Emberá dance rumba in Darien, where Emberá dancing has been more established. Very conveniently, the new style of dancing was also easier for the tourists to follow and has facilitated tourist participation.

More importantly, while older dance patterns become features of everyday dance practice, new dance moves are introduced through rehearsal and improvisation, and the Emberá dance tradition, which was declining until the introduction of tourism, is undergoing a revitalization. This is apparent also in the Emberá animal-dances, the other major type of Emberá dancing, which encourages improvisation as part of imitating the movement and attributes of native animal species. The introduction of tourism has motivated the residents of Parara Puru to dance a much greater number of animal dances than ever before, and introduce a wide variety of new dance moves and choreographed patterns into their existing repertoire. The degree of improvisation has been accelerated by tourism, inspiring the Emberá to realize new avenues of artistic expression.

Similar examples of improvisation and experimentation that result in new patterns and designs can be found in the context of the Emberá art of basket and

54

mask construction. The wider Emberá society in Panama – not merely the communities that entertain tourists – are involved in the production of cultural artefacts that eventually find their way into the tourist market (Velásquez Runk 2001). With the increase in material culture production, new designs emerge out of older patterns, while new colours are introduced using old and well-established dyeing techniques (cf. Callaghan 2002). As the art of Emberá basketry continues to evolve, new natural dyeing mediums are introduced to produce more colours and accommodate a greater variety of designs.[7] My respondents in Parara Puru welcome this creative freedom and the new possibilities that it encourages, and state that they prefer work invested in constructing cultural artefacts to labouring for cultivation-related undertakings.

As we have already seen, the desire to anticipate the expectations of tourists has inspired creativity and cultural improvisation among the Emberá who are involved with tourism. In the context of work invested in cultural performances for tourists, the established authenticity of older practices merges with the spontaneous discovery of new motifs. The reorganization of new and old elements emerges organically in daily life as the Emberá adapt to new circumstances, but does not contradict older practices – that is, what the Emberá themselves see as 'Emberá traditions'. The latter remain, as I have argued elsewhere, true to the spirit of Emberá social organization and process (Theodossopoulos 2010). In this respect, however stereotypical or unrepresentative the expectations of some tourists might be, they have stimulated, to a smaller or larger extent, the production of creative solutions to a new set of challenges.

Conclusion

While at the beginning of their engagement with tourism the residents of Parara Puru simply relied on their readily available knowledge about their culture (that is, what most Emberá more or less know), in a relatively short period of time, and through frequent practice in working with tourists, they started refining their skills at presenting Emberá culture. During their first steps as entertainers of tourists they attempted to provide their guests with an indigenous experience, a spectacle (see Urry 1990). With the passage of time, however, the Emberá of Parara Puru identified some dimensions of their culture that the tourists were likely to appreciate more, collected additional information about these cultural dimensions, and improved their skill in practising them. Having learnt how to anticipate some of the tourists' expectations, and equipped with this knowledge, they started guiding the tourists into and around their culture, instead of merely participating in a spectacle. As with other Amerindian ethnic groups, they now exercise a certain degree of control over their self-presentation (cf. Bunten 2008: 392; this volume).

Presently, the Emberá who live in communities that regularly receive tourists spend more time than ever before discussing, being concerned with, and practising the performative and artistic aspects of their culture. Month after month, year after year, they become more experienced as artists, dancers, storytellers and guides to the Emberá tradition. Through daily practice, they share more opportunities to spontaneously improvise, introduce new patterns or designs to established motifs, incorporate new materials into traditional techniques, and include additional information into customary sets of knowledge and narratives. Small fragments of partly forgotten information about Emberá history and tradition are collected and integrated into new narratives, or used to authenticate contemporary practices. However, new adaptations and improvisations taking place in Parara Puru are not challenging the conventions of Emberá culture, but they evolve 'from within the local cultural matrix' (Bruner 2005: 5). As such cultural improvisation is 'intrinsic to the very processes of social and cultural life' (Ingold and Hallam 2007: 19).

So, the Emberá improvise and experiment as they try to meet the expectations of their visitors. In this process, they feel committed to respecting 'the ways of their parents and grandfathers' through a conscious attempt to reproduce dances, artefacts, and body decoration in accordance with established cultural patterns. Yet, through the spontaneous combination of new forms with old structures – which inevitably occur in everyday practice – they restructure their cultural representations. This 'restructuring' often involves, as Stewart has suggested in his discussion of creolization and mixture, 'an internal reorganization of elements' (2007: 18). This is why I argue that a more systematic appreciation of the internal reorganization of cultural expressions can help us circumvent the obstacles of the binary distinction between authenticity and inauthenticity, an opposition that implies a static and limiting understanding of culture as a fixed and self-contained entity. In everyday life there is no single genuine Emberá culture; culture, as Bruner (1993, 1994, 2005) argues, always evolves and adapts to new challenges, just one of which is indigenous tourism.

But while the dialogue with the tourists' expectations is inspiring creativity, it also brings to the surface a few contradictions inherent in the tourists' imagination of contemporary indigenous people. The tourist expectations oscillate between a yearning to preserve an uncontaminated version of indigeneity – an expectation of unshakeable cultural integrity and purity (Ramos 1998: 70) based on 'an ontological and essentialist vision of exotic cultures' Salazar (2010: xviii) – and an implicit desire to introduce Western civilizational benefits into the indigenous experience, such as education in schools or medical care in hospitals. These contradictory expectations match comparable tensions experienced by the Emberá in the non-tourism-related dimensions of their lives – such as the commitment to hold fast to a distinctive indigenous tradition and the responsibility of participating in the life of a modern nation. In this respect, the efforts of the Emberá to understand and anticipate the expectations of tourists closely relate to, and often complicate, similar concerns they tackle – independently of tourism – as citizens of their nation and inhabitants of a changing world.

At the same time, however, the expectations of the world towards the Emberá are also changing. The residents of Parara Puru are able to detect these changes through their negotiation of tourist expectations in the tourism encounter. Up until twenty years ago, the Emberá were discriminated against by their nation's non-indigenous majority on the grounds of their cultural distinctiveness (which was stereotyped as primitiveness). Now, foreigners from the most powerful and prosperous nations of the world approach Panama's indigenous communities with respect and care. Even Panamanian visitors are willing to appreciate Emberá culture in positive terms, adopting their government's official perception of cultural diversity as an asset to the nation (more generally) or the development of tourism (more particularly) (cf. Guerrón-Montero 2006a; Pereiro Pérez 2010). In this regard, the Emberá have come a long way from their old strategy of avoiding contact with the outside world to their current accelerated contact with the global community, which has resulted in increased recognition and respect from outsiders.

The Emberá residents of Parara Puru are continually polishing their skill in deciphering and anticipating contradictory tourist expectations. The tourists undeniably add an additional level of ambiguity to the hazy interface of tradition with modernity. My Emberá respondents, however, are keen to face and resolve the problems arising from this ambiguity and, without any doubt, they declare their desire to take advantage of the tourist economy. They now wish to reach out to the world and enhance the representation and visibility of their culture (Theodossopoulos 2009; Strathern and Stewart 2009), to derive some benefit from the globalizing economy (Loker 1999), and to renegotiate – as other Panamanian ethnic groups have done (cf. Howe 1998, 2009; Guerrón-Montero 2006a, 2006b; Tice 1995; Young and Bort 1999) – their relationship with the wider national and international community. In Parara Puru, the tourists' expectations, despite their contradictory nature, have simultaneously inspired both cultural improvisation and the revitalization of older indigenous practices, encouraging the Emberá to adapt – as they have done in the past (cf. Kane 2004; Williams 2005) – to new challenges and opportunities. The dialogue with the international community, as this is realized through the negotiation of expectations in the tourist encounter, has facilitated this process, repeatedly reminding the Emberá that the outside world is curious about their unique culture.

Notes

The conclusion and parts of this chapter were presented in a plenary lecture during the ASA09 conference held at Bristol. I would like to thank the British Academy (small grants SG-49635 and SG-54214) and the ESRC (research grant RES-000-22-3733) for supporting the fieldwork upon which this chapter is based. I would also like to thank the residents of Parara Puru for being my patient teachers of the Emberá way of life, and my co-editor, Jonathan Skinner, for his valuable and detailed comments and suggestions.

1. Where I undertook anthropological fieldwork in August and September 2005, February, March and April 2007, March and April 2008, July and August 2009, February, March, April and May 2010 and January, February, March and April 2011. The first draft of this chapter was written in 2009, but during revision benefited from later fieldwork.
2. An idealized image that coexisted in an ambivalent relationship with contrasting perceptions of physical danger and moral degradation lurking in the tropical jungle (Frenkel 1996).
3. For a detailed description of these dances, and their importance for Emberá cultural representation, see Theodossopoulos n.d.
4. The Panamanian Ministry of Education has recently produced a couple of textbooks of the Emberá language for primary education, a project that is (at the time of writing) at an experimental stage.
5. The textiles used for the Emberá *parumas* are different from those used by Kuna women for their traditional costumes, although both are often – and especially nowadays – manufactured in Asia. The origin of both the Kuna and Emberá traditional women's outfit 'cannot be credited to any single outside source'; both contain 'elements that can be traced back several hundred years, and others that have developed as the result of contact' and as adaptations to the arrivals of new materials (Salvador 1976: 169).
6. For a detailed description of rumba- and cumbia-Emberá, and the significance of improvisation in Emberá dancing, see Theodossopoulos n.d.
7. For comparative examples of indigenous arts, new designs and older patterns, see Graburn 1976, Smith 1989; and among the Kuna (the neighbours of the Emberá) see Tice 1995, Salvador 1976.

References

Abram, S., J. Waldren and D. Macleod (eds). 1997. *Tourists and Tourism: Identifying with People and Places*. Oxford: Berg.

Bendix, R. 1997. *In Search of Authenticity: The Formation of Folklore Studies*. Madison: University of Wisconsin Press.

Boissevain, J. (ed.). 1996. *Coping with Tourists: European Reactions to Mass Tourism*. Oxford: Berghahn Books.

Bruner, E.M. 1993. 'Epilogue: Creativity Persona and the Problem of Authenticity', in S. Lavie, K. Narayan and R. Rosaldo (eds), *Creativity/Anthropology*. Ithaca, NY: Cornell University Press, pp. 321–34.

Bruner, E.M. 1994. 'Abraham Lincoln as Authentic Reproduction: A Critique of Postmodernism', *American Anthropologist* 96(2): 397–415.

Bruner, E.M. 2005. *Culture on Tour: Ethnographies of Travel*. Chicago, IL: University of Chicago Press.

Bunten, A. 2008. 'Sharing Culture or Shelling Out? Developing the Commodified Persona in the Heritage Industry', *American Ethnologist* 35(3): 380–95.

Callaghan, M.M. 2002. *Darien Rainforest Basketry: Baskets of the Wounaan and Emberá Indians from the Darién Rainforest in Panamá*. Arizona: HPL Enterprises.

Clifford, J. 1986. 'On Ethnographic Allegory', in J. Clifford and G.E. Marcus (eds), *Writing Culture: The Poetics and Politics of Ethnography*. Berkeley: University of California Press, pp. 98–121.

Coleman, S. and M. Crang (eds). 2002. *Tourism: Between Place and Performance*. Oxford: Berghahn Books.

Conklin, B.A. 1997. 'Body Paint, Feathers, and VCRs: Aesthetics and Authenticity in Amazonian Activism', *American Ethnologist* 24(4): 711–37.

Conklin, B.A. and L.R. Graham. 1995. 'The Shifting Middle Ground: Amazonian Indians and Eco-Politics', *American Anthropologist* 97(4): 695–710.

Edensor, T. 1998. *Tourists at the Taj: Performance and Meaning at a Symbolic Site*. London: Routledge.

Ellen, R. 1986. 'What Black Elk Left Unsaid: On the Illusory Images of Green Primitivism', *Anthropology Today* 2(6): 8–12.

Ewart, E. 2007. 'Black Paint, Red Paint and a Wristwatch: The Aesthetics of Modernity among the Panará in Central Brazil', in E. Ewart and M. O'Hanlon (eds), *Body Arts and Modernity*. Wantage: Sean Kington Publishing, pp. 36–52.

Frenkel, S. 1996. 'Jungle Stories: North American Representations of Tropical Panama', *The Geographical Review* 86(3): 317–33.

Gow, P. 2007. 'Clothing as Acculturation in Peruvian Amazonia', in E. Ewart and M. O'Hanlon (eds), *Body Arts and Modernity*. Wantage: Sean Kingston Publishing, pp. 53–71.

Graburn, N.H. (ed.). 1976. *Ethnic and Tourist Arts: Cultural Expression from the Fourth World*. Berkeley: University of California Press.

Guerrón-Montero, C. 2006a. 'Tourism and Afro-Antillean Identity in Panama', *Journal of Tourism and Cultural Change* 4(2): 65–84.

Guerrón-Montero, C. 2006b. 'Can't Beat Me Own Drum in Me Own Native Land: Calypso Music and Tourism in the Panamanian Atlantic Coast', *Anthropological Quarterly* 79(4): 633–63.

Herlihy, P.H. 1986. 'A Cultural Georgraphy of the Emberá and Wounaan (Choco) Indians of Darien, Panama, with Emphasis on Recent Village Formation and Economic Diversification, Louisiana State University: PhD dissertation.

Herlihy, P.H. 2003. 'Participatory Research: Mapping of Indigenous Lands in Darien, Panama', *Human Organisation* 62: 315–31.

Howe, J. 1998. *A People Who would not Kneel: Panama, the United States and the San Blas Kuna*. Washington: Smithsonian Institution Press.

Howe, J. 2009. *Chiefs, Scribes, and Ethnographers: Kuna Culture from Inside and Out*. Austin: University of Texas Press.

Ingold, T. and E. Hallam. 2007. 'Creativity and Cultural Improvisation: An Introduction' in E. Hallam and T. Ingold (eds), *Creativity and Cultural Improvisation*. Oxford: Berg, pp. 1–24.

Kane, S.C. 2004. *The Phantom Gringo Boat: Shamanic Discourse and Development in Panama*. Christchurch, New Zealand: Cybereditions Corp. (Originally: 1994, Washington, DC: Smithsonian Institution).

Kirtsoglou, E. and D. Theodossopoulos. 2004. '"They are Taking our Culture Away": Tourism and Culture Commodification in the Black Carib Community of Roatan', *Critique of Anthropology* 24(2): 135–57.

Lindholm, C. 2008. *Culture and Authenticity*. Oxford: Blackwell.

Loker, W.M. 1999. 'Grit in the Prosperity Machine: Globalization and the Rural Poor in Latin America', in W.M. Loker (ed.), *Globalization and the Rural Poor in Latin America*. Boulder: Lynne Rienner, pp. 9–39.

Milton, K. 1996. *Environmentalism and Cultural Theory: Exploring the Role of Anthropology in Environmental Discourse*. London: Routledge.

Morris, B. 1981. 'Changing Views of Nature', *The Ecologist* 11: 130–37.

Pereiro Pérez, X. 2010. *Estudio Estratégico del Turismo en Kuna Yala: Primera Versión del Informe de investigación 2008–2010*. Panama: SENACYT.

Ramos, A.R. 1998. *Indigenism: Ethnic Politics in Brazil*. Madison, WI: University of Wisconsin Press.

Rosaldo, R. 1989. *Culture and Truth: The Remaking of Social Analysis*. London: Routledge.

Salazar, N.B. 2010. *Envisioning Eden: Mobilizing Imaginaries in Tourism and Beyond*. Oxford: Berghahn Book.

Salvador, M.L. 1976. 'The Clothing Arts of the Cuna of San Blas, Panama', in N.H. Graburn (ed.), *Ethnic and Tourist Arts: Cultural Expression from the Fourth World*. Berkeley: University of California Press, pp. 165–82.

Santos-Granero, F. 2009. 'Hybrid Bodyscapes: A Visual History of Yanesha Patterns of Cultural Change', *Current Anthropology* 50(4): 477–512.

Selwyn, T. (ed.). 1996. *The Tourist Image: Myths and Myth-Making in Tourism*. Chichester: Wiley and Sons.

Smith, V.L. (ed.). 1989. *Hosts and Guests: The Anthropology of Tourism*. Philadelphia, PA: University of Pennsylvania Press.

Stewart, C. 2007. 'Creolization: History, Ethnography, Theory', in C. Stewart (ed.), *Creolization: History, Ethnography, Theory*. Walnut Creek, CA: Left Coast Press, pp. 1–25.

Strathern, A. and P.J. Stewart. 2009. 'Shifting Centres, Tense Peripheries: Indigenous Cosmopolitanisms', in D. Theodossopoulos and E. Kirtsoglou (eds), *United in Discontent: Local Responses to Cosmopolitanism and Globalization*. Oxford: Berghahn Books, pp. 20–44.

Swain, M.B. 1989. 'Gender Roles in Indigenous Tourism: Kuna Mola, Kuna Yala and Cultural Survival', in V.L. Smith (ed.), *Hosts and Guests: The Anthropology of Tourism*. Philadelphia, PA: University of Pennsylvania Press, pp. 83–104.

Taussig, M. 1993. *Mimesis and Alterity: A Particular History of the Senses*. London: Routledge.

Theodossopoulos, D. 2009. 'Introduction: United in Discontent', in D. Theodossopoulos and E. Kirtsoglou (eds), *United in Discontent: Local Responses to Cosmopolitanism and Globalization*. Oxford: Berghahn Books, pp. 1–19.

Theodossopoulos, D. 2010. 'Tourism and Indigenous Culture as Resources: Lessons from the Emberá Cultural Tourism in Panama', in J.G. Carrier and D.V.L Macleod (eds), *Tourism, Power and Culture: Anthropological Insights*. Bristol: Channel View, pp. 115–33.

Theodossopoulos, D. n.d. 'Dance, Visibility and Respresentational Self-awareness in an Emberá Community in Panama', in H. Neveu-Kringelback and J. Skinner (eds), *Knowledge, Transformation and Identity in the Anthropology of Dance*. Oxford: Berghahn Books.

Tice, K.E. 1995. *Kuna Crafts, Gender, and the Global Economy*. Austin, TX: University of Texas Press.

Urry, J. 1990. *The Tourist Gaze: Leisure and Travel in Contemporary Society*. London: Sage.

Velásquez Runk, J. 2001. 'Wounaan and Emberá Use and Management of the Fiber Palm Astrocaryum Standleyanum (Arecaceae) for Basketry in Eastern Panama', *Economic Botany* 55(1): 72–82.

Velásquez Runk, J. 2009. 'Social and River Networks for the Trees: Wounaan's Riverine Rhizomic Cosmos and Arboreal Conservation', *American Anthropologist* 111(4): 456–67.

West, P. and J. Carrier. 2004. 'Ecotourism and Authenticity: Getting Away from It All?', *Current Anthropology* 45(4): 483–98.

Williams, C.A. 2005. *Between Resistance and Adaptation: Indigenous Peoples and the Colonisation of the Choco 1510–1753*. Liverpool: Liverpool University Press.

Young, P.D. and R. Bort. 1999. 'Ngóbe Adaptive Responses to Globalization in Panama', in W. Loker (ed.), *Globalization and the Rural Poor in Latin America*. Boulder, CO: Lynne Rienner, pp. 111–36.

Chapter 4
THE PARADOX OF GAZE AND RESISTANCE IN NATIVE AMERICAN CULTURAL TOURISM: AN ALASKAN CASE STUDY

Alexis Celeste Bunten

❦

Introduction

Drawn from a case study of a tribally owned cultural tourism venue in Southeast Alaska, this chapter explores the paradox of representation that Native American tour guides face in commoditizing their living cultures. Operating in an industry governed by Western tropes of representation, Native American tour guides feel enormous pressure to deliver a competitive product that appeals to perceived consumer desires, yet they do not openly accept themselves as objects on display, an human commodity, and therefore resist being objectified according to stereotypes that persist in popular culture. These conflicting motivations are played out during the tourism encounters between the Native American hosts and non-Native guests.

Within the political economy of tourism, market forces typically demand hosts to perform their cultures simplified to meet nostalgic and iconic readings of a place and its inhabitants. Still, Native American tourism workers find ways to challenge the tourist gaze covertly, while maintaining the persona of good-natured host. These acts shift the power to define local identity from the consumer, who often unwittingly represents a hegemonic viewpoint, to an Indigenous one. The host's imaginings of tourist expectations play a central role in the social repositioning that takes place throughout the touristic encounter. This chapter argues for a practice-based[1] perspective on the processes of self-commodification[2] that take place at the tourism site through an exploration of the interplay between tourist gaze and host resistance. This approach 'restore[s] the actor to the social processes without losing sight of the larger structures that constrain (but also enable) social action ... opening up the space for questions of power and inequality' (Ortner 2006: 3).

The concept of the 'tourist gaze' can be used as a diagnostic of power manifest in the structures of inequality reflected in the touristic encounter. According to John Urry's framework, locals play back desired images to satisfy the customers. 'What people gaze upon', Urry explains, 'are ideal representations of the view in question that they internalize from postcards and guidebooks (and increasingly from television programmes)' (Urry 1990: 86). Simply put, tourists who sign up for a Native American cultural tour expect a guide that fits their ideas of how a Native American should appear and act. Within this framework, tourists may unwittingly have the power to shape the outcome of cross-cultural encounters by giving preference to locals who look and behave in ways that are, in their minds, 'authentic'.[3] The tourist gaze foists an additional 'burden of representation' (Ginsburg 2002: 48) upon cultural producers who must create an Indigenous presence in an industry dominated by non-Indigenous institutions and agencies. Repeatedly meeting tourist expectations can attract more tourist dollars, but may run the risk of irrevocably altering the hosts, a process Dean MacCannell (1984) refers to as 'reconstructing ethnicity'. I argue that these types of identity-altering repercussions of the tourist gaze are largely superficial, operating on those flexible aspects of the self that are offered for tourist consumption in the first place, as appearance. Rather, the tourism industry should be regarded as one of many mainstream pressures to conform to Western culture that has the opposite effect of motivating hosts to maintain local values rather than abandon them.

Too often, ethnic minorities involved in cultural tourism are described as being coerced into participating in the creation and performance of an 'inauthentic' product,[4] a view that strips both them and the tourists who pay to encounter them of any honourable intentions when the cross-cultural experience mediated through tourism is much more complex. In fact, tour guides representing their ethnic cultures are often very sophisticated culture-brokers who thoughtfully put together a product performance drawn from cross-cultural understandings of their clients' desires and expectations. The case study presented in this chapter challenges simplistic critiques of self-commodification as 'selling out' or 'being exploited' and argues instead for an agentic perspective on the processes involved, one which emphasizes the complicated and often contradictory nature of host/guest interactions.

Edward Bruner (2005) refers to the cultural tourism venue as a 'touristic borderzone', or a performative space within which tourists and locals meet. At this juncture, local people must decide for themselves what aspects of their cultures are alienable and how to commodify these things in order to participate (and even thrive) economically by taking advantage of the worldwide tourism industry. In touristic borderzones around the world, locals are aware of the potential political, financial and cultural benefits of participation in tourism. They are also wary of the cultural degradation that can result from packaging culture according to outside tastes and consumptive patterns.

Destinations that play host to cross-cultural tourism venues often witness Western desires for 'the Other' through colonialism, salvage ethnography, popular imagery and tourism. This case study is concerned with one such place that has captured the imagination of the West since early contact between fortune-hunters working for the Russian American Company at the turn of the nineteenth century and local Natives. This place is Sitka, Alaska, the ancestral homeland of the Tlingit Indians located in the heart of the Northwest Coast of North America. Living in a lush, temperate rainforest abundant in resources, the Tlingit are world renowned for their intricate formline designs carved on totem poles and woven into their chilkat blankets, their enormous dugout war canoes, and their complex ceremonial life that includes elaborate multi-day feasts for the dead. The hosts discussed in this chapter, who work for Tribal Tours, present their tangible and intangible heritage to visitors from around the world.

Tribal Tours

Established in 1994, Tribal Tours is a subsidiary of Sitka Tribe of Alaska (STA), a U.S. federally recognized tribal government. STA has approximately four thousand members of primarily Tlingit, Haida, Aleut and Tsimpsian ancestry. Sitka Tribe of Alaska's local membership makes up well over one-third of Sitka's population of just under nine thousand. Tribal Tours employs up to approximately fifty staff throughout the year, of which the vast majority are Alaska Native, primarily Tlingit in origin. A number of them have mixed ethnic backgrounds with other tribal affiliations, as well as Euro-American, Pacific Islander, Filipino, other Asian, or Hispanic descent. Being of mixed ancestry is not uncommon among Sitka's Native population, but as such, these individuals identify themselves and are mutually recognized by tribal members as Native Alaskan.

Although they share a common Native identity, Tribal Tours' workers and cultural consultants are by no means a uniform group. Taken as a whole, they represent every demographic: young and old, male and female, Indigenous and Western-educated,[5] wealthy and poor,[6] with differing heritages and backgrounds. Nearly all of Tribal Tours' employees grew up in Sitka, and have ties to the local Tlingit clan system. Some were born in Sitka to highly traditional families, and others have returned (some for the first time) to their ancestral homeland with little to no life experience within the Native community. All employees are involved in cultural activities in some facet beyond the workplace, whether it be through participation in dance groups, traditional subsistence activities, art making or participation in ceremonial life. While there are local Natives who choose to have little involvement with tourism, the industry affects the entire Native population through the circulation of tourist dollars, the dissemination of Indigenous knowledge, the upkeep of culturally important sites, and the physical presence of visitors for some one hundred and thirty years!

Sitka Natives have shared the legacy of tourism since the first tourist-specific steamship carried sightseers to Sitka in 1884 (Raibmon 2005: 140). The accessibility of the Tlingit 'village' to downtown Sitka made it a popular attraction for Victorian-era visitors, who did not hesitate to walk into Native homes uninvited and observe their inhabitants without respect for their privacy. One such visitor observed, 'In all the houses the Indians went right on with their breakfasts and domestic duties regardless of our presence; and the white visitors made themselves at home, scrutinized and turned over everything they saw with an effrontery that would be resented, if indulged in kind by the Indians' (Scidmore 1885: 60 in Kan 2004).

Sitka's white, civic leaders knew that Native peoples and their cultures attracted visitors, and that tourism could serve as a sustainable economic enterprise. As such, they encouraged tourists to marvel upon the accomplishments of missionary and educational institutions established shortly after the 1867 sale of Alaska from Russia to the United States. Sergei Kan writes, 'a visit to the Sitka Industrial School [established to assimilate Natives to a Christian, white way of life] … was part of every tourist's itinerary (e.g., *The Alaskan*, 5/7/1890: 2). Thus, a visitor to Sitka could literally make a journey from "savagery", the old Indian Village, to "civilization", the Industrial School and the cottages, in less than half-hour' (Kan 2004: 214–15). Sheldon Jackson, territorial Alaska's first General Agent of Education, invited tourists to see the many artifacts on display at the museum he founded in his namesake on the campus of the Industrial Training School in the 1890s. He encouraged Native students to make souvenirs and entertain tourists as a source of extra cash and an alternative to engaging in 'antisocial' behaviour. Still, Natives were largely barred from owning local businesses and participating in areas of civic life, and thus were relegated to serving as an unpaid spectacle and selling handmade souvenirs on the streets or to white middlemen.

While early Tlingit entrepreneurial efforts were stymied by American settlers' Victorian sensibilities and institutionalized racism, the twentieth century witnessed a major transformation of the political landscape for Sitka's Native population. Tlingit political mobilization combined with the passing of several state and Federal laws set the stage for all Alaska Natives to control their own economic destiny and representation. Tribal Tours has trodden a steady uphill course against this historical backdrop to where the business is now an important player in Sitka's local economy and an international model for best practices in Indigenous tourism.

Tribal Tours' products consist primarily of Tlingit dance performances and various city tours conducted by local, Native Alaskan guides. Although it is not the only conduit to encountering Native American cultures in Sitka – the Sheldon Jackson Museum, the Sitka National Historical Park and the Southeast Alaska Indian Cultural Center all showcase objects of material culture as well as staff Native Alaskan artist demonstrators – Tribal Tours' marketing strategy is to differentiate itself from other local tour businesses by delivering its product from the Native point of view. Despite this point of difference, Sitka Tribe of Alaska may only participate in the tourism industry under the constraints of existing structures that dictate the framework in which Tribal Tours may operate.

For cultural tourism venues, this takes the form of staging the world as a museum in which non-Western cultures are experienced in a uniform, sanitized, synchronic design, regardless of location, ethnicity and history.[7] This is why almost all cultural tourism venues involve some modicum of 'traveling back in time' before the taint of colonizing contact achieved through devices such as constructing models of traditional housing, speaking an ancestral language, and performing dances in customary dress. Scholars (Kirshenblatt-Gimblett 1998; Handler and Saxon 1988) have remarked upon this 'museumizing' through the paradigm of tourism, noting that heritage politics are, according to Arjun Appadurai (1990: 304), 'remarkably uniform throughout the world'. Perhaps most visitors are more likely to tour 'the Other' when they are presented in a familiar and comfortable mode. (However, at this point it is unknown as very few Indigenous-owned venues violate standard trends.) Tribal Tours has worked, in part, to fit this mould by constructing the Sheet'ka Kwaan Naa Kahídi Community House, a modern replica of a traditional Tlingit clan house, to serve as a performance venue for their Sheet'ka Kwaan Naa Kahídi dance group and host community-wide events. Its tours showcase iconic images of Northwest Coast Native cultures with stops at local sites of interest including the Sitka National Historical Park where visitors can view totem poles, the Sheldon Jackson Museum with its world class collection of Native Alaskan material culture, and the living Tlingit 'village'.

Generating Expectation

Marge and Helen,[8] sixty-something, retired Euro-American sisters from the Midwest United States step off the tender (a transportation boat) that brought them from the cruise ship anchored in the bay to the dock in Sitka, Alaska. Sitka is their third and final port of call on their seven-day cruise through Southeast Alaska's famed 'Inside Passage'. Over the past five days, Marge and Helen have eaten mountains of food, walked through the temperate rainforest, observed glaciers calve, experienced a historic 'gold rush' district, and shopped 'till they dropped'. Earlier that morning, the sisters watched an informational video circulated on board the cruise ship; this video presented the day's port as the quaint, historic capital of Russian America, established after the Russians defeated the Tlingits in the historic battle of 1804 that took place on the grounds of what is now the Sitka National Historical Park. The sisters already knew to expect Russian heritage when they arrived in Sitka, based on the brochures they had studied when they decided to travel by cruise ship. In fact, they specifically chose to travel Alaska by cruise ship for the comfort and convenience this mode of travel offers. With accommodation, meals and various amenities all included, they decided taking a cruise would be the best way to stretch their retirement incomes on a nice vacation.

The cruise lines and their local vendors have crafted a product that delivers 'big', 'wild' Alaska with little discomfort and minimal expenditure.[9] Market research reports that visitors to Alaska hope to experience the wilderness, wildlife and scenic beauty, followed by experiencing Native Alaskan cultures (McDowell Group 2001). Jennifer Craik points out that 'cultural experiences offered by tourism are consumed in terms of prior knowledge, expectations, fantasies, and mythologies' generated in the tourist's origin culture rather than by the cultural offerings of the destination (1997: 119). Alaska carries an image that appeals to visitor desires for – to use phrases found in one cruise line's marketing brochures – 'the great land', 'the last vast wilderness', and the 'land of adventure' as an antidote to the modern, suburban, even 'tame', day-to-day life of the average cruise passenger.

These desires are reinforced by the marketing efforts of tour operators whose advertisements simultaneously feed off and construct popular notions attached to a place (King 1997; Nuttall 1997; Silver 1993). Cruise line advertising campaigns represent Alaska with images of glaciers, bears, whales, Native Alaskans, gold and fish. According to cruise industry marketing materials, each port of call has its own unique charm. Skagway transports visitors back in time to the Alaskan gold rush. Juneau is known for its massive glacier, whale watching, and gold mining history. Ketchikan is a rugged fishing port and the place to see Saxman Native Village, as if there is only one Native settlement to visit in Southeast Alaska.[10] In this schema, Sitka is primarily marketed as 'the Russian capital of America,' and secondarily as the ancestral homeland of the Tlingit people. At each port, vendors whose products tap into these narratives make contracts with the cruise lines to sell their tours on board the ship. These vendors save on marketing, and the cruise lines take a percentage of each sale made on board the ship. City officials cooperate with the cruise industry to uphold this system to the extent that they rely upon tourist spending, and the political clout that these multinational corporations wield.

This strategy is part of a larger system of representation in the U.S., in which the hegemonic forces of industry and government (Traube 1996) work together to control cultural production for the masses. An Alaska state-funded marketing survey (Nichols and Gilstrap 2000) noted, 'because of dwindling state commitments to marketing, the cruise ships have essentially become the primary sources of Alaska's "image" advertising by spending millions of dollars marketing the destination'. Through this process, local history and culture(s) are made into commodities, refurbished and sanitized through state funds, erasing[11] more complex historical processes. Cruise lines that promote Sitka as Russian America do not tend to highlight Sitka's Alaska Native heritage. Instead, their advertising emphasizes local attractions featured on the Russian America tour pre-sold on board the ships.

One cruise line describes Sitka as:

> The onion domes of St Michael's Cathedral are your first clue that Sitka was once a Russian settlement – the colonial headquarters of Count Baranof, no less. Discover the echoes of its heyday at a performance by the New Archangel Dancers. Be greeted by Tlingit native people, then stand on the spot where the United States took possession of Alaska in 1867 for $7.2 million, less than two cents per acre. The dramatic setting in the shadow of Mt Edgecumbe is one of the loveliest in the Great Land. Take a stroll through old growth forest in Sitka National Historical Park, shop the downtown district, and poke around the Sheldon Jackson Museum for a close-up look at some of the city's most prized arts, crafts and Russian relics.

Messages like these inform passengers about what is important to consume while in Sitka for a day, namely Russian heritage. The percentage of passengers on this cruise line pre-booking 'Russian History' tours for their arrival in Sitka vastly outnumbers those seeking out and booking a tour from the Native Alaskan perspective. Based on visitor feedback collected by Tribal Tours, it seems visitors are neither made aware that Sitka is a hub of regional Native culture, nor are they offered the opportunity to experience it through off-shore excursions sold on board most ships.[12] The majority of cruise line passengers arriving in Sitka are primed to experience 'Russian America'.

The Architecture of Desire

At one time, Sitka was indeed the capital of Russian America, but the Russian period only represents a small, though relatively important, fraction of Sitka's history of human habitation. The ancestors of Sitka's Tlingit population migrated from the Nass River area of present-day British Columbia, drawn to Shee (now Baranoff) Island by the flickering lights of L'ux (renamed Mt Edgecumbe) volcano, last active some ten thousand years ago. By contrast, the Russians occupied the area between 1799 and 1802, and from 1804 to the 1867 sale of Alaska from Russia to the U.S. In fact, there were never more than a few hundred Russians residing in Sitka at any given time during the entire Russian American period. The Russian Czars knew Alaska was too distant to maintain a permanent colony, and the territory was primarily used for resource extraction and trade.

The marketing of Sitka as 'the capital of Russian America' is what Rossel (1988: 5) describes as 'exaggerations, misleading statements, and lies' that provide a certain way of understanding reality, and that offers the 'tourist view'. While the Alaskan tourism industry does not market outright lies, it tends to reinvent the relationship between Sitka's past and present in a very physical, experiential way. In tandem with the dominant marketing strategy, several cultural edifices have been constructed or restored in Sitka to preserve Sitka's Russian history.[13] St Michael's Russian Orthodox Cathedral stands in the middle of the town, rebuilt in 1976 according to its original 1844 plans after a 1966 fire burned down the original building, at the time the longest standing Russian Orthodox Church in America.[14]

The Russian Bishop's House, constructed in 1841–43, was purchased by the U.S. Parks Service in 1972 and restored to its original appearance over a ten year period. The Russian blockhouse, part of the stockade built in the 1820s to keep the local Natives from entering the Russian part of the city, was reconstructed in 1962. Today, the preservation of the blockhouse and the Russian Orthodox cemetery behind it falls under the purview of the Bureau of Land Management who erected interpretive devices to commemorate the Russian colonial influence. Even the sites of the historic battles between the Tlingits and the Russians took place on what are now public grounds, commemorated through interpretive plaques. At the site of the 1802 battle, where the Tlingits massacred inhabitants of the original Russian fort in resistance against mounting Russian transgressions, a Russian Orthodox grave marker has been erected.

The paving of a steep hill overlooking central Sitka and the surrounding bay, is a more recent and balanced reconstruction of a site of cultural and historical importance. Long before the arrival of Europeans, the Tlingits recognized the strategic value of this place they called 'Noow Tlein' for spotting enemies arriving by canoe and defending the fortified clan houses that once stood there. After the Russians drove away Tlingit dissenters in the historic 1804 battle for Sitka, Noow Tlein became the headquarters of the Russian American Company. Today, interpretive panels give relatively equal attention to the site in regard to its use by local Tlingits, the Russians, and the site of the 1867 transfer of Alaska from Russia to the United States.

In comparison, tourism may be an important or auxiliary facet of Sitka's 'Native' structures, but they do not service tourists to the extent that monuments to Russian America do (with the exception of St Michael's Cathedral, whose active congregation includes members of the Native community). Sitka Tribe of Alaska constructed and maintains the Sheet'ka Kwaan Naa Kahídi, home of the Sheet'ka Kwaan Naa Kahídi dancers and the 'Made in Alaska' gift shop, and used for various events by the entire community. In 2010, the State of Alaska agreed to fund the renovations for Sitka's Alaska Native Brotherhood Hall, the birthplace of the Alaska Native civil rights movement. The Tlingit 'village', marked by signs painted with Northwest Coast designs, is home to the Sitka Tribe of Alaska headquarters, and a very active traditional clan house. These buildings are usually part of Tribal Tours' itinerary, and recently featured in the Sitka Convention and Visitors' Bureau and the National Trust for Historic Preservation websites, alongside 'Russian' and 'American' content.[15] This 'balanced' cultural/historical approach to marketing Sitka has been a recent development since the mid-2000s, resulting from shifting local politics and widespread recognition of the contributions Tribal Tours has made to the community.

Supported by government agencies such as the National Park Service, the Bureau of Land Management, the National Trust for Historic Preservation, the State of Alaska, Sitka Tribe of Alaska, as well as private entities, edifices that pay tribute to Sitka's complex and diverse cultural history appear to proportionally complement the attention paid to them in marketing materials. It is not clear which came first, entrepreneurs who realized they could benefit by bringing customers desiring to experience physical reminders of Sitka's unique past, or agencies and organizations who recognized the merit of preserving this place so instrumental in Alaska and United States history. Sitka tourism grew in part out of the physical reminders of its past, while efforts to preserve these structures may have been born of a marriage between the tourism industry and government programmes to preserve America's physical and historical resources. Though a discussion of the maturation of Sitka tourism is beyond the scope of this chapter, it is clear that the marketing of Sitka as 'Russian America' matches what tourists both expect and experience while visiting Sitka, and that Sitka has much more to offer than what is advertised on board many of the cruise lines.

While many visitors take advantage of pre-packaged excursions developed in tandem with the marketing of Alaska, they are not entirely passive consumers. The marketplace responds to visitors' various tastes and demands creating new products and taking advantage of other resources the destination has to offer as opportunities arise. In places such as Sitka, where most tourism businesses are under local ownership, the result is a diverse array of services and goods for consumption that enhance the visitor's experience. In this case, hosts and guests are not pawns manipulated by the capitalist economic structure; the same forces that shape the tourist gaze respond to agency.

Selling the Native Experience

Despite the opportunity to pre-book a Russian historical tour on board the cruise ship, Marge and Helen decide to improvise their day in Sitka. As they walk the length of the dock after disembarking the tender, the sisters are not disappointed by the multitude of local tour options. Vendors flank each side of the jetty, standing next to their clapboard signs, buses, bikes and kayaks all competing to meet tourist demands for an 'authentic Alaska'. A young woman, dressed in a black felt vest designed with a beadwork appliqué of a frog, approaches the sisters. Marge and Helen are taken with the striking good looks of the young lady; they admire her long, shiny black hair, and liquid brown eyes.

'Would you like to buy a city tour today?' the young lady asks.

'What kind of tour is it?' Marge replies.

'I am offering a cultural and historic one hour city tour of Sitka from the Native point of view. The tickets are only twelve dollars, and by buying them you will be supporting our local Sitka Tribe of Alaska, the parent of Tribal Tours. That lady over there, Sandy [she points to another attractive but older woman wearing a similar vest, silver jewellery and a smart, black skirt] will be your tour guide. Her next tour leaves in 15 minutes.'

'Well, we were hoping to learn about Russian America,' Helen responds.

'Oh, this tour covers it all,' the salesgirl quips, and further explains: 'On tour, you will learn about the history of Russian America as you'll see the Russian blockhouse, the Russian Cemetery, the Russian Orthodox Church, and the Russian Bishop's House, still standing from the Russian period. You will also experience Sheet'Ka as my people have known it since time immemorial'.

'What do you mean?' Marge asked.

'Well,' the salesgirl responds, 'our guides will take you to see Japonsky Island, where an air station was built during World War II. There is currently a Native boarding school where kids from all over the state come for high school. I go there, and that's where my parents met when they went there twenty five years ago! My dad is Inupiaq Eskimo from Nome and my mom is *Lingít* from here. It's also a good place to watch for marine wildlife. I saw two stellar sea lions in the channel the other day. I also go there to harvest black seaweed.' She pulls out a plastic sandwich bag of dried seaweed. 'It's high in iodine, and beta carodines'. Then lowering her voice, she adds, 'it's good for treating menstrual problems'.

'Well, we don't have to worry about that!' Marge laughs.

'Immune problems and also arthritis, which runs in my family,' the salesgirl adds.

'Wait a minute, where did you say we can get some of that?' Marge jokes.

'Want to try some of mine?' The salesgirl offers her seaweed to the women who crunch the crispy, salty, dried seaweed between their teeth. 'There are other subsistence foods that you'll learn about on the tour. The land and sea kept our people alive. Everywhere you look, there are things to eat. Your guide will probably show you.'

'What else do you see on tour?'

'The tour goes to the Sitka National Historical Park where Sandy will take you on a nature walk to see the salmon run up Indian River. You should see a lot of berries along the trail this time of year. The park is also the location of the historic 1804 battle between the Russians and the Tlingits. We didn't lose the battle. My clan's ancestors left after our ammunition got blown up. But we eventually came home, and we are still here long after the Russians have gone. The park also stores our *at.óow*, clan regalia that we still use in ceremony today. If you go with Sandy, she can talk about several pieces there as they belong to her clan. They are like her family, with names, stories attached, and special meanings to her clan. She will also take you to Sandy Beach where you can see *L'ux* the volcano that drew our ancestors here. On a nice day like today you might see locals swimming in the water.'

'We'll take it!' Helen pulls out her wallet and purchases the tickets, pleased that she and Marge have saved about 30 per cent of what they would have paid for the Russian historical tour sold on board the cruise ship.

'The tour either drops off back here, or at the Sheet'ka Kwaan Naa Kahídi Community House. If you get off there, you can go see the Native dance show performance this afternoon. The show takes a half hour. The dancers perform a number of different style dances, and teach about the Tlingit culture. You will even get an opportunity to join us during our invitational! People really like it. And if you want your shopping to reflect the real Sitka and support local artisans, there is also a 'Made in Sitka' gift shop that showcases pieces of original art that are locally made.'

Marge and Helen board their motorcoach, excited about the prospect of meeting an 'authentic' Alaska Native. 'How are you doing this morning?' Sandy greets them as the women take their seats. 'Great!' Helen responds. 'We weren't necessarily going to take a tour today, but when that nice young lady told us about your tour, we couldn't resist!'

'We are sisters,' Gail continues, 'and we are really excited to learn about your people. We are actually Sioux Indians too! Our great grandmother was an Indian princess, but she had to hide her identity because, you know, the times were too racist back then.' 'Well, I am happy you are on board then, and I hope that you enjoy your tour today,' Sandy responds with a wry smile.

Meeting the Tourist Gaze

Once the coach is filled to capacity, Sandy begins her tour: '*Aan Yát Kusaani, Lingit x'einax Name yóo xát duwasaakw. Dleit kaa x'einax Sandy yóo xát duwasáakw. Sheet'ka kwaan áyá xát. Tlingit naax xát sitee. L'uknax.ádi áyá xát ...*' She continues in the Tlingit language for about five minutes, then finishing the monologue asks 'Did you all understand that?' Everybody laughs. 'What I just said was 'good morning. My Tlingit name is [*name withheld*]. My name in English is Sandy and I am from Sitka Alaska. I am a member of the Tlingit nation. Welcome to Sheet'ka Alaska and Tribal Tours. I am delighted you have chosen to join me on tour today. In our language we call this place Sheet'ka. Can all of you try and say that? "Sheet'ka".'

The tour group repeats, 'Sheet'ka'.

Sandy continues: 'Roughly translated, it means "the village behind the little islands". As you can see [gestures with a wide sweeping arm motion] we have a lot of little islands all around Sitka. They are like a protective barrier for us. I also introduced myself. My name given to me at birth is [*name withheld*]. I am *L'uknax̱.ádi* of the raven Coho clan. I am the child of a *Wooshkeetaan* eagle shark and a grandchild of the *Kaagwaantaan* eagle wolf. I also told you about my clan house, *Kayaash Ka Hít*, which is the Coho house and my clan crest, which is the Coho salmon as you see here on my vest. [Sandy turns around revealing a magnificent, multicoloured Coho salmon beaded on the back of her vest.] If you have any questions, feel free to ask me.'

From the beginning, Sandy took command of her group's expectations for a Native-themed tour. She established her identity by speaking the Tlingit language and outlining her clan lineage.[16] Sandy prepared them to be alert and listening, ready to respond to their guide. With over a decade of experience giving tours, Sandy knew exactly how to fill an hour with 'edutaining' content that appealed to tourists' curiosity about living in Alaska, and what it means to be Native Alaskan. She knew what tourists wanted of her, and how to deliver it.

In Sitka and mass tourism destinations around the world, local guides accommodate perceived tourist expectations as part of their product performance to deliver the people, history and culture of a unique destination. As described on their website, Sitka Tribe of Alaska's Tribal Tours offers an 'opportunity to experience Alaska with real Alaskans ... Our Alaska Native guides have a personal connection to Sitka's history and culture, and you can feel the difference.' A company whose point of difference is cultural, Tribal Tours prides itself in delivering an 'authentic' experience. The website content continues, 'Sitka Tribal Tours employs guides that are residents of the Sitka community. Our entire community participates in annual training with Tlingit elders and local historians. This guarantees Native cultural authenticity and historical accuracy within our program' (www.sitkatribe.org/sitkatours/about.html).

From the first impression, Sandy marked herself as a member of an 'exotic' culture. Although her features physically marked her as different from her largely Euro-American audience, Sandy's beaded vest, Northwest Coast Native designed silver bracelets, and earrings polished off her striking appearance. Beyond the visual, Sandy clearly demonstrated her 'Native-ness' through her strategic use of the Tlingit language indexing her identity as a member of the Tlingit Nation. After introducing herself, Sandy drew the group's attention to an island just across the bay, the site of her family's ancestral fish camp, and described what it is like to harvest fish as part of a traditional subsistence lifestyle. This comment substantiated her ties to place by asserting that generations of Tlingits have lived here, and played upon the stereotype that Native Americans are somehow closer to nature by living off the land. Through her looks, language, and the content of her speech, Sandy established herself as somebody who can deliver an insider's view of Sitka from an 'authentic' Tlingit viewpoint within the first few minutes of her tour.

In order to market and sell culture, it must be packaged to showcase sufficient signs of 'the Other' corresponding to consumer desires. In the same way that Native arts can be simplified for tourist consumption (Graburn 1976), culture itself can be presented in bits and pieces, easily digested in the format of a tour. Tour guides play the role of 'the Other', moulding their performance into bite-size, consumable bits, performing a simplified version of themselves that conforms to what they think fits the tourist gaze. Performing 'the Other' is a critical activity that reflects the double consciousness implicit in the representation of ethnic identity through the hegemonic encounter. The cultural tourism worker keenly experiences this 'double consciousness', or the idea that 'one is always looking at one's self through the eyes of others', as she struggles between her identity as lived outside of the workplace and the identity she commoditizes to satisfy the tourist gaze. Ultimately, the tour guide expresses free choice over the way she constructs and performs an identity, but these choices affect the market value of the self as a commodity. In this manner, the tourist gaze can more accurately be theorized in terms of the interplay between hosts and guests.

Resisting the Tourist Gaze

As Sandy continues her tour, she takes the group to the Indian 'village' part of town. As she slowly drives past the parallel rows of austere, two-story wooden houses, Sandy points out where she and her relatives grew up, telling stories of her childhood in the village. Suddenly, Sandy stops and directs the group's attention to a house decorated with multiple, crudely executed Northwest Coast Native art designs and exclaims sarcastically, 'the man who lives here would lose his Indian blood if he got a nosebleed'. As the other passengers around them laugh, Marge and Helen look at each other puzzled; they do not understand that Sandy's joke was covertly directed at them. This joke seemed to indicate Sandy's feelings that despite the sisters' 'family myth' of a Sioux Indian grandmother, the women did not grow up in a Native American community and as such, they could not 'share' a Native identity with her.

To claim Native American ancestry, yet not enough to carry any personal memories of this identity and to claim it 'lost' generations back, is a popular way to identify oneself as truly 'American', to feel a part of the American historical and cultural fabric, and as such, family myths arise.[17] Those who vocalize such 'family myths' often echo the American Indian of the popular imagination – the fringe dress Cherokee princesses, feather headdress generic plains Indian chief – and because these legends are so far removed from the contemporary Native experience, they are easy to identify. Historian Melissa Meyer (1999: 241) points out, 'The Indians who populate the American popular imagination bear absolutely no relationship to real native people either in the past or in the present ... [allowing] Americans and people over the world to sustain highly romanticized notions of Indianness'.

Sandy's joke directed at the two sisters demonstrates that just as tourists size up their Native guides with the power of the tourist gaze, tourism workers return the gesture with what could be considered, 'the tourism worker's (or host) gaze'. The 'tourism worker's gaze' and 'the tourist gaze' are a heuristic device, dichotomous frames of reference that mediate interactions between hosts and guests in the touristic borderzone. Dichotomous ends on a continuum of subjectivities, the tourism worker's gaze is as covert as the tourist gaze is overt. If the tourist gaze is a front stage activity, the tourism worker's gaze belongs in the backstage. As the tourist gaze is informed by stereotypes circulated in mainstream society about the culture being consumed, the tourism worker's gaze is informed by the day-to-day interactions with tourists that generate 'reverse stereotypes'. Just as the tourist gaze reproduces asymmetrical power relations between Western tourists and members of minority cultures on display, the tourism worker's gaze is an attempt to take back a modicum of power to define herself and have a say in her working conditions.

Operating in direct conflict with the demands of the hospitality industry to always remain friendly, approachable and polite, turning the gaze back onto tourists is a form of resistance. Discussing the psychological ambivalence that subordinates feel, cultural anthropologist, Sherry Ortner, writes, 'in a relationship of power, the dominant often has something to offer, and sometimes a great deal (though always of course at the price of continuing in power). The subordinate thus has many grounds for ambivalence about resisting the relationship' (1995: 175). Likewise, Native American cultural tourism workers have strong feelings of ambivalence towards their clients. On one hand, workers experience a fulfilling sense of pride in sharing cultural excellence with admiring tourists. On the other hand, facing the demands of service work coupled with negative stereotyping associated with the tourist gaze tears at positive feelings of self-worth, and may invoke deep-seated intergenerational psychological trauma. Rather than internalize feelings of alienation and low self-worth that can result from negative interactions with tourists, tour guides use a number of strategies from avoidance to confrontation to protect themselves from the self-destructive aspects of playing to tourists' harmful expectations.

For many, standing up for themselves while playing to the tourist gaze means simultaneously resisting it, albeit covertly. As James Scott (1990) points out, resistance can be hidden behind a mask of compliance utilized as a way to live through, but not necessarily resolve, problematic power relations. Tourism workers' resistance usually goes undetected by those to whom it is directed; it varies in gradation and intensity as it is 'continually negotiated in the discourse and practice of everyday life' (Valaskis 1993: 238). At its most basic and unconscious level, tour guides practise resistance simply by portraying themselves within a trope of cultural persistence in the face of dominant society. At its most consciously directed level, tour guides actively challenge tourists' stereotypes about Native Americans through rehearsed or spontaneous commentary.

Resistance in the cultural tourism setting is part of a larger struggle among Native American people to control their representation in the dominant society. Just a few generations ago, Southeast Alaska Native community leaders and activists spoke out against Jim Crowe era segregation in Alaska's cities built on top of their ancestral village grounds. They fought with state and federal governments to be treated as equal citizens of the U.S. and for the return of their lands. Against this historical backdrop of colonialism, racism, and segregation, Native tour guides do not simply stand by and listen to tourists occasionally make ignorant comments at the expense of their pride. Out of respect for their relations, living and dead, who fought for equality and social justice, they resist as part of an overall mission to present themselves as fully rounded human beings, beyond the flattening effect of stereotyping.

Native tour guides resist past stereotypes they are a part of by positioning themselves as firmly entrenched in modernity, as multifaceted individuals who are a part of the contemporary American mainstream. For example, while discussing local bear-sightings on a tour, a guide explained:

> They eat salmon berries, blueberries and huckleberries, but a major part of their diet comes from the salmon. They will rip the heads off and they will eat the fatty part of the body. They will eat thirty-five to forty salmon a day until they reach what they call their fat content and then they will go into a waking hibernation and then into sleeping hibernation. Do you want to know where I learned all of that from? ... The Discovery Channel!

In telling this joke, the guide positioned herself as someone who learns about nature by watching television (just like the tourists) rather than by an innate oneness with nature, or through the lessons of a wizened elder.

By presenting alternative visions of their lives outside of the tourism context, guides strive to change the commonly held stereotype, deeply rooted in the reinvention of America's past as a nation-building tool, that Native people are multigenerational victims of the narrative of manifest destiny in which 'Indians' subsume themselves to the 'natural' progression of 'America' into their territories. To counteract tourists' hegemonic readings of the past, tour guides present history from a Native point of view. Another guide named Jimmy tells the story of the battle of 1804 between the Russians and the Tlingits, and is careful to point out that at the outcome of the battle, the Tlingits only granted the Russians rights to a small parcel of land in present-day Sitka, called *Noow Tlien*. Following this interpretation, the Russian government never had the right to sell the territory of

Alaska to the U.S. in 1867, because the Russian American Company never had a legitimate claim to the land. Jimmy concludes this story with the remarks: 'We may have lost the Battle of 1804 against the Russians, but we have not lost the war. We were here before the Russians and we were still here after they left. We were here when the Americans came. And we will still be here after everyone else is long gone.'

With this statement, the guide drives home the point that the battle of 1804 is not just a story. Rather, it is part of an ongoing narrative in which the Tlingit people persist despite outside forces that seek to destroy their way of life. This interpretation of the battle of 1804 makes a powerful political statement that compels non-Native audiences to reassess preconceived ideas they may have concerning the victimization of Native peoples or that Native cultures are frozen in the past.

Native American tour guides' presentations of history from a subaltern point of view are powerful political expressions of identity. Stuart Hall writes, 'Identities are the names we give to the different ways we are positioned by, and position ourselves within, the narratives of the past' (1992: 225). By telling the story of the Battle of 1804, Jimmy asserts that he is not just a guide exploiting tourists to profit from his identity. Rather, he is a member of a powerful and persistent tribe whose message is greater than an hour of entertainment on tour. Within this framework, tourists ought to feel honoured to be privy to learning about what it means to be Tlingit from the point of view of an 'authentic' Native. Jimmy's account of the Battle of 1804 is not simply fashioned to entertain tourists according to the tourist gaze. In his role as cultural ambassador, Jimmy takes an active role in refashioning tourists' conceptions of Native peoples from passive victims to active survivors.

Conclusion

Exiting the bus, Helen discretely hands Sandy two crumpled dollar bills, 'Thank you so much Sandy! That is the best tour I have taken on this whole cruise'.[18] Turning to Marge, she exclaims, 'I did not expect that to be so interesting did you?'

The cultural tourism industry is often criticized for reproducing oppressive, neocolonial structures of power.[19] Tribal Tours workers are not oppressed to the extent that they choose to commoditize their identities, exploiting mainstream ideologies of what it means to be Native American and their clients' desires to consume 'the Other'. On the other hand, Tribal Tours' workers are constrained by their clients' expectations regulated by dominant archetypes for consumption (and mutual exploitation) that fabricate and maintain the image of 'the Other'. Tribal Tours' employees would probably agree with Vine Deloria's statement that 'Not even Indians can relate themselves to this type of creature, who, to anthropologists [and tourists], is the "real" Indian. Indian people begin to feel that they are merely shadows of a mythical "super Indian"' (Deloria 1970: 86). In response to this paradox, Michael Harkin (2003) writes:

> An ideological dialectic exists in Western culture, in which Indians are portrayed – and frequently portray themselves – as alternatively of the past and very much with us today, as living in noble simplicity and mastering the world of technology and global capitalism, as authentic representatives of alternative life ways and crass practitioners of hucksterism. This ideological matrix informs the tourist encounter, whether it takes place in a casino complex or a culture center in a remote village. Increasingly, Indians and other aboriginal groups will attempt to seize control of it by playing against type, by explicitly addressing stereotypes, and above all, by introducing irony into the equation.

Tribal Tours' employees willingly enter into a line of work where they are subjected to the tourist gaze, but they use the touristic encounter as an opportunity to shift dominant paradigms, actively refuting stereotypical notions through what Barbara Babcock (1978, 1994) calls 'symbolic inversion' or subtle moments of resistance within an overall scheme of cultural exchange. Unpacking activities of 'symbolic inversion' at Seattle's Tillicum Village Native American dinner-theater attraction, Katie Johnson and Tamara Underiner (2001) suggest that what is needed is a re-theorization of the producer's role in representing 'the Other' that applies a dialogic approach 'which includes Native subjectivity along with the vexed colonial frame'. Laura Peers builds on this theoretical stance, suggesting that the exchanges between Native American/First Nations hosts and non-Native guests at historical reenactment attractions along in the Great Lakes region of North America are potentially transformative cultural performances that provoke tourists to rethink assumptions 'buried within visitors' nostalgia about the unimportance and inferiority of Native peoples' (2007: 131). By simply sharing their worldviews in contrast with dominant histories, Native American interpreters challenge existing structures of power while asserting their rights to exist in the contemporary world on their own terms.

Cultural tourism businesses such as Tribal Tours represent a different relationship between cultural producers and their audiences, one in which struggles between locals, middlemen and tourists over representation (and the assumptions that go along with them) adjust according to an amplified agency on the part of cultural producers. Native American tourism workers do not blindly accommodate the tourist gaze, fulfilling clients' desires for the exotic American Indian and all the stereotypes that accompany it. Rather, they often see their jobs as part of a personal mission to share, with dignity and respect, aspects of their cultures that they choose. Through face-to-face interaction with non-Natives, Native American tourism workers dispel negative stereotypes and address historical inaccuracies. They make a powerful statement that they can and will control their representation on their own terms through a careful balance of sharing and secrecy. Native American tourism venues should not be understood as purpose-built to suit tourists' imaginations and fulfil the tourist gaze, but rather as a shared experience between locals and visitors, albeit one that is occasionally infected with intercultural tension. After all, the tourism experience unites the tour guide and the tourist; both parties are insiders to this experience, but they conceive and experience it differently. By coming together, hosts and guests create a dynamic space for the creation of new expectations of themselves and each other.

Notes

1. This chapter calls for a praxis-based approach following Ortner's (1984, 2006) formulation of it, in which cultural meanings and values are not subsumed by or merely a byproduct of economic and material conditions, rather co-constructed through social interaction.
2. The author defines self-commodification as 'a set of beliefs and practices in which an individual chooses to construct a marketable identity product while striving to avoid alienating him or herself' (Bunten 2008: 381).
3. My use of 'authenticity' here refers to the tourists' ideas of the concept, not postmodern deconstructions of it. In this case, tourists' expectations of cultural authenticity are derived mainly from dominant narratives and ideologies developed at some point in the past or present by those in power to justify the treatment and political situation of Indigenous populations. Sometimes these narratives are no longer particularly useful, such as America's 'manifest destiny' used to justify the mistreatment, removal and genocide of millions of Native Americans, but they remain in the minds of tourists. These dominant narratives trickle down to the popular consciousness through folk transmission and hegemonic devices such as the educational system, museums, and other sites of heritage.
4. Dean MacCannell (1973, 1976) claims that the tourist's desire for authenticity is disrupted through the commercialization and commodification of culture through touristic display. Nick Stanley refers to this perspective as 'the tradition of melancholia' in which ethnographic display is situated within a hegemonic global system that does not allow for plural meanings to emerge for both host and guest participants in the cultural encounter. According to the tradition of meloncholia, cultural demonstrations in the tourism setting are inherently exploitative, and inauthentic. Alternatively, Stanley proposes to view ethnographic display as a positive thing, 'preferring instead to enquire whether and under what conditions individuals and groups may sustain their sense of identity through performance in a postmodern world' (Stanley 1998: 151). Erik Cohen (1988: 382) shares this perspective. He writes, 'One has to bear in mind that commoditization often hits a culture not when it is flourishing, but when it is actually already in decline, owing to the impingement of outside forces preceding tourism. Under such circumstances, the emergence of a tourist market frequently facilitates the preservation of a cultural tradition, which would otherwise perish. It enables bearers to maintain a meaningful local or ethnic identity which they might have otherwise lost.'
5. Most employees over the age of eighteen have a high school diploma. Of these, many have had some college, and/or post-high school vocational training.
6. The qualifiers 'rich and poor' are extremely subjective in this case. Some Tribal Tours workers refer to their co-workers as 'rich', when they might fit in a middle-class, median-income bracket. Tribal Tours workers' incomes range from poverty-level to above the median household income of $51,901 (City and Borough of Sitka website). Also, many workers hold additional jobs across a variety of fields and industries.

7. For more discussion of this phenomenon, which I term, 'cultural uniformity as a simplifying trope', see Bunten 2008.
8. While all names are fictional in this chapter, the scenarios they describe occurred.
9. The cultural tourism formula requires the tourism site to have most or all of these elements: 1) the greeting, 2) the guide, 3) demonstrated use of the heritage language, 4) traditional architecture, 5) a performance, 6) a gift shop or souvenirs for sale, and often 7) demonstrations of traditional Native crafts. Throughout the experience, all communication follows Western performative, oratorical standards. The guide narrates in a linear fashion, presenting and discussing what tourists are seeing at each moment. A Master of Ceremonies narrates the dance performance explaining what the tourists are about to hear and see. These elements make up the structural backbone of cross-cultural commodification in the cultural tourism setting. Cultural tourism workers learn to navigate, work with, and maintain these aspects of ethnographic display as critical components to their labour (Bunten 2006).
10. Although there is a certain element of simulacra associated with marketing each Southeast Alaskan city as a port known for some aspect of their histories, each of these cities are genuinely unique in respect to their advertising. For example, Skagway really was an entry point for the Alaskan gold rush, and Sitka was the Russian capital of America as advertised.
11. 'Erasure is a process in which ideology renders some persons or activities invisible. Facts that are inconsistent with the ideological scheme either go unnoticed or get explained away' (Irvine and Gal 2000: 38).
12. Since the time this chapter was written, additional cruise lines have contracted to sell Tribal Tours products onboard their ships.
13. Although it could be argued that if the real history is that these places decayed or were destroyed over time, would it not be more 'authentic' not to rebuild them? Are rebuilt historical edifices such as St Michael's Russian Orthodox Cathedral more 'authentic' than newer attractions such as the Sheet'ka Kwaan Naa Kahidi Community House?
14. The local Tlingit community, who made up some of the church's congregation, offered a great deal of support to rebuild St Michael's Cathedral.
15. Although a multi-vocal approach to marketing Sitka's rich heritage is a step forward from presenting a one-sided history that exaggerates Russian America, the marketing of Sitka does not capture Sitka's complexity – for example, the impact of Sitka's 'Russian' and 'American' past on today's Sitka Native population.
16. It is important to note that even though most guides give an introduction in Tlingit, none of them are fluent in the language. In fact, the language is moribund, with fewer than five hundred fluent native speakers, all of whom are over the age of fifty.
17. Identity politics surrounding who is and is not considered Native American are complex and hotly contested. Some of the factors utilized in discerning Native identity include family, blood quantum, experience, and the geopolitics of location. This chapter does not aim to enter this debate, but merely to illustrate one tour guide's ownership and protection of her own identity while simultaneously commoditizing it. For more discussion, see Jackson 2002, Meyers 1999, and Sturm 2002.
18. This is a common comment that Tribal Tours guides receive from visitors.
19. For more discussion, see Crick 1996, Bruner and Kirshenblatt-Gimblett 1994, and Pratt 1992.

References

Anderson, B. 1991. *Imagined Communities: Reflections on the Origin and Spread of Nationalism.* London: Verso.

Appadurai, A. 1990. 'Disjuncture and Difference in the Global Economy', in M. Featherstone (ed.), *Global Culture*. London: Sage Publications, pp. 295–310.

Babcock, B. 1978. *The Reversible World: Symbolic Inversion in Art and Society*. Ithaca: Cornell University Press.

————. 1994. 'Pueblo Cultural Bodies', *Journal of American Folklore* 107(423): 40–54.

Bruner, E. 2005. *Culture on Tour, Ethnographies of Travel*. Chicago: University of Chicago Press.

Bruner E. and B. Kirshenblatt-Gimblett. 1994. 'Maasai on the Lawn: Tourist Realism in East Africa', *Cultural Anthropology* 9(4): 435–70.

Bunten, A.C. 2006. "'So, How Long Have You Been Native?" Self-Commodification in the Native-Owned Cultural Tourism Industry', Ph.D. dissertation. Los Angeles: University of California, Los Angeles.

————. 2008. 'Sharing Culture or Selling Out? Developing the Commodified Persona in the Heritage Industry', *American Ethnologist* 35(3): 380–95.

City and Borough of Sitka. n.d. 'About Sitka'. Retrieved 13 September 2010 from http://www.cityofsitka.com/residents/about/index.html.

Cohen, E. 1988. 'Authenticity and Commoditization in Tourism', *The Annals of Tourism Research: A Social Sciences Journal* 10(1): 371–86.

Craik, J. 1997. 'The Culture of Tourism', in C. Rojek and J. Urry (eds), *Touring Cultures: Transformations of Travel and Theory*. London: Routledge, pp. 113–36.

Crick, M. 1996. 'Representations of International Tourism in the Social Sciences: Sun, Sex, Sights, Savings, and Servility', in Y. Apostopoulos, S. Leivadi and A. Yiannakis (eds), *The Sociology of Tourism: Theoretical and Empirical Investigations*. London: Routledge, pp. 15–50.

Deloria Jr, V. 1970. *Custer Died for Your Sins: An Indian Manifesto*. New York: Avon Books.

Ginsburg, F. 2002. 'Screen Memories: Resignifying and Traditional in Indigenous Media', in F. Ginsberg, L. Abu-Lughod and B. Larkin (eds), *Media Worlds: Anthropology on New Terrain*. Berkeley: University of California Press, pp. 39–54.

Graburn, N. 1976. *Ethnic and Tourist Arts: Cultural Expressions from the Fourth World*. Berkeley: University of California Press.

Hall, S. 1992. *Culture, Media, Language: Working Papers in Cultural Studies 1972–79*. London: Routledge.

Handler, R. and W. Saxon. 1988. 'Dyssimulation, Reflexivity, Narrative, and the Quest for Authenticity in Living History', *Cultural Anthropology* 3(3): 242–60.

Harkin, M. 2003. 'Staged Encounters: Postmodern Tourism and Aboriginal People', *Ethnohistory* 50(3): 575–85.

Holland America Line. 'Explore Cruise Ports'. Retrieved 20 May 2005 from http://www.hollandamerica.com/cruise-destinations/PortDetail.action?portCode=SIT.

Irvine, J. and S. Gal. 2000. 'Language Ideology and Linguistic Differentiation', in P.V. Kroskrity (ed.), *Regimes of Language*. Santa Fe, NM: School of American Research Press, pp. 35–83.

Jackson, D. 2002. *Our Elders Lived It: American Indian Identity in the City*. DeKalb, IL: Northern Illinois University Press.

Johnson, K. and T. Underiner. 2001. 'Command Performances: Staging Native Americans at Tillicum Village', in C. Jones Meyer and D. Royer (eds), *Selling the Indian: Commercializing and Appropriating American Indian Cultures*. Tucson: University of Arizona Press, pp. 44–61.

Kan, S. 2004. "'Its Only Half a Mile from Savagery to Civilization": American Tourists and the Southeastern Alaska Natives in the Late 19th Century', in M. Mauzé, M. E. Harkin and S. Kan (eds), *Coming to Shore, Northwest Coast Ethnology, Traditions, and Visions*. Lincoln and London: University of Nebraska Press, pp. 201–20.

King, J. 1997. 'Marketing Magic: Process and Identity in the Creation and Selling of Native Art and Material Culture', in M. Mauzé (ed.), *Present is Past; Some Uses of Tradition in Native Societies*. Lanham, MD: University Press of America, pp. 81–94.

Kirshenblatt-Gimblett, B. 1998. *Destination Culture: Tourism, Museums, and Heritage*. Berkeley: University of California Press.

MacCannell, D. 1973. 'Staged Authenticity: On Arrangements of Social Space in Tourist Settings', *American Journal of Sociology* 79: 589–603.

———. 1976. *The Tourist: A New Theory of the Leisure Class*. New York, NY: Schocken Books.

———. 1984. 'Reconstructed Ethnicity Tourism and Cultural Identity in Third World Communities', *Annals of Tourism Research* 11: 375–91.

McDowell Group. 2001. 'Cultural Theater Market Demand Estimate' from a report prepared for Shee Atika Incorporated.

Meyer, M. 1999. 'American Indian Blood Quantum Requirements: Blood is Thicker than Family', in V. Matsumoto and B. Allmendinger (eds), *Over the Edge: Remapping the American West*. Berkeley: University of California Press, pp. 231–50.

National Trust for Historic Preservation. 2010. 'Dozen Distinctive Destinations: Sitka'. Retrieved 14 July 2010 from http://www.preservationnation.org/traveland-sites/sites/western-region/sitka-alaska.html.

Nichols and Gilstrap, Inc. 2000. Strategic Marketing Analysis and Planning for Alaska Tourism.

Nuttall, M. 1997. 'Packaging the Wild: Tourism Development in Alaska', in S. Abram, J. Waldren and D. MacLeod (eds), *Tourists and Tourism; Identifying with People and Places*. Oxford and New York: Berg, pp. 223–38.

Ortner, S. 1984. 'Theory in Anthropology since the Sixties', in N. Dirks, G. Eley and S. Ortner (eds), *Culture/Power/History: A Reader in Contemporary Social History*. Princeton: Princeton University Press, pp. 372–411.

———. 1995. 'Resistance and the Problem of Ethnographic Refusal', *Comparative Studies in Society and History* 37(1): 173–93.

———. 2006. *Anthropology and Social Theory: Culture, Power and the Acting Subject*. Durham, NC: Duke University Press.

Peers, L. 2007. *Playing Ourselves: Interpreting Native Histories at Historic Reconstructions*. Lanham, MD: Alta Mira Press.

Pratt, M. (1992) *Imperial Eyes: Travel Writing and Transculturation*. New York: Routledge.

Raibmon, P. 2005. *Authentic Indians: Episodes of Encounter from the Late-Nineteenth-Century Northwest Coast*. Durham, NC: Duke University Press.

Rossel, P. (ed.) 1988. 'Potlatch and the Totem: the Attraction of America's Northwest Coast', in P. Rossel (ed.), *Tourism: Manufacturing the Exotic*. Copenhagen: IWGIA Document No. 61.

Scott, J. 1990. *Domination and the Arts of Resistance: Hidden Transcripts*. New Haven, CT: Yale University Press.

Silver, I. 1993. 'Marketing Authenticity in Third World Countries', *Annals of Tourism Research* 20: 302–18.

Sitka Convention and Visitors Bureau. n.d. 'Attractions'. Retrieved 12 September 2010 from http://sitka.org/things-to-do/attractions/html.

Sitka Tribe of Alaska. 'About Us'. Retrieved 15 January 2010 from http://sitkatours.com/about.html.

Stanley, N. 1998. *Being Ourselves for You: The Global Display of Cultures*. London: Middlesex University Press.

Sturm, C.D. 2002. *Blood Politics: Race, Culture and Identity in the Cherokee Nation of Oklahoma*. Berkeley: University of California Press.

Traube, E. 1996. 'The "Popular" in American Culture', *Annual Review of Anthropology* 25: 127–51.

Urry, J. 1990. *The Tourist Gaze: Leisure and Travel in Contemporary Societies*. London: Sage.

Valaskakis, G. 1993. 'Parallel Voices: Indians and Others – Narratives of Cultural Struggle', *Canadian Journal of Communication* 18(3): 283–98.

Chapter 5
FORWARD INTO THE PAST:
'DIGGING' THE BALEARIC ISLANDS

Jacqueline Waldren

Introduction

At the airport we never had any difficulty identifying 'the diggers'. Backpacks and dufflebags bursting with sheets and towels and sturdy gear for their two-week 'dig' and stay at the Deia Archaeological Museum. Middle-aged men and women sporting all-weather shirts, pants, hats and hiking boots, or young college students in the scantest of summer wear. Quickly introducing ourselves we gathered them together in the Land Rovers and set out for their adventure and our daily work. Once off the motorway from the airport the scene of olive and almond trees, the blue sky and the sight of the imposing Mediterranean Sea as the cars drove the winding road to Deia was more than any of them had expected. No pictures could capture the scenes before them. For those from the United States, 24 hours without sleep and the excitement of what lie ahead was dizzying.

This chapter is concerned with the negotiation of expectations surrounding an archaeological dig in one of the most tourist-oriented areas of the Mediterranean, where the commoditization of present and past cultures and the environment is highly developed. Excavating and restoring ancient monuments and preserved relics on the islands of Majorca offer these volunteers an experience of another place and time which allows them to become physically (and spiritually) involved in an unwritten past and to view their own lives in contrast. Outside their usual milieu and unconstrained by normal rules of conduct the volunteers experience a sense of freedom and escape from their ordinary lives. Seeking a connection with the past, with nature, and long-dead unknown people, their motivations and imaginings of participating in the unravelling of ancient lives through the study of artifacts, landscapes and human remains will be blended with the aims and goals of archaeology and contrasted to varied local perceptions of place, time and space.

Reimagining the past – glorifying it, making up things or interpreting them in different ways – may be people's way of expressing either a desired or nostalgic image of a harmonious past and/or a recent present that never really existed. Thus the element of fantasy, or the imaginary, enters into the way in which local people conceptualize their history, visitors observe sites, and specialists interpret prehistory. Monuments are cleaned and made accessible to the public and the tourism industry relies on such images to attract people to adventure into the past. In Majorca, land and buildings owned by elites, and cared for by locals, have been modernized into hotels and landscaped gardens. A few archaeological sites have been purchased from the owners and opened to the public. However, many locals, land owners, residents and farmers, may not identify in any way with these changes, and in contrast to those who make their living from tourism, have little interest in the distant past and are not willing to open their lands for public access.[1] Many landscapes where ancient monuments can be found are on private estates and have never had public access.

Setting the Scene

Having been the administrator of an archaeological project directed by my husband, Dr William Waldren, in Majorca for the past thirty years, I would like to use the volunteers who have participated in this project as my study group to gain some deeper insights into the motivations, expectations and satisfactions they have experienced during their fortnight visit to our archaeological project. The Deia Archaeological Museum and Research Centre (DAMARC) was formed by the Waldrens from 1960 to 1974, and includes a museum, laboratory, lecture room and conservation lab, and provides accommodation and meals for twenty volunteers and staff. The 'dig' I am discussing is composed of three sites located in the high Jurassic mountains of the island and each differs greatly in geology and environment. Together they have provided the oldest record of human occupation of the Balearic Islands (Majorca, Menorca, Formentera and Cabrera) and human association with endemic extinct fauna. The 'digs' (plus a hundred other projects) are marketed by a non-profit environmentally concerned organization, Earthwatch, to members (who pay an annual fee to join and receive three brochures a year). 'Prehistoric Societies of Majorca' is presented as follows:

> Majorca, a sun-soaked, scenic isle, with terraces of olive, fig, almond, and lemon groves climbing steep slopes from the blue Mediterranean Sea, has been a cultural melting pot for six thousand years. Prehistoric cultures immigrated from every direction in succession, bringing their own advances in architecture, agriculture and metallurgy.

You can help investigate the activities of various cultures that used the Son Mas Sanctuary, among the oldest known ritual sites in the Western Mediterranean and help to interpret the migrations of peoples to this crossroads of the Mediterranean, from the mists of prehistory until Roman times, and their impact on the ecology and development of the island. Deia, a quaint village in the northern sierras of Majorca steeped in history, provides a timeless backdrop for your exploration. (Earthwatch catalogue 2006)

This invitation to participate in an archaeological dig on Majorca draws on the visual, social, intellectual and adventurous curiosities of the individual contemplating this project. The prospective participants are drawn from a captive 'members' audience. The above description has been designed to entice people to join the archaeologist in this beautiful setting to aid in unravelling the prehistoric past of Majorca. Their participation provides the funding needed to realize this work. The archaeologist's acceptance of non-professional volunteers aged 16–75 is motivated by their essential financial and physical contribution to the realization of the project.

Many of the participants (mostly American, a few British and European, an occasional Chinese or Japanese) come from backgrounds as diverse as train drivers, lawyers, doctors, teachers, students, actresses, or directors. Some of the older participants expressed that they 'had always dreamed of becoming an archaeologist', a profession considered in the 1930s to 1960s, when they were growing up, as a risky career choice. Many of these amateur lovers of archaeology came to Majorca with the illusion of 'living their dream'. One 70-year-old woman explained:

For me it was my retirement present. From the time I was a young girl and read of the Leakey's exploits in Africa, I wanted to work in the field. But it was not possible to support three children and finish my degree at the same time. So it was put on the shelf until I retired and had the funds to go on this adventure.

Another, who was a retired doctor, added:

The description of the project reawakened my childhood dream and allowed me to imagine what life as an archaeologist was like. The setting in a mountain village with terraced landscape supporting olive trees, streams running from the mountains to the sea, sunny days and social evenings in local cafés made it even more attractive.

Not all volunteers arrive in Majorca with the same degree of excitement. Some are overcoming traumatic experiences (widowhood, divorce, illness), life changes between children leaving home, jobs, gap year or starting college. For them the dig is a rite of passage from one stage to another in their lives. Their separation from all that was familiar, among strangers in a foreign land, subject to new and different conditions, allows them time and space to reflect upon their everyday lives and expectations for the future. The PI (Principal Investigator) encourages everyone to keep involved with the project after they leave and some saw this as their new direction. For example, a number of middle-aged men and women decided to go back to college to read archaeology, students previously undecided on their major or considering reading archaeology made up their minds. Many returned as staff in later years and went on to teaching careers.

Impressions and Expectations from Life on the Dig

During their participation in the dig, the participants live communally in a unique artist-built home, sharing dormitory accommodations, home-cooked meals and daily field and lab activities. Their briefing material gave them the schedule, described the facilities as 'rustic simple comforts unlike those at home', and listed the clothes and special items (e.g., Swiss knife, torch, sleeping bag) they would need. These preparations were the beginning of their adventure, so that weeks before their departure they were entering into the feel of what was ahead. It was always surprising to see how conscientious participants were in keeping to the lists, leaving behind their preferred mode of dress or make-up, and instead bringing old T-shirts, multi-pocketed pants and waistcoats à la Indiana Jones.[2] Each new group was collected at the airport on the first day, and even though we had no pictures beforehand we could spot the intrepid volunteers from afar. 'Diggers' are recognized by their khaki trousers or 'Bermudas', dusty T-shirts and heavy shoes in the midst of the tourist's sandals and bright colours.

During their first day in Majorca, after settling into their dormitory rooms, participants are 'let loose' on the village so they can stretch their muscles, find their way around, relax after their long flights, begin to chat with their new colleagues and get a personal sense of landscape and local life. Reunited before dinner they are given an orientation in the hope that they will adapt to the routine (both domestic and scientific) that will fill the next fortnight. The next day, after introductory lectures on concepts of prehistoric, seasonal, generational and life cycle time, volunteers are taken on a tour of the sites. To returnees and staff the guided tour tends to comprise a given repertoire of objects, stories and other highpoints, yet allow for embellishment and anecdotes (Bouquet and Porto 2006: 13). Participants work daily in the field from 9 A.M. to 2 P.M., returning to the centre for lunch and afternoon pottery washing, classifying, counting, numbering and drawing. The repetitiveness of the lab work often leads to them volunteering to do the entire day in the field, despite temperatures of 30–40 degrees in July and August. Needless to say, the supervising archaeologists are thrilled by this as more can be accomplished. However, the backlog of lab work increases.

In the evenings, the volunteers join ordinary tourists, expat residents and locals in the few village cafés where they can compare their experiences.[3] The contrast between the volunteers' involvement in a scheduled work project and the sun, sea, poolside and sangria days of 'normal' tourists often becomes the main topic of discussion. Reactions from those that the diggers meet may vary from 'Are you crazy, spending your holiday digging up Majorca and paying to do it?' to 'Wow, how exciting…!' In their reply to such comments the diggers reveal their own motivations for joining the project. As some honestly admit, the desire to have a vacation away from home, a change of routine, and some leisure time, are compatible with their participation in the dig. Yet, for most, the archaeological dimension of the project was the primary attraction. As they explain, 'being the first person to uncover a past relic is like fulfilling a life dream' or 'we were looking for a participatory, group experience, an opportunity to contribute to science'.

It is clear that through the comraderie and esprit de corps that develops over the fortnight's duration that both the professional archaeologist and the volunteers gain knowledge and pleasure (beyond their expectations) from the overall experience. Instant friendships develop and many people who meet on a team maintain contact with one another and the project over many years, often returning to once again share in its progress. Two women returned nine times, one man eleven times. During a year when the dig was not active, 72-year-old Sandra wrote:

> While I was in Savannah, Hilda (another digger now 88) and I both observed that Majorca's Copper Age is still not listed with Earthwatch. Does that mean you have not been able to complete your transformation? What about future digs? We think of all of you often and dream of our tenth return to Deia and to working 'in the field' once more … Hilda and I send you our love. Here's to a future for staying and excavating with the Waldren enterprise!

Landscape, the Thrill of Archaeology and Nostalgia

The success of the dig in meeting the expectations of the volunteers was the combined outcome of different but interrelated experiences: the beauty of the physical environment, the charismatic leader, the intense communal living and dining, but maybe above all, the thrill of the archaeological investigation, that opens the gate for imagining a landscape of ancient stone buildings, undiscovered social spaces, and rituals of life and death in a world removed from the mundane reality of everyday life. More importantly, this combination allowed the imagining of the past to take place within the physicality of the present, as part of real experiences lived through the senses. The combination of the imagined with the real transformed the 'archaeological holiday' to a dream come true.

Participants commented on their sensation that whatever had transpired on this landscape over the centuries had and continues to involve enormous human efforts. Even today, stone walls (terraces) criss-cross the mountains, supporting olive trees and earth and the stone houses built there.

During the first days, once introduced to the huge stone monuments on the site, the volunteers did what the archaeologist called 'site cosmetics' – cutting back weeds and bush to reveal the megalithic monuments they were to excavate within. The many tedious jobs associated with excavation were taken up with enthusiasm, which was rewarded when a sherd was uncovered after extensive scraping, sifting and carrying buckets of earth. Although the volunteers were not professional archaeologists, the PI running the project always made a point of letting them know that he respected their life experience and knowledge from other fields, and appreciated their willingness to 'get in the dirt and dig'. Unfettered by academic expertise, their questions and insights were valued contributions to making the sites, bones and artefacts come alive. The PI was the epitome of the intrepid archaeologist: tall, muscular, intense and incredibly enthusiastic about everything he said. For him, excavation was 'not a profession' but 'a way of life'. He lived, breathed and dreamed archaeology. And his enthusiasm touched all those who came to the project.

Filmed over four days for the television series *Time Team* (Channel 4 UK) the sites and activities were theatricalized and the searches for 'lost' epochs were aimed at catching viewers' imagination and allowing them brief encounters with the excitement of archaeology. Tony Robinson, the well-known commentator, introduced the programme as follows:

> The Team's foray abroad this year was to Deia on the island of Majorca, in pursuit of the 'Beaker folk', an enigmatic culture – dating from about 2,500 to 1,300 BC during the Copper Age – thought by some to have been responsible for the introduction of metalwork into Britain. Here, the traces of them are few, but on Majorca, Professor Bill Waldren has uncovered Son Oleza, a virtually complete prehistoric settlement the size of a football pitch. He has found foundations for buildings, both domestic and communal, and perimeter walls; clay-lined water channels to supply the houses; and a large quantity of finds including 127,000 pieces of Beaker pottery – more than have been found in the whole of Britain. The Team also investigate a 'maze' that presents them with some difficulties – not least the removal of over a ton of rubble from a promising wall line – and a temple site that may have astronomical implications. (Time Team 2001)

The viewers' imaginations are aroused as they follow the work, potential meanings given to artefacts and areas uncovered before their eyes. Television documentaries such as Time Team provide visual reality and offer vicarious consumption of untrod territories, prehistory or other periods and all that each site evokes. Many tropes about travel and sociological theories (including those about tourists) refer to the idea of an idyllic life located away from the here and now (see for example, Urry 1990). There is much discussion today about the 'modern' disengaged person and it is suggested that for them current social migrancy (movement, travel) provides the 'vantage point from which one is best able to come to know oneself' (Andrews 2000). Ritual journeys outside of everyday space and time propel the search for self. Projects such as this dig provide for needs in modified forms of *communitas* and *animus loci*. People of different social backgrounds, perfect strangers joined together for this project, form a 'normative *communitas*' (as described by Turner 1982). Rapport and Dawson argue that people share a yearning for inclusion, emotion and displacement, in a word notions of 'home' and that is dependent on estrangement (1998: 7). Other theorists are in agreement about this nostalgic quest, emphasizing its territorial and fabricated nature.

The Dig from the Local Point of View

The mediation of tourism encounters in Deia over extended intervals of time and space has evolved to the point that 'the diggers' are identified in local vernacular as *els oses* (those who dig up grave-bones). Nicknames are an important indication of a person's place – and incorporation – in village life (Waldren 1996). By the second day of their stay in Majorca the volunteers are greeted in the local shop or café and often asked 'How is it going? Did you find anything today?' As the evening progresses staff relate how their local friends say, 'We know you go out at night and plant the stuff they find … you have to make sure they get their money's worth'.

This is a relevant comment as it clearly indicates the commercial quality associated with tourism. Although not all transactions between foreigners and locals are oriented around business, it is difficult to separate commercial exchange from other forms of interaction. Everyday exchanges with a multitude of strangers depersonalizes the usual local exchanges. Global economic and social trends are reflected in local encounters and, most of all, new forms of education and employment have made major gender differences in the experiences of children, young adults and pensioners. Cosmopolitan, after years of 'hosting' tourists, retirees, artists and writers from around the world, Majorcan's are trying desperately to maintain, recapture and reinvent their history, environment and culture while participating fully in the global social, material and economic advances at their disposal. Young single men and women share social activities with regular visitors after continued encounters; they will buy drinks for one another, maybe go climbing together, and as time and knowledge of the other increases, they might visit the home country of their non-local friends, even travel with them. Older generations, however, do not mix so easily and many do not mix at all.

The dig is made possible by monetary transactions yet the essence is *communitas* and discovery of self and the past, a joining of diverse people, motivations and goals all of which seem to be beyond the commercial. The contribution made to village life socially and economically is most valuable for all concerned, from other visitors, residents, locals, the café and shop owners, to food and service providers. The impact of the dig reflects local and global interdependence between human cultures and their environments and the effects that changes in one have on the other. Among some of the older locals in Deia and nearby villages, where caves and rock shelters as well as megalithic constructions abound, there is a scepticism about the authenticity of these ancient sites, the value of their excavation or the artefacts found. Meanings of ruins and engagements with remains of the past have been perceived differently over the past fifty years by farmers, land owners, archaeologists, young people, foreign residents and government bodies.[4] The interaction with monuments has impacted in diverse ways with the present, and the reality behind conservation and preservation issues reveals changing political, social and economic concerns. The active digs in Deia made locals more aware of their prehistoric past although they were more involved with the contemporary social and cultural impacts.

While the harshness of the landscape left little leisure for mere admiration for those who must wrest their living from the land, local people both appreciated and resented their environment. Their relationship with it involved farming work – often experienced as 'struggle' (see Theodossopoulos 2003) – but also opportunities to admire the transforming result of this work on the land. This encouraged the appreciation of the land's beauty, not merely as pristine nature, but as the product of generations of hard work inscribed on the landscape. It also involved an intimate, experiential knowledge of the island, its climate, its textures, the contrasts of stone and earth, seasonal changes, mountains and sea. It was conducive to producing ample crops, but required many months of arduous labour, fears of nature's unpredictable effects (unseasonal rain, hail, dry spells, insects) during the further months of waiting to collect and process the products. Land used for agriculture, owned by elites, cared for by locals and converted into job-producing development (hotels, construction, etc.) was seen in the 1970s to 1990s as a positive form of environmentally aware modernization. However, climactic conditions are unpredictable, and as more building occurred natural resources were stretched and greater planning and building restrictions needed to be created and enforced.

The use and abandonment of the archaeological sites reflects similar constraints: water access, climatic changes, different religious and social concepts, and the importance of considering the long-term patterns of change that have created a particular socio-cultural, political and material landscape over time. During their stay, as familiarity with materials, objects, site details and teaching progresses, participants' interpretations and imaginings of the life that might have transpired on the sites are often more colourful and ethnocentric than that unravelled by the archaeologists over decades, yet add to evening discussions animated by local wine. Prehistoric archaeology identifies and studies cultures displaced in place and time in the absence of documentary accounts. It is between the direct interaction of individuals and objects that the culture is mediated; the objects have embedded within the materiality of their design and manufacture a series of cultural values that shape the practices, both body and mind, by which those objects were used. They have been shaped for instrumental purposes and designed to fit in with particular types of cultural practice. Where a successful cultural form provides an ongoing framework for interpreting and generating experience, boundaries are easily discernable, symbols are neatly situated, and sequence is explicitly controlled (Rabinow 1977).

Thus the potential for interpretation is open and often alters as more evidence is uncovered. Like Wordsworth's majestic white mountain, Mont Blanc, imaginings turn out to be a disappointment: 'The clouds cleared, the peak was unveiled, and we grieved to see it'. The realities of past lives are often revealed to be less romantic than imagined through artefacts, stratigraphies, bones and stones. This element of risk and discovery and reinterpretation adds to the excitement of the dig.

Different Landscapes, Different Myths, Different Expectations

In anthropology, landscape has been used to refer to the meaning imputed by local people to their cultural and physical surroundings – how a particular landscape looks and feels to its inhabitants (Bender 1993, 1998; Hirsch and O'Hanlon 1995; Ucko and Layton 1999). It is important to clarify from the beginning that the landscape in Deia means different things to the diverse population of this cosmopolitan village. To 'locals' it is not just land but people, families, work, leisure, time, space and location carried in the mind and mediated in experience. It is formed and reformed over time according to the social, political, economic and ecological developments within and beyond the village. The landscape is redolent with past actions, history, ancestors and myth, which are used in defining social groups.

Tourists, visitors, 'diggers' and foreign residents view the village from various perspectives: romantic, idealistic and spiritual, and liken it to a paradise that reflects timeless permanence. The relationship between place and space, insiders' and outsiders' images and representations are dependent on cultural and historical context (Waldren 1996). Global and local perceptions and social relations have formed the place we call Deia today. I will suggest that a 'myth' of Deia has developed and been enhanced by the idealized visions of visitors and expatriate residents, and has encouraged Majorcans in general to see the value of past cultures and their own fading culture, rugged terrain and rural settings as products to be consumed rather than as a burden or remnant of pre-modern existence.

This myth is a composite of various allusions by long-time resident Robert Graves and other poets and artists that have portrayed the village as 'like Delphi', 'home of the White Goddess' (Graves 1948), full of archaeological ruins and a magic they feel pervades Deia's landscape. These esoteric fantasies have combined with elements from old Majorcan *rondalles* (oral tales) many of which concern heroes who rise from humble origins to a higher destiny through the aid of strangers. These stories help to convey the ethos of Deia, its history of eccentric visitors seeking self-knowledge and artistic fulfilment and their long-suffering but condoning hosts. An imaginary landscape peopled by exotic others is articulated in the telling of these stories and a myth is developed, enhanced and perpetuated by each retelling to visitors and tourists.

Deia's landscape reveals the input of prehistoric communities, Romans, Moors, Catalans and today's Majorcans and international residents. These people have engaged with it, reworked it, appropriated it and altered it. The landscape one finds today is quite different than in the past. In the words of Tilley 'the landscape is socialized through interconnections with settlements, houses, mountains, trees, roads and sea and drawn into the domain of human negotiations' (1993). Every inch of Deia is privately owned, often named after its original owners, characteristic landmarks, elements of the area or activities carried on there. These names are metaphors of social relations past and present and reveal the social, economic and cultural history of the village (Waldren 1996: 78).

With tourism now a major economic and social force in most of the islands bordering the Mediterranean, culture is often commoditized. However, what is ultimately consumed is not objects or places, but each person's expectations, sensations or imagination of them. Places are often imbued with magical or mythical qualities by those who observe them, even more than by those who inhabit them. Archaeologists lead our diggers down unmarked roads helping them to 'discover' new sights, sounds and feelings far removed from their usual recognizable habitat. The traveller's imagination is offered a wide span. Romance, corporeal experiences, intimacy with nature or among locals or other participants or with tourists all contribute to the construction of a new conceptualization of place. In this process, the volunteer is an active agent involved through physical exertion rather than a detached observer.

Anthropology and archaeology share an interest in the study of the landscape that has brought the two disciplines together (see Ucko and Layton 1999). A common denominator in the approaches from both disciplines is that landscape is no longer the backdrop for human activity, but an active force in their lives. Archaeological remains and local people are part of the landscape but their interests on issues of monuments, ploughed fields, grazing animals, seasonality or development are quite diverse, leading to what Lucia Nixon described as 'a landscape of contested identity' (2006).

In Deia, those who remain to work the land are seen as backward by their peers, out of step with modernization and opportunities. However, landowners rely on their labour and expertise to maintain cultivations, while archaeologists glean insights from their knowledge of the terrain. Here, the archaeologist is interested in 'the construction of the monument, social differentiation as expressed in the ability to mobilize manpower [*sic*] and the degree to which social competition may be expressed through the construction, use and abandonment of the monument'

(Chapman, Waldren and Von Strydonck 1993). The excavations reveal prehistoric constructions of great interest to the archaeologists while the mountains of earth and rock removed create obstacles for animals that graze in the area.[5] The landscape is reformed by the excavations. The farmer warns the archaeologist against leaving deep holes that his sheep might fall into, while the landowner wants to avoid trespassing tourists searching out the monuments.

The archaeologist's knowledge and experience combined with the creative influence of the archaeological interpretation of partial material remains often leads to the imagination of a privileged landscape only archaeologists can read.[6] It is as though they form an X-ray vision of what a particular landscape meant over time in the hope of uncovering the underpinnings they imagined with the help and enthusiasm of the volunteers. These privileged, imagined archaeological landscapes coexist with the landscapes experienced by the locals, but in a separate, parallel, imagined reality. The volunteers gradually enter this imagined reality, as they learn how to read, inhabit and embody the landscapes of archaeological knowledge.

It is in this respect that the volunteers learn, in a short period of time, how to hold several Majorcan landscapes at the same time (cf. Bender 1993). Their journeys of discovery at the excavation site set free their imagination, opening a portal to the worlds of the past. This is combined with the embodied, sensual experience of an enchanting physical landscape, new tastes and new acquaintances. The overwhelming nature of these experiences often leads the volunteers to develop an esoteric, idealized connection with Deia, to approach the archaeological site as a magical, mysterious, or spiritual domain. Lacking the empirical and technical knowledge of the professional archaeologists, and the long-term, dwelling perspective of the locals, they walk in between parallel, enchanted worlds, the archaeological landscapes of the past, and the landscapes of their new and diverse social acquaintances in the present.[7]

Conclusion

As William Waldren wrote in his article on Warehouses of Prehistory for the travel book *Inside Guides: Majorca & Ibiza, Menorca & Formentera*, 'Islands are not just vacation paradises, but important places in which all nature of evolution, prehistory and history have taken place' (1989: 28). Today's visitors to Majorca have many choices: city, country, beach, pool, walking, biking, mountains, culture, history, prehistory. Most of these can be combined, as modern roads, infrastructures and services criss-cross the island. Archaeological sites and museums are open to the public and the vast span of expectations and imaginings of those who arrive on the island continue to foster new activities and projects.

The perception and promotion of the island's 'natural' landscapes, climate and agricultural past includes all of these choices and more. Historical and contemporary myths of the Mediterranean continue to attract a multitude of visitors. Among these are the volunteers who participate in a particular archaeological dig in Majorca, the protagonists of the ethnography presented in this chapter. I have explored the articulation of the expectations of the volunteers with their discovery of a highly idealized Majorcan landscape, one that encompasses separate layers of historical time in parallel. During this process of discovery, the diggers gain new insights and actively construct new imaginings or perspectives of the Majorcan landscape. As Philip Duke (2008) argues with respect to the construction of archaeological discourse on another Mediterranean island (Crete), the tourists – and in this case, the tourist-volunteers – reconstitute the present in the past, drawing extensively from their experiences in the present to imagine a comparable past.

As the volunteers spend more time among the ruins and artefacts left by prehistoric peoples and/or excavated by other volunteers before them, they challenge themselves, put their physical, social and cognitive abilities to the test, and enlarge their view of the past. While they adapt to these multiple new experiences, they compare the parallel landscapes of the past with their 'ordinary' life back home, and they find the former much more exciting. We can acknowledge that all life involves the construction of agreed-upon fictions and that the least harmful are those that assert self-worth. The desire of the volunteers to return to what has become an idyllic place, is based on the expectation that everything will be 'the same' and as exciting as before. Not surprisingly, most volunteers yearn to return to Majorca, to reconnect with the idiosyncratic landscapes they created in their minds during their previous visits. In order to maintain the memory and expectation of this self-discovered, imagined world, they often compartmentalize their experiences in Majorca from their ordinary lives back home (see Theodossopoulos and Skinner, in this volume), even from the lives of the local Majorcan and the 'other', ordinary tourists. Their persistent desire to uphold to their personal, enchanted landscapes of Majorca is a testimony to the agency of the contemporary tourist to actively construct and control the tourist experience.

Hilda, a multiple returnee, reminds me each time she leaves that she wants 'the same downstairs room next time' and 'please don't let anyone dig in my trench'. Her expectations, like those of many other volunteers, indicate a romantic relationship with Majorca and its history, the excavation site and the individuals who participated in the dig. This does not necessarily include an awareness of the production and logistics of the excavation as a realistic operation. Still, the experience of each volunteer has been unique and allowed a pause and reflection about the self and everyday life 'back at home'. When the departing diggers arrive at the airport, they reiterate their excitement and fulfilment; their sadness at having to end a fortnight of digging, gazing, sensing, and learning is palpable; their eyes, hugs and warm goodbyes expressing the sense that some of their expectations have, after all, been realized.

It was a glorious golden September when I landed on the island of Majorca, one of eleven volunteers to report for some of the dirtiest duty you have ever seen on a vacation. But, I dug the place. I mean, really dug it. I've got the broken nails, the photos of broken pots and the memories to prove it … It was a fun lesson in instant archaeology. The thing that caught my imagination was a tiny green bead. 'That's not a bead, it's probably a bit of copper', Waldren said upon examining it. Now I could picture copper being melted and one of the precious drops escaping to end up in my hand thousands of years later. (Vicki, a journalist-volunteer, writing in *The Seattle Tribune*, 5 September 1999)

I will never be the same after this experience. (Vicki, a 40+ year-old volunteer)

Notes

1. Philip Duke's *The Tourists Gaze, the Cretans Glance: Archaeology and Tourism on a Greek Island* (2008) suggests that modern class issues and the creation of European identities have been, and still are, normatized by the discourse of Minoan archaeology. The development of the past for such purposes in Majorca is quite different.
2. The impact of such film versions of the search, challenges and discovery of ancient sites or treasures feeds the imagination and raises expectations.
3. The Deia population fluctuates from 750 winter residents of which 30 per cent are foreigners to 1,000–1,200 summer residents and visitors (second-home owners, holiday rentals and hotel guests) of which almost 50 per cent are foreign.
4. Duke (2008) suggests that the middle-class status of visitors influences the Cretan government's presentation of the past to attract more revenue, thus excluding the local Cretans from the Minoan past, despite it being a National Heritage site. Archaeologists, heritage councils and local owners influence or impede such presentations in Majorca.
5. The monuments were impediments rather than curiosities for the sheep herder who used these sites. As Bender notes for Stonehenge, 'the strange shapes and sizes of the hedged fields bore no resemblance to the present day needs of the small dairy farmer who worked the land' (1998: 184).
6. A Spanish archaeologist attributes the megalithic monuments on the Balearic island of Menorca to giants. He is not alone in such unproven hypotheses. Barry Fell, an accomplished marine biologist at Harvard 'University', was best known for his books, which claim that many centuries before Columbus 'discovered' America, Celts, Basques, Phoenicians, Egyptians and others were visiting North America. http://en.wikipedia.org/wiki/Marine_biology.
7. A participant sent the following comment to sum up his experience: 'while increasingly shaped by science, archaeology retains the quality it had when it was created in the 19th century: it tells a story'.

References

Andrews, H. 2000. 'Consuming Hospitality on Holiday', in C. Lashley and A. Morrison (eds), *Search of Hospitality: Theoretical Perspectives and Debates*. Oxford: Butterworth Heinemann, pp. 235–54.

Bender, B. (ed.). 1993. *Landscape: Politics and Perspectives*. Oxford: Berg.

Bender, B. 1998. *Stonehenge: Making Space.* Oxford: Berg.

Bouquet, M. and N. Porto (eds). 2006. *Science, Magic and Religion: The Ritual Processes of Museum Magic.* Oxford: Berghahn Books.

Chapman, R., W. Waldren and M. Von Strydonck. 1993. 'Radiocarbon Dating and Talayots: The Example of Son Ferrandell Oleza', *Antiquity* 67: 108–116.

Duke, P. 2008. *The Tourists Gaze, the Cretans Glance: Archaeology and Tourism on a Greek Island.* Walnut Creek, CA: Left Coast Press.

Graves, R. 1948. *The White Goddess: A Historical Grammar of Poetic Myth.* London: Faber & Faber.

Hirsch, E. and M. O'Hanlon (eds). 1995. *Anthropology of Landscape: Perspectives on Place and Space.* Oxford: Oxford University Press.

Nixon, L. 2006. *Making a Landscape Sacred: Outlying Churches and Icon Stands in Sphakia, Southwestern Crete.* Oxford: Oxbow.

Rabinow, P. 1977. *Reflections on Fieldwork in Morocco.* Berkeley: University of California Press.

Rapport, N. and A. Dawson (eds). 1998. *Migrants of Identity: Perceptions of Home in a World of Movement.* Oxford: Berg.

Theodossopoulos, D. 2003. *Troubles with Turtles: Cultural Understandings of the Environment on a Greek Island.* Oxford: Berghahn Books.

Tilley, C. 1993. 'Art, Architecture, Landscape [Neolithic Sweden]', in B. Bender (ed.), *Landscape: Politics and Perspectives.* Oxford: Berg, pp. 49–84.

Turner, V. 1982. *The Ritual Process.* New York: Cornell University Press.

Ucko, P.J. and R. Layton (eds). 1999. *The Archaeology and Anthropology of Landscape: Shaping Your Landscape.* London: Routledge.

Urry, J. 1990. *The Tourist Gaze: Leisure and Travel in Contemporary Societies.* London: Sage.

Waldren, J. 1996. *Insiders and Outsiders: Paradise and Reality in Mallorca.* Oxford: Berghahn Books.

Waldren, W. 1989. 'Warehouses of Prehistory', in A. Eames (ed.), *Inside Guides: Majorca & Ibiza, Menorca & Formentera.* UK: APA Publications, pp. 25–30.

Chapter 6
ON DIFFERENCE, DESIRE AND THE AESTHETICS OF THE UNEXPECTED: *THE WHITE MASAI* IN KENYAN TOURISM

George Paul Meiu

ം⚹ം

Introduction

In 1998, Swiss author Corinne Hofmann published *The White Masai*, recounting her four-year experience in Kenya as the wife of a Samburu warrior. The narrator, a 27-year-old middle-class Swiss woman, arrived in December 1986 on a vacation in the coastal town of Mombasa, Kenya, accompanied by her Swiss boyfriend, Marco. There, Corinne met the Samburu warrior Lketinga. She fell in love instantly. 'I can't explain, even to myself,' she reflected, 'what secret magic there is about this man' (Hofmann 2005: 14). Her desire for the 'tall, dark brown, beautiful exotic man' (2005: 2) came suddenly and unexpectedly. Corinne confessed that '(i)f anyone had told me two weeks ago I would fall in love with a Masai [*sic*] warrior, I would have laughed out loud' (2005: 14). From then on, 'my whole life has been thrown into chaos' (loc.cit.). Upon return to Switzerland, she broke up with Marco. In July 1987, she flew back to Kenya to find Lketinga. Mesmerized by this 'strange and alien' warrior (2005: 7), Corinne decided to give up her bridal gown store, her apartment, and her car in Switzerland, and move to Kenya. The couple married and settled in a Samburu village in the north of the country, where they opened a small store. Later, they moved to Mombasa to start a tourist souvenir business. The narrator describes the hardship of her life in the bush, her illnesses, her conflicts with Lketinga, and the birth of their daughter,

Napirai. Because of Lketinga's growing jealousy, excessive drinking, and violent behaviour, Corinne eventually decides to run back to Switzerland with her daughter, never to come back.

The White Masai became an international bestseller. In the ten years following its publication, it was translated into twenty-eight languages, and sold more than four million copies. The book also played an important role in shaping the expectations and desires of numerous European female tourists travelling to Kenya and developing intimate relationships with Samburu men. The historical context of these relationships, however, emerged more than a decade prior to the publication of the book. Already in the 1980s, young Samburu men from northern Kenya had begun travelling seasonally to the town of Mombasa, on the coast of the Indian Ocean. There, they earned money by performing 'tribal' dances, selling souvenirs, and developing relationships with female tourists. Corinne's relationship with Lketinga had itself been a product of this context. The publication of *The White Masai* and the international media popularization of the author's story furthered the growth of these intimate exchanges in Kenyan tourism. For many women travelling to Kenya, experiencing 'culture' in the style of *The White Masai* came to refer to a desire for intimacy, love and sex, which were perceived as a self-fulfilling pilgrimage beyond the market and the world of tourist consumption.

Throughout the narrative of *The White Masai*, the primitivist expectations that shaped Corinne's desires for Lketinga and for life in the African bush seem to collapse repeatedly in the face of her 'unexpected' encounters with the everyday realities of contemporary Kenya. The 'unexpectedness' of such encounters, I wish to suggest, carries a double-potentiality. It can further marketable percepts of 'cultural difference' at the same time that it can also offer a critical lens for their historical interrogation. If, for Corinne, falling in love with a Samburu warrior has 'thrown (her) life into chaos', the very possibility of the chaos, of the unknown and the unexpected came later to possibly hold value for some of the tourists developing relationships with Samburu men. The ambiguities generated by the tensions between the production of expectations and the desire for the unexpected are at the core of the present analysis.

In this chapter, I argue that a critical examination of the 'unexpected' outcomes of embodied experience can unveil some of the hegemonic mechanisms through which marketable stereotypes of cultural difference are reproduced. To illustrate my argument, I read the narrative of *The White Masai* against the plot of the Swiss documentary *Wiedersehen in Barsaloi* (Reunion in Barsaloi). This documentary, which celebrates Hofmann's return among the Samburu fourteen years after she fled, actively produces an 'expectation for the unexpected' among consumers of cultural difference. I contextualize these elements of public discourse through ethnographic data of my own. This will raise important questions with regard to the production of expectations in tourism: what are the ways in which the unexpectedness of experience – its unpredictability – resists and reinforces processes of commodification and consumption? What are the political implications of commodifying the 'unexpected', by generating an expectation for it? And what do the ambiguities surrounding the 'unexpected' tell us about the constitution of the ethnic and cultural commodity?

Commodifying Culture

By emphasizing how the consumption of cultural difference is generative of unexpected experience, I wish to reveal some of the subtle processes through which commodified culture, or the 'ethno-commodity' (Comaroff and Comaroff 2009) is reconfigured in historical context. Herein, the dialectical relationships between difference and desire, expectation and the unexpected, reshape the particular phenomena that tourists consume as 'culture'.

The White Masai is part of a wider historical moment, in which popular and academic representations increasingly approach cultural difference as an essential reality and as explanatory principle for contemporary phenomena. In contrast to this trend, postcolonial theorists showed that cultural difference and categories of alterity are discursive mechanisms which define positions of power and legitimize various forms of domination and exploitation. Discursive figurations of the Other constitute conditions of possibility for modern, Western sovereignties and subjectivities (Fanon 1952; Fabian 1983; Said 1978; Trouillot 1991). Social domination works, herein, through particular media to create the effect of distance, objectification and inherent difference (Ahmed 2000; Stallybrass and White 1986; McClintock 1995; Magubane 2004; Masquelier 2005). Since the eighteenth century, visual and textual representations played an important role in European figurations of the Orient as an object of contemplation, or in the construction of a 'world *as* exhibition' (Mitchell 1989). By the late twentieth century, international travel and tourism had facilitated growing venues for the cultivation of a 'hegemonic gaze' that reproduced representations of alterity in contexts of inequality and exploitation (Little 1991; Lutz and Collins 1993; Kratz 2002). Anthropological studies of tourism showed how visual and textual representations mediate the asymmetrical relationships between tourists and hosting communities (e.g. Bunten 2008; Bruner 2002, 2005; Kasfir 2007; Phillips and Steiner 1999). While, on one hand, such representations reflect tourists' expectations and desires for cultural authenticity, on the other, they also constitute emblems through which indigenous peoples can brand and market their cultures (Chanock 2000). In late capitalism, cultural difference is often reproduced on the market, through commodified representations of alterity (Comaroff and Comaroff 2009).

Nevertheless, marketable representations of the Other also carry the possibility of incommunicability, miscommunication, or other kinds of unintended readings. Because such representations are always rooted in the concrete practices of subjects, they are never fully determined in terms of their indexical properties. Homi Bhabha (1994) argues that stereotypes of cultural difference must be perpetually reiterated in the face of their inability to fully reflect actuality. The disarticulation between actuality and abstraction is generative of a certain excess, of a certain material ambivalence (1994: 66, 77; see also Comaroff and Comaroff 2009: 23–24). Embodied encounters with various particular Others can both reassert and subvert established representational paradigms. Sara Ahmed (2000) maintains that encounters with strangers 'involve both fixation and the impossibility of fixation'. Such encounters have a 'surprising nature' premised on the 'possibility that *we may not be able to read the bodies of others*' (2000: 8). I build on these approaches to understand unexpected experience as a challenge to consuming cultural difference. Unexpected experience constitutes an excess produced by the failures of both commodity fetishism and the fetishism of cultural difference to fully obscure the historical relations of their production. Faced with unexpected experience, consumers can resituate the locus of cultural difference to new forms of experience, bodily qualities and contexts. Such reconfigurations of the ethno-commodity generate new desires and produce new sources of value.

In the narrative of *The White Masai*, unexpected experience perpetually reorients the narrator's desires away from some of the objects and events where cultural difference is initially presumed to rest. In the plot of the documentary *Wiedersehen in Barsaloi*, however, the 'free play' of unexpected experience is commodified, becoming itself an object of desire, a new source of value. I will draw on Deleuze and Guattari's notion (1983) of 'deterritorialized desire' to suggest that the desires produced by unexpected experience mark at once a limit of the commodity, and a new source of surplus value. I will also revisit Terry Eagleton's definition of aesthetics to argue that the realm of unexpected experience, like the bourgeois world of art, represents both a space of critical potentiality and an ideological condition for the commodity form (1990). In this sense, I refer to an emerging 'aesthetics of the unexpected' among consumers of culture.

Samburu Men, European Women and *The White Masai* in Kenyan Tourism

In order to understand the political implications of *The White Masai* for Kenyan tourism, we must first familiarize ourselves with the historical context in which its narrative emerged. British colonialists as well as traders and travellers to Kenya had long depicted the Samburu people as primitive, exotic, and change-reluctant pastoralists (Kasfir 2007). Following Kenya's Independence in 1963, such images continued to attract travellers and tourists from West European countries, while also generating new contexts in which the Samburu could produce capital.

Meanwhile, as I shall suggest, the shifting forms of intimacy between local youth and European travellers also shaped representations of Samburu cultural difference. Herein, *The White Masai* was to play an important role.

Tourist ads and ethnographic texts typically describe the Samburu as a Maa-speaking ethnic group of semi-nomadic cattle pastoralists, inhabiting the semi-arid savannahs of northern Kenya. These texts often specify that the Samburu are closely related, culturally and linguistically, to the internationally more famous Maasai people of southern Kenya. Drawing on the visual resemblance of Maasai and Samburu dress, decorations, and bodily postures, tourist agencies and publishers of coffee-table books and postcards often brand representations of Samburu people with the highly marketable label of the 'Maasai'. Many tourists, thus, come to know the Samburu as 'a clan of the Maasai' – hence also the title of Hofmann's book. Most strikingly, nationalist discourses and tourist advertisements index Samburu ethnicity through the emblematic image of the tall, slim, light-skinned, half-naked, exotic young male warrior (*moran*), carrying a spear and a club, his hair dyed with ochre, his body adorned with colourful beads. Borrowed from the representations of early travellers, colonial officials and anthropologists, the image of the moran became an icon of tradition and a core brand of Kenya as an international destination (see also Bruner 2005: 35; Kasfir 2007). According to the website of *Kenya Cultural Profiles*,

> the Samburu still cherish and retain the customs and ceremonies of their forebears, unlike most other tribes in Kenya who have been influenced by Western civilization. … The moran, or warriors, are the most striking members of Samburu society and are inevitably attractive to young girls. They enjoy a convivial and relatively undemanding life with permissive sex for roughly 14 years. Most of them will at one time or another have many lovers who demonstrate affection with lavish gifts and beads.[1]

As the 'most striking members of the Samburu society', the anachronistically perceived moran not only index the Samburu 'tribe' as a whole, but their beauty, so 'inevitably attractive to young girls', and their 'permissive' sexuality is associated with the 'liberated' desire of a lost paradise. The moran become an element of a primitive past that carries value for tourists and travellers because it holds the transformative potential of a temporal and cultural transgression, the possibility of 'becoming different'.

With the spectacular rise of the Kenyan tourist industry throughout the 1980s, 1990s, and early 2000s,[2] being a Samburu or Maasai moran became a way of embodying value on the market. Beginning in the early 1980s, numerous young Samburu men migrated seasonally some thousand kilometres, from their home communities in northern Kenya to the tourist resorts of the coast. There, they sold spears and beads along various beaches, and performed dances in hotels and cultural villages. Meanwhile, more and more female tourists from Germany, Switzerland, Netherlands, France, Belgium and England, among other European countries, began developing intimate relationships with Samburu moran.

Samburu Men in Coastal Tourism

Faced with the economic challenges of a rapidly declining pastoral economy, and a receding national labour market, many young Samburu men decided to earn money in tourism. Young men initiated, through circumcision, in the age-grade of the moran benefited from twelve to fifteen years of relative independence from their families, before marrying and settling down as elders. During this time span, the community expected them to provide for themselves (usually by living apart, in the forests), and to begin accumulating some capital for future bridewealth payments. While many moran achieved capital by raiding neighbouring ethnic groups for cattle, many others, increasingly since the 1950s, entered the labour market as soldiers, policemen or watchmen. Meanwhile, the Samburu have also come to be aware of possessing capital that is globally marketable, by virtue of the distinctiveness of their ethnic identity. The growing demand for things Samburu, regardless of whether visual depictions (Askew 2004; Kasfir 2004), spears (Kasfir 2007), necklaces (Straight 2002), dances and lovers (Meiu 2009), intensified the attempts of many Samburu to take their cultural and ethnic identity to the market. As neoliberal economic reforms in East Africa placed the possibility of social reproduction in uncertainty and unpredictability (Comaroff and Comaroff 2000: 306; see also Weiss 2004; Ferguson 2006; Smith 2008), young Samburu men came to envision liveable futures through the commodification of their cultural difference and ethno-sexuality in tourism.

Among young Samburu men, intimate relationships with European female tourists held the potential of securing a future. Through such relationships, they could achieve the prestigious commodities associated, in their home communities, with 'development' (*maendeleo*), respectability, and high status. For them, the Otherness of white women came to signify the possibility of 'overnight' wealth accumulation. A Samburu man told me that he decided to go to Mombasa when he 'saw (that) some people came into white women and built houses'. 'I saw they had a good life,' he added, 'and that's why I decided to go.' Numerous men of Lketinga's age-set (the *Lkuroro* moran, circumcised in 1976) and, even more so, of the following age-set (the *Lmooli* moran, circumcised in 1990) enriched themselves through relationships with European women. Men received money, more or less regularly, from their foreign partners, through Western Union. With this money they bought themselves various goods, from goats and bicycles, to cows and cars, even houses and hotels. Some also managed to use this money to pay bride prices for one or two Samburu wives. They also opened stores, bought land, and built commercial spaces for rent in their home area of Maralal. Many of them owned televisions and videocassette recorders, mobile phones, cars, large cattle herds, and had at some point travelled to Europe. All these were indications of wealth and prestige that marked them out in their home communities (Meiu 2009).

In a context that is characteristic of the manifestations of the neoliberal market in East Africa, where increased unemployment and the growing gap between the rich and the poor fuel the insecurities of everyday life, the possibility of success came to be associated with an ethos of gambling (Weiss 2004: 9). For many young Samburu men, the figure of the white woman seeking to 'become different' offered itself as a prize to some of those who managed to successfully perform neo-imperial fantasies for tourist consumption, and who were ultimately lucky enough to attract tourists' desire. 'My family was very poor,' one Samburu man told me, 'so I went to Mombasa to try my luck with a little bit of business.' 'I (had) also heard,' he explained, 'that if you get a white woman, you will never lack anything again.' However, the neoliberal market and its gambling-like contexts of value production generated high anxieties among moran in tourism. The large number of men returning home without any capital or aging in poverty on the coast added an air of urgency to finding a white woman.

European Women in Kenya

Female tourists on the Kenyan coast encountered Samburu moran on the beaches, in hotels, in bars and clubs, or on the streets of towns such as Mombasa, Mtwapa, Ukunda or Malindi. Many of them viewed the distinctive attire and the proud demeanour of the young moran as more 'originally African' than those of other locals. 'The morans,' a German woman told me, are not only 'naturally beautiful', but 'they are all that Africa is about; they are its essence'. Therefore, many women desired intimate relationships with the moran as a way to authenticate their own travelling experiences. The Samburu moran, many women knew, came to the coast from far-away places of the country, and, therefore, seemed less 'corrupted' by the commercialized nature of the everyday in tourist resorts. By developing intimate relationships with Samburu moran, by visiting their home villages in northern Kenya, and by establishing strong affective ties with their families and friends, female tourists hoped to escape the seeming artificiality of the tourist market, for a more 'authentic', more 'real' Africa. A woman from France, who had been visiting Kenya for over fourteen years, told me that after meeting her Samburu partner on the coast on her first visit, she never returned again to coastal tourist resorts. 'I always come directly here, to the Samburu District,' she explained, '(because) this is real Africa, not the Africa of tourists.' 'Real Africa' appeared to offer a sense of affective community that seemed to have been lost in the West, and appeared to be only superficially mimicked in tourism.

There is a wide variety of types of relationships that European women developed with Samburu men. While many sought the company of moran for one-night stands, or for the duration of their vacation, many others engaged in long-term relationships or even marriages. In the latter case, women sometimes moved permanently to Kenya, at other times, more rarely, their partners moved to Europe. Most often, the partners visited each other regularly, preferring to maintain separate residences. In all cases, however, women were more likely to determine how the relationship would unfold, because they were the ones financing their male partners. Although most women were older than their partners (by ten to thirty years), and only few had children with them, they often adopted or sponsored one or several children of their partners' lineage. While all women arrived to Kenya firstly as tourists, many eventually returned to work for NGOs, or to start various small businesses while living with their partners. Relationships usually, but not always, ended when women were no longer able to finance their partners, or when men decided to also take on wives from their own communities.

European women, who were in long-term relationships with Samburu men, often saw themselves as having come to embody cultural difference. This added a sense of value and authenticity to their lives. Numerous times, women actualized their sense of authenticity by writing autobiographic poems and memoirs, by giving interviews about their lives to journalists and film-makers, or by merely narrating their experiences to families and friends in Europe. All these modes of articulating experience cultivated a Western subjectivity that produced the truth of the self through the power of confession (see Foucault 1978; Gusdorf 1980). Although not all women wrote, and although there were many women who regularly refused to be interviewed about their lives in Kenya, numerous other women had already published their memoirs (e.g. Bentsen 1989; Oddie 1994; Mason 1995; Hofmann [1998] 2005, 2006; Cain, Postlewait and Thomson 2004; Hachfeld-Tapukai 2004, 2009; Wiszowaty 2009). Overall, these writings share a set of presuppositions and rhetorical techniques. For example, authors often depict socio-economic inequalities as 'cultural difference', and figure material poverty as a source of authenticity. They also often avoid reflecting on their own capacities to freely enter and exit sites of cultural difference, thus trying to authenticate their experiences in the African bush. Meanwhile, there is an overarching presumption that the narrating subject can have the Other, carnally or otherwise. The Other often appears to be perceived by the narrator as raw material to which she adds value in the writing process. But, besides this, as we will see with *The White Masai*, these narratives are, in fact, much more complex.

'The White Masai'

Hofmann's memoir was first published in German in 1998 and was soon to become a bestseller. In German-speaking countries, the book was part of a wider genre of women's life writings that celebrated the authentic experiences of cross-cultural romances or marriages to foreign men. Most widely read among these are, for example, Betty Mahmoody's (1987) *Not Without My Daughter*, the story of an American woman trying to escape her oppressive marriage to an Iranian man, and Hachfeld-Tapukai's (2004) *Mit der Liebe einer Lowin* (With the Love of a Lioness), the story of a German woman married to a Samburu man in Kenya.

Next to such titles, *The White Masai* was widely available in book stores and 'Flohmarkts', and appealed mostly to a female readership. Elise, a German traveller I interviewed in the Samburu District in 2009, said that she first received the book from a relative, long before deciding to come to Kenya. The book, she said, was a favourite topic of debate in women's circles in recent years and was known to provoke both positive and negative reactions. With its translation into English, in 2005, the book also became available at stores in Kenya, where it was sold mostly to tourists, along with postcards, coffee-table books and other souvenirs.

Most women travelling to Kenya and developing relationships with Samburu men read the book, at some point, and often compared and contrasted their own experiences with those of the narrator. For example, some women criticized Corinne for 'misunderstanding her husband' or 'misrepresenting Samburu culture', while others tried to learn, from her experiences, ways to deal with their own relationships. Meanwhile, Samburu people knew of 'Lketinga's story' more by word of mouth rather than through the book itself. This story was part of a growing genre of folk narratives about the failed relationships between moran and *muzungu mamas* (white women). However, with the book's translation into English, the story had a second coming. Suddenly numerous journalists visited the district in search of Lketinga and of white women who had married Samburu men and had been living there. These journalists wanted to capture the 'sensationalism' of such cross-cultural marriages. In 2004, the German company Constantin Film went to the Samburu District to make a film after Hofmann's book. In this context, many Samburu were hired either as extras or as members of the cast. Furthermore, since 2005, several copies of *The White Masai* also circulated among school-educated people in Maralal. Meanwhile, Samburu men in tourism often heard about the book from their European partners. Joseph, a young Samburu man, recalled how his British girlfriend once told him 'Oh, I read about Lketinga and *The White Masai* and I love your culture.' She told him: 'I want you to make me experience it like that.' By 2008, Samburu men in tourism had already begun occasionally to refer to any foreign woman in a relationship with a moran, as 'a white Maasai'.

In this context, Hofmann's memoir has important implications with regard to the commodification of cultural difference, the production of tourist expectations, and the reconfiguration of desires and intimacies. In what follows, I outline some of the potentialities of unexpected experience, by critically reading *The White Masai* and the documentary *Wiedersehen in Barsaloi* in relation to the context outlined above.

Unexpected Experience in *The White Masai*

In the eyes of Western readers, Hofmann's memoir unquestionably makes an argument for cultural difference as an irreconcilable ontological reality (Berman 2005: 211, 214). However, *The White Masai* does more than just reiterate cultural difference. Because Corinne's unexpected encounters with the everyday realities of contemporary Kenya continuously disrupt the desiring process, her inability to locate and consume the desired difference becomes a recurring theme. In the process, the narrator perpetually resituates cultural difference to new realms of embodiment and experience as a way of explaining incommunicability or miscommunication.

Corinne's desire for intimacy with Lketinga destabilizes, from the outset, the visual paradigm through which the body of the moran is marketed in Kenyan tourism. At the beginning of their relationship, Corinne contemplates Lketinga's bodily beauty in terms of its visual aspects. She sees a 'tall, dark brown, beautiful exotic man' who 'is wearing almost no clothes – just a short red loincloth'. He wears beads, '(h)is long red hair has been plaited into thin braids, and his face is painted with symbols' (Hofmann 2005: 2). However, the visual beauty of the iconic moran soon generates a desire for tactile proximity. Corinne explains that 'all that is running through my mind is how I can make contact with the breathtakingly beautiful man,' because 'just staring at him isn't going to get me anywhere' (loc.cit.). For Corinne, expectations of cultural difference gradually move away from the stereotypical visual idiom to a realm of synesthesia and affect. This is reflected, for example, in her desire to engage the moran through bodily proximity: 'I want to stroke his face and know what it's like to kiss him' (2005: 19). But, before she finds out from a local woman that 'Masai [*sic*] men ... don't kiss (because) (t)he mouth is for eating, and kissing ... is contemptible' (2005: 21), Corinne undergoes a deep sense of disappointment when Lketinga unexpectedly refuses to kiss her:

> At long last I dare to come close to his beautiful mouth and softly touch my lips to his. All of a sudden I feel all of his body go rigid, and he's staring at me in horror. 'What you do?' he asks and takes a step backwards. Brought down to earth with a bang I stand there, understanding nothing; then, suddenly ashamed, I turn around and run into the hotel distraught. In bed I'm overcome by a fit of crying. (2005: 19)

The sense of communicational failure, the initial impossibility of establishing a common ground for an embodied engagement with each other comes unexpectedly, disrupting desire.

Throughout the narrative, Corinne experiences various circumstances pertaining to sex, food sharing, sleeping practices, defecation, disease, bureaucratic corruption, or the expression of emotions in similarly unexpected and disruptive manners. Initially, she had imagined her life with Lketinga as a true 'romance'. Said Corinne, 'in my mind's eye I'd lain in this man's hands often, imagined kisses and the wildest of nights' (2005: 19). Yet, every expectation can produce something unexpected. After her first attempts at intimacy, she is faced with the challenge of an embodied difference that needs to be overcome if a common premise of pleasure and intimacy is to be established between the partners. This becomes more obvious in Corinne's reflection on her first sexual encounter with Lketinga, narrated in a typically confessional mode:

> When it gets dark and we can no longer hold off the moment of physical contact, I sit down on the narrow little cot and wait with pounding heart for the minute I have longed for. Lketinga sits down beside me and all I can see is the mother-of-pearl button on his forehead, the ivory rings in his ears, and [the] whites of his eyes. All of a sudden everything happens at once. Lketinga presses me down to the cot, and already I can feel his erection. Before I can even make up my mind whether or not my body is ready for this, I feel a pain, hear strange noises and it's all over. I feel like bursting into tears of disappointment. *This was not at all what I had expected. It's only now that I realize that this is someone from a completely alien culture.* But my thoughts don't get any further than that when suddenly the whole thing happens again. It happens again several times during the night, and after the third or the fourth time we 'do it', I give up trying to use kisses or caresses to prolong the experience. Lketinga doesn't seem to like it. (2005: 21; emphasis added)

Corinne confesses her experience in detail not only as a way to speak the truth about the Self (cf. Foucault 1978), but also to suggest that difference is deep-rooted. The narrator comes to understand all that which she encounters unexpectedly as a difference in culture. Cultural difference always emerges in a new, unexpected form, irritating and frustrating the desiring subject. For example, when Corinne realizes that Lketinga constantly refuses to eat with her, she asks Priscilla, a young Maasai woman, for an explanation. Priscilla tells Corinne that the moran are not allowed to eat in the presence of women; neither, for that matter, anything that a woman has touched or looked at (Hofmann 2005: 21). This upsets Corinne:

> So Lketinga can't even eat with me and I can never cook anything for him. Funnily, this is something that shakes me even more than the idea of never having good sex. ... I'm speechless. All my romantic fantasies of cooking and eating together out in the bush or in a simple hut collapse. I can hardly hold back my tears. (2005: 24)

Expectations of primitivist romance collapse, once again, in the face of the unexpected. But Corinne does not give in to the initial disappointment, instead trying to learn about Lketinga by translating unexpected experience into cultural difference. In this way, initial reasons of disappointment become new sources of excitement. For example, increasingly stimulated by the 'savage perfume of his long red hair' (hair dyed with ochre), Corinne notes that 'the wholly alien' and 'the barriers' begin to appear less distant, and that she feels a 'whole new sense of joy' (2005: 25). Hence, unexpected experience produces new expectations and new objects of desire. Ironically, however, Corinne's desire to overcome the cultural difference of her partner, as a condition for the realization of their love, is premised on her fetishistic desire for the very same Otherness that Lketinga seems to embody. This central contradiction sets in motion the dialectics between expectation and the unexpected: unexpected experience produces new expectations, while every expectation can have unexpected outcomes.

The perpetual disruption and regeneration of desire as a result of unexpected experience carries an important critical potential for the historical analyst. Unexpected experience upsets desire in ways that can indicate limitations in the consumption of the ethno-commodity. Such desire, I suggest, can be imagined in terms of what Gilles Deleuze and Felix Guattari (1983) refer to as 'deterritorialized desire'. Deleuze and Guattari argue that, in order to function, all societies must structure, limit, and 'code' infinite, interminable flows of desire. But, they explain, structures are never fully determinate, and every structural organization produces its forms of excess or 'deterritorialized' desire. In capitalism, such forms of desire (as evidenced, for example, in alcoholism or schizophrenia) often resist coercion into the productive process, and thus facilitate a terrain from which the system can be critically engaged (1983: 140; see also Roffe 2005). For us, unexpected experience deterritorializes desire, in that it allows it to slip away from its structurally established, normative object. In this sense, unexpected experience opens up a space from which we can begin to question the objects of our desires, and to investigate historically the hegemonic mechanisms through which these objects are reproduced.

Deterritorialized desire reshapes both the Other and the desiring subject. The stereotypically perceived moran melts away in the face of Corinne's desire for proximity, destabilizing the consumptive process. The unexpected, therefore, not only unfixes the Other, but also threatens the boundaries of the subject. Throughout the narrative, the tensions between the solid and the fluid moments of Corinne's self-perception are a recurring theme. In her first meetings with Lketinga, the narrator perceives her own body becoming fluid: 'My knees have gone weak, I can hardly stand. Sweat is flowing from every pore. I have to hold on to a pillar on the edge of the dance floor to stop myself collapsing' (Hofmann 2005: 6). But when Lketinga leaves, the terra firma returns under her feet (2005: 3). The initial loss of the terra firma is pleasant yet annoying, ecstatic yet dangerous. It pushes the subject off her limits, making her 'a complete wreck' (2005: 3). The subject and her capacity to desire and consume can only reemerge by reestablishing the boundaries between herself and the Other. Discovering cultural difference anew, the narrator also shapes these boundaries in new forms. For instance, Corinne sees herself as gradually coming to embody Otherness. She is no longer just a white woman, but a 'white Maasai'. 'I feel myself at one with this man,' Corinne reflects of her intimacy with Lketinga, 'and now, this night, I know that despite all the barriers between us, *I have already become a captive of his world*' (2005: 25; emphasis added).

In the narrative of *The White Masai*, unexpected experience reconfigures the ethno-commodity. The desiring subject is initially faced with the impossibility of concretely locating and consuming the cultural difference that is abstractly marketed through the visual image of the moran. But, eventually, she rediscovers difference in new media and new contexts. Unexpected experience, therefore, unveils, here, an experiential limitation of the consumption of cultural difference, from which the ethno-commodity can reemerge in new ways.

The Commodification of the Unexpected in *Wiedersehen in Barsaloi*

If, on one hand, unexpected experience destabilizes the ethno-commodity, on the other hand, the unexpected can also become a new source of surplus value. In this section, I turn to the Swiss documentary film *Wiedersehen in Barsaloi* (2005), to show how unexpected experience is commodified in the representations that foreground the popularity of Hofmann's book. Such representations now produce and market an 'expectation for the unexpected'.

The film *Wiedersehen in Barsaloi* (Reunion in Barsaloi) documents Corinne Hofmann's experience while returning to Kenya, to 'her African family', fourteen years after she had fled with her daughter. The film was to serve as documentation for a further memoir of her experience in Kenya (Hofmann 2006). Corinne is now accompanied on her trip by her publisher and by a cameraman and film producer. The two men carefully capture and document every step of her trip. The film begins with her flight into Nairobi, her short stay in the Kenyan capital, and continues with her gradual move towards the Samburu District in northern Kenya. The documentary reaches its peak with Corinne's actual reunion with Lketinga and his family. Towards the end of her stay in Samburu District, Corinne visits an Italian missionary who had helped her on her first trip. She also visits the set of a movie that is now being shot after *The White Masai*. In the end, she returns to Mombasa to revisit the place where she had first met Lketinga. Celebrating the authentic image that Hofmann had built for herself, the film is entirely based on her confessions. At almost regular intervals, Corinne appears in the focus of static scenery, confessing her perceptions and emotions to the camera. Although, at first sight, the confessional mode of the documentary resembles that of Hofmann's memoir, the film actually stages and commodifies unexpected experience by inscribing it into well-known colonial representational paradigms.

The documentary opens with Corinne sleeping in the aeroplane on her way to Kenya. Suddenly, she wakes up, notices the camera, and confesses: 'I was calm and now I get cramps in my stomach again (and) wet palms. I am nervous (*gespannt*) to find out what will happen. Man, it's been almost fourteen years. I am anxious to see how everything has changed and how the people will react. I am anxious.' (My translation from German). The German verb *gespannt* (nervous or anxious in anticipation of something that will happen), produces the unexpected as that which gives value to the film, effecting the viewer's tension in the face of the unknown.

The suspense grows. Sitting down on the terrace of a lodge, with an exotic savannah scenery at her back, Corinne confesses on the morning of the day when she was supposed to meet Lketinga: 'I am nervous. I am also a little down, because all this can excite you. One doesn't know what to expect. I don't know if I should laugh or cry. We will see what wins out.' (My translation from German.) The impossibility of predictability, the fact that 'one doesn't know what to expect' fuels the viewer's tension, generating strong contradictory emotions. However, the outcomes of Corinne's trip to Kenya were, in fact, more predictable than the film will have us believe. She was visiting Kenya as a special guest of the set of the movie *The White Masai*. She had earned extensively both from her book and the movie and had also sent money to Lketinga and sponsored his community throughout those years. Consequently, the remaining anxieties associated with the reunion are amplified in a confessional mode, producing a marketable version of the unexpected.

The film stages unexpected experience within a highly recognizable narrative structure, by using colonial stereotypes, such as the rehearsal of a modernist temporality and of the visual paradigms associated with it. The film begins with a scene from the plane, a sign of Western modernity to which Corinne and her companions belong. The plot then gradually descends the evolutionary ladder, from Kenya's capital of Nairobi, a chaotic middle space between tradition and modernity, to the authentic, 'primitive' space of the savannah and the Samburu villages. There, Lketinga continues to live in an archaic past, in a traditional 'mud' hut. Leaving Nairobi, and reaching a cliff of spectacular scenery on the Rift Valley, Corinne confesses that '(y)esterday, Nairobi still wasn't really it'. 'There,' she explains, 'I wasn't yet at home.' But, faced with the exotic beauty of the landscapes of the Rift Valley, she suggests that this 'looks much more like that which I know, like I used to live'. 'We are approaching my homeland (*Heimat*),' she adds, '(a)nd I'm nervous about what is waiting for me.' Similarly, when she visits her missionary friend in the romantic landscapes of the Samburu lowlands, she explains that we arrived 'for real, at the end of the world'. The film orders the visually objectified sceneries on a modernist temporal axis, so that Corinne's return to 'her African family', is also a return in time (see Fabian 1983). Through a well-known imperialist archetype, 'the journey is figured as proceeding forward in geographical space but backward in historical time' (McClintock 1995: 30). Using stereotypical images and stylistic modalities, the film brings unexpected experience into the 'secure' space of recognition and marketability.

The film not only commodifies unexpected experience, but, in doing so, it also tries to foreclose the disruptive effects that the unexpected can have on the desiring subject and on the consumptive process. This can be imagined in terms of what

Deleuze and Guattari (1983) refer to as the commodification of deterritorialized desires. This is a way for the economic system to transform that which is anti-productive into a new source of value. Deleuze and Guattari argue that, under the guise of 'liberation', late capitalism cultivates a regime of unrestricting ('decoding') flows of desire (e.g. 'the liberation of sexuality'), only to assign them monetary value (1983: 140; see also Roffe 2005: 36). For this purpose, such unruly desires cannot remain anti-productive, but must 'throw themselves into desiring production' (Pronger 2002: 106–7). In the narrative of *The White Masai*, unexpected experience entertains, to some extent, deterritorialized desires that are anti-productive, disrupting the consumption process and threatening the desiring subject. The plot of the documentary, however, attempts to 'tame' such desires, reorienting them towards economic productivity.

Through commodification, unexpected experience becomes a fetish, disconnected from any critical potentialities.[3] What is marketed here, then, is particularly the 'fascinating' experience of cross-cultural incommunicability and miscommunication. It is not ironic then, that, when Corinne finally 'reunites' with Lketinga and 'her African family', few words are exchanged. Instead, the silence that emerges between them becomes itself a cause for tension and suspense, a product of cultural difference, and a new source of value.

Towards an Aesthetics of the Unexpected

In the previous two sections, I set up an analytical contrast between the narrative of *The White Masai* and the plot of the documentary *Wiedersehen in Barsaloi*. I suggested that, in the former, unexpected experience reconfigures cultural difference, whereas, in the latter, the unexpected offers itself for consumption, as a desirable product of difference. The narrator of *The White Masai* seeks Otherness at the same time that she tries to overcome it; she continuously resituates cultural difference, at the same time that she needs to stabilize it, in order to consume it. In this way, she allows objectified notions of difference to shift in the fluidity of embodied experience. This experiential fluidity, I suggest, carries critical potential, because it helps us question those forces that intervene to restrict and commodify experience, in order to make it valuable to the larger system of production. Such forces become visible with the hegemonic reproduction of marketable expectations in *Wiedersehen in Barsaloi*. Through the rehearsal of colonial stereotypes, the film attempts to capitalize on overwhelmingly diverse desires and experiences by shaping them in ways that are commensurable with the commodity form. Read against each other, the memoir and the film show how the unruly desires produced by unexpected experience can, firstly, emerge as a limitation of the commodity, then, as a new source of value.

Nevertheless, from a different analytical viewpoint, the memoir and the film might not be that different after all. Both are forms of public discourse that circulate representations of cultural difference to a wide audience. Both are also commodities generative of desires among Western consumers. Therefore, one can go a step further and argue that both the book and film can share similar contrasting potentialities. First, looked at from the perspective of the market, the memoir, like the film, also commodifies the unexpected. Because its narrative is circulated as a commodity, the described unexpected experience reaches the reader in the 'secure' space contained between the two covers of the book. For the reader, Corinne's experiences might as well confirm previous assumptions of unbridgeable cultural difference (Berman 2005: 214), and figure the unexpected as a pleasurable addition to the quality of travelling experience. Not unlike the film, the book can, then, also produce an 'expectation for the unexpected'. For example, Elise, a German traveller I interviewed in the Samburu District in 2009, explained that 'the most important thing I took from *The White Masai* was that you should never have too strong ideas about what to expect when you come here'. The book had inspired Elise to travel with an appreciation for surprise, the unknown, and the unexpected. 'I always think,' she added, 'that the best moments of travel are those that you seek least.'

Second, the commodification of the unexpected is itself never fully determined. The marketable experience of the unexpected can itself be disrupted in various contexts of consumption, producing new desires and new expectations. For example, when I discussed the book and the film with Sabrina, a French woman who had been married to a Samburu man for over twenty years, she offered to explain that 'everything is so surprising for (Corinne) because she is stupid: she doesn't speak Samburu (language) and she doesn't realize (that) the people around her only want her money'. Sabrina spoke the Samburu dialect of Maa language fluently and also considered herself knowledgeable on issues pertaining to Samburu culture. For her, the marketable appeal of the unexpected was of little importance, because it was premised on Corinne's ignorance of local issues. Here, Sabrina's desire to assert the authenticity of her own experience over that of Corinne disrupted marketable notions of the unexpected in new ways.

Therefore, in a more dialectical analytical lens, in which expectations and the unexpected perpetually reconfigure each other, unexpected experience can be at once an experience generative of surplus value, and an anti-economic space from which the hegemonic reproduction of the ethno-commodity can be critiqued. In order to capture this double-potentiality of unexpected experience I speak of an 'aesthetics of the unexpected'. Aesthetics, Terry Eagleton (1990) argues, came about in the struggles of the Western bourgeoisie to account for the lives of bodies (1990: 15). It attempted to produce a new type of human subject that would not threaten political unity, 'one which, like the work of art itself, discovers the law in the depths of its own free identity, rather than in some oppressive external power' (1990: 19). The commodification of the unexpected, similarly, has the capacity to cultivate a consuming subject who does not question the historical forces that have shaped objects of desire, but rather seeks meaning in fetishized subjective experience. However, Eagleton suggests, as much as the domain of aesthetics reflects bourgeois ideas of subjectivity and political unity, it also offers itself as a refuge to the bourgeoisie from their own repressive values. Therefore, aesthetics produces, at once, a body repressed by law, and a sensuous body fuelled by creativity and the revolutionary energy of anti-instrumentalist thought (1990: 8–9). Similarly, one can read unexpected experience, in the instances of public discourse analyzed above, as a new aesthetic space of the tourist and traveller at the turn of the millennium. This aesthetic space of unexpected experience can be simultaneously subordinated to the laws of exchange value and commodity fetishism, while also maintaining a realm of indeterminacy, from which the hegemonic abstractions of capital can be questioned and critiqued.

Conclusion

The White Masai is the product of a context in which Samburu male bodies have become highly valuable in Kenyan tourism, in which European female tourists desired more authentic lives through intimate relations with moran, and in which Samburu young men imagined futures by capitalizing on their ethnic sexuality. In this context, *The White Masai* is also productive of new expectations, new desires, and new ways of imagining cultural difference. In this chapter, I mapped some of the political potentialities of the book for its historical context. Further ethnographic research should also show what role the book plays in shaping diverse forms of desire and intimacy among tourists, more particularly. By reading the narrative of Hofmann's memoir in relation to the film *Wiedersehen in Barsaloi*, I identified an emerging aestheticization of the unexpected. The aesthetics of the unexpected, I argued, is an experiential realm based on the indeterminacy of representations of cultural difference, on their possible incommunicability, or, for that matter, on the limits of commodity fetishism. This aesthetic realm entertains shifting forms of desire which can also regenerate and reconfigure cultural difference and the ethno-commodity.

Marketable forms of cultural difference are, therefore, perpetually shaped, in historical context, through the dialectical relationships between particular forms of difference and desire, and between expectation and unexpected experience.

Acknowledgments

I wish to thank Jean Comaroff, John L. Comaroff, Jennifer Cole, Judith Farquhar, Anita Hannig, Larisa Jasarevic, Fred Ketchum, Willam Mazzarella, Kathryn McHarry, Erin Moore, Nancy Munn, Jen Smith, and the participants in the *Medicine, the Body, and Practice Workshop* at the University of Chicago, for their thoughtful comments on earlier versions of this chapter.

Notes

1. Kenyan Cultural Profiles website (http://www.enchanted-landscapes.com/profiles/Samburu.htm, accessed on 22 October 2004).
2. Although tourists were coming to Kenya as early as the 1900s (Kibicho 2009: 63), their numbers boomed in the last three decades of the century. Following Independence, in 1963, the government of Kenya embraced tourism as a main path to economic development, establishing, for this purpose, the Kenyan Tourism Development Corporation (1965), and the Ministry of Tourism and Wildlife (1966). Throughout the 1970s, the number of visitors levelled at 350,000 per annum. However, following global economic reforms, in the 1980s the number increased twofold (Schoss 1995: 36–38). Throughout the 1990s and early 2000s, the number of tourists visiting Kenya increased further (by 94.4 per cent), reaching in 2004, 1,361,000 per annum. Wildlife safaris, coastal beaches, cultural villages, and historical sites were some of Kenya's main tourist attractions (Schoss 1995; Bruner 2005; Kasfir 2007); sexual relations with locals were yet another (Kibicho 2009).
3. Elizabeth Povinelli (2001) encounters a similar situation among the Wadeye of Australia. She shows how the indigenous Australians of Wadeye are caught up in situations wherein they are pivotal to the production of surplus value for national and global tourist industries, and yet stand to benefit little, if at all, from their pursuits. Povinelli observes how, in Wadeye, a growing sense of trauma and panic in the face of contrasting social obligations comes to be commodified as Aboriginal spirituality – as *Geist*, and Dreaming – in response to tourist desires. And, if panic marks here 'a limit to capital internal to the subject' (2001: 249, 251), 'such moments are quickly fetishized as authentic culture – as the valuable "real stuff" of culture' (2001: 252).

References

Ahmed, S. 2000. *Strange Encounters: Embodied Others in Post-coloniality.* London: Routledge.
Askew, K.M. 2004. 'Striking Samburu and a Mad Cow: Adventures in Anthropollywood', in A. Shryock (ed.), *Off Stage/On Display: Intimacy and Ethnography in the Age of Public Culture.* Berkeley: University of California Press, pp. 33–68.
Bentsen, C. 1989. *Maasai Days.* New York: Doubleday, Anchor Books.
Berman, N. 2005. 'Autobiographical Accounts of Kenyan-German Marriages. Reception and Context', in E. Ames, M. Krotz and L. Wildenthal (eds), *Germany's Colonial Past.* Nebraska: University of Nebraska Press, pp. 205–26.
Bhabha, H.K. 1994. *The Location of Culture.* New York: Routledge.
Bruner. E.M. 2002. 'The Representation of African Pastoralists: A Commentary', *Visual Anthropology* 15: 387–92.
Bruner, E.M. 2005. *Culture on Tour: Ethnographies of Travel.* Chicago: University of Chicago Press.
Bunten, A.C. 2008. 'Sharing Culture or Selling Out? Developing the Commodified Persona in the Heritage Industry'. *American Ethnologist* 35(3): 380–95.
Cain, K., H. Postlewait and A. Thomson. 2004. *Emergency Sex and Other Desperate Measures: A True Story from Hell on Earth.* New York: Hyperion.
Chanock, M. 2000. '"Culture" and Human Rights: Orientalising, Occidentalising, and Authenticity', in M. Mamdani (ed.), *Beyond Rights Talk and Culture Talk. Comparative Essays on the Politics of Rights and Culture.* New York: Saint Martin's Press, pp. 15–36.
Comaroff, J. and J.L. Comaroff. 2000. 'Millennial Capitalism: First Thoughts on a Second Coming', *Public Culture* 12(2): 291–343.
Comaroff, J.L. and J. Comaroff. 2009. *Ethnicity, Inc.* Chicago, IL: University of Chicago Press.

Deleuze, G. and F. Guattari. 1983. *Anti-Oedipus: Capitalism and Schizophrenia.* Minneapolis: University of Minnesota Press.

Eagleton, T. 1990. *The Ideology of the Aesthetic.* Oxford: Blackwell.

Fabian, J. 2002 [1983]. *Time and the Other: How Anthropology Makes its Object.* New York: Columbia University Press.

Fanon, F. 2008 [1952]. *Black Skin, White Masks.* New York: Grove Press.

Ferguson, J. 2006. *Global Shadows: Africa in the Neoliberal World Order.* Durham, NC: Duke University Press.

Foucault, M. 1978. *The History of Sexuality,* Vol. 1. New York: Pantheon Books.

Gusdorf, G. 1980. 'Conditions and Limits of Autobiography', in J. Olney (ed.), *Autobiography: Essays Theoretical and Critical.* Princeton: Princeton University Press, pp. 28–48.

Hachfeld-Tapukai, C. 2004. *Mit der Liebe einer Löwin: Wie ich die Frau eines Samburu Kriegers wurde.* Bergish Gladbach: Luebbe.

———. 2009. *Der Himmel uber Maralal: Mein Leben als Frau eines Samburu-Kriegers.* Bergish Gladbach: Ehrenwirth.

Hofmann, C. 2005. *The White Masai.* London: Bliss Books.

———. 2006. *Reunion in Barsaloi.* London: Bliss Books.

Kasfir, S.L. 2004. 'Tourist Aesthetics in the Global Flow: Orientalism and "Warrior Theatre" on the Swahili Coast', *Visual Anthropology* 17: 319–43.

———. 2007. *African Art and the Colonial Encounter: Inventing a Global Commodity.* Bloomington: Indiana University Press.

Kibicho, W. 2009. *Sex Tourism in Africa: Kenya's Booming Industry.* Farnham: Ashgate Publishing Group.

Kratz, C.A. 2002. *The Ones That Are Wanted: Communication and the Politics of Representation in a Photographic Exhibition.* Berkeley: University of California Press.

Little, K. 1991. 'On Safari: The Visual Politics of a Tour Representation', in D. Howes (ed.), *The Varieties of Sensory Experience: A Sourcebook in the Anthropology of the Senses.* Toronto: University of Toronto Press, pp. 149–63.

Lutz, C. and Collins, J.L. 1993. *Reading National Geographic.* Chicago: University of Chicago Press.

Magubane, Z. 2004. *Bringing the Empire Home: Race, Class, and Gender in Britain and Colonial South Africa.* Chicago: University of Chicago Press.

Mahmoody, B. 1987. *Not Without My Daughter.* New York: St Martin's Press.

Mason, C. 1995. *White Mischief: The True Story of the Woman Who Married a Kenyan Tribesman.* Sussex: Summersdale.

Masquelier, A.M. (ed.). 2005. *Dirt, Undress, and Difference: Critical Perspectives on the Body's Surface.* Bloomington: Indiana University Press.

McClintock, A. 1995. *Imperial Leather: Race, Gender, and Sexuality in the Colonial Contest.* New York: Routledge.

Meiu, G.P. 2009. 'Mombasa Morans: Embodiment, Sexual Morality, and Samburu Men in Kenyan Tourism', *Canadian Journal of African Studies* 43(1): 105–28.

Mitchell, T. 1989. 'The World as Exhibition', *Comparative Studies of Society and History* 31(2): 217–36.

Oddie, C. 1994. *Enkop Ai: My Life With the Maasai.* Sydney: Simon and Schuster.

Phillips, R.B. and C.B. Steiner (eds). 1999. *Unpacking Culture: Art and Commodity in Colonial and Postcolonial Worlds.* Berkeley: University of California Press.

Povinelli, E.A. 2001. 'Consuming Geist: Popontology and the Spirit of Capital in Indigenous Australia', in J. Comaroff and J.L. Comaroff (eds), *Millenial Capitalism and the Culture of Neoliberalism.* Durham: Duke University Press, pp. 241–70.

Pronger, B. 2002. *Body Fascism: Salvation in the Technology of Physical Fitness.* Toronto: University of Toronto Press.

Roffe, J. 2005. 'Capitalism', in A. Parr (ed.), *The Deleuze Dictionary*. New York: Columbia University Press, pp. 35–37.

Said, E.W. 1978. *Orientalism*. New York: Pantheon Books.

Schoss, J.H. 1995. 'Beach Tours and Safari Visions: Relations of Production and the Production of "Culture" in Malindi, Kenya', Ph.D. dissertation. Chicago: University of Chicago.

Smith, J.H. 2008. *Bewitching Development: Witchcraft and the Reinvention of Development in Neoliberal Kenya*. Chicago: University of Chicago Press.

Stallybrass, P. and A. White. 1986. *The Politics and Poetics of Transgression*. London: Methuen.

Straight, B. 2002. 'From Heirloom to New Age Artifact: The Cross-Cultural Consumption of Mporo Marriage Beads', *American Anthropologist* 104: 1–15.

Trouillot, M. 1991. 'Anthropology and the Savage Slot: The Poetics and Politics of Otherness', in R. Fox (ed.), *Recapturing Anthropology: Working in the Present*. Santa Fe: School of American Research Press, pp. 17–44.

Weiss, B. 2004. 'Introduction. Contesting Futures: Past and Present', in B. Weiss (ed.), *Producing African Futures: Ritual and Reproduction in a Neoliberal Age*. Leiden: Brill, pp. 1–19.

Wiszowaty, R. 2009. *My Maasai Life: From Suburbia to Savannah*. Vancouver: Greystone Books.

Chapter 7
DISPLEASURE ON 'PLEASURE ISLAND': TOURIST EXPECTATION AND DESIRE ON AND OFF THE CUBAN DANCE FLOOR

Jonathan Skinner

༺᭥᭥᭥᭥᭥᭥᭥᭥᭥᭥᭥᭥᭥᭥᭥᭥᭥༻

Introduction and Niche Tourism

This chapter looks at tourist expectations in a niche tourism vacation, to the mismatch between sold package and received tourist experience, or the lack of congruity between advertising and reality – 'negative disconfirmation' (Oliver 1997) as the post-experience cognition fails to live up to the pre-experience expectations. It is a given that tourist satisfaction is critical to the success of the tourism industry and that it is needed for industry-sustaining levels of tourist consumption. And yet, one frequently hears of tourist holidays becoming nightmares as the ludic and liminal time away from the rigours of everyday life – haptic pleasures in the sun – turn into tourist nightmares of cancellations, bad weather, bad service, or cheapskate consumption that does not live up to pre-vacation expectations.

Crouch et al. (2001: 265) call for tourism studies to be 'interactive' with the researcher fully involved in the researched to fully understand and appreciate the tensions of practice, identity and context, 'the doing of tourism', and to fully assess the various subject positions the tourists go through before, during, and after their vacations: variously the imagination and expectation, constitution and execution, satisfaction and recognition phases. This is a call to arms for an immersed anthropology of tourism first proposed by anthropologist – and occasional tour-guide – Edward Bruner (1989a, 1989b, 2005; see also Malone, this volume). This chapter 'enlists' by way of a presentation and examination of the packaging and consumption of a 'failed' 'dance tourism' niche package holiday by an anthropologist of dance, dance enthusiast and tourist immersed in his study.[1] The chapter first examines the nature of the package holiday company and its niche activity. It then goes on to explore and assess the problems with the particular holiday in question, and how it failed to live up to expectations.

This is a case of niche tourism gone awry as a disjunction forms between how the tourist operators imagine and plan the holiday, and what the clients expect and receive. As an experience, it is one of failure to anticipate or enchant the tourists in a highly specific market. It is perhaps even highlighted and exaggerated by the recent changes in the tourist industry to do with de-differentiation in a post/modern climate. The tourism industry has turned recently to the marketing of alternative or niche tourism as the reactionary new form of tourist development in the twenty-first century (Carlisle 2000; Weaver 1995; Smith and Eadington 1995). This development is not entirely new: one just has to look at the evolution of tourism from Roman aristocratic mountain boltholes to eighteenth-century Grand Tour of Europe (Casson 1974; Walton 1982, 1983). But more recently, from the latter quarter of the twentieth century, it has picked up as a reaction – or 'counterpoint' (Robinson and Novelli 2008: 1) – to the mass tourism with its Fordist mass market standardized leisure services (Burkart and Medlik 1981).

As Waldren exemplified earlier in this volume, niche tourism is a special interest tourism often run by small tourism operators. Their packages can be individualized and tailored to the tourists; flexible and small in number, they can offer the personalized touch. There are now a plethora of niche tourisms ranging from romance and sex tourism in the Caribbean and South East Asia (Pruitt and LaFont 1995; Cohen 1993) to rural and farm tourism in Spain, California and Scotland (Perales 2002; Momsen and Donaldson 2001; Morris and Gladstone 2001), book tourism in the United Kingdom (Seaton 1996a), solidarity tourism in Israel (Beirman 2002) and disaster and dark tourism around the battlefields and in the terrorism destinations found throughout the world (Lennon and Foley 2000; Skinner 2003a; Seaton 1996b; Robertson 2002; Iles, this volume). Generally, they cater for small market groups. But this does not necessarily mean that their tourist numbers are small.

Niche tourism, or rather 'adjective tourism', also alludes to the exoticization and re-branding of tourism itself, and not just the tourist destination (cf. McCrone, Morris and Kiely 1995). According to Carlisle (2000), in the context of tourism, the 'niche' refers to the opposite of mass-market tourism. Niche tourism is synonymous with alternative tourism in the sense that they refer to a reaction to the tackiness of the 'Golden Hordes' tourism to places such as the Costa Brava, Blackpool and Disneyworld (cf. Turner and Ashe 1975; Butler 1995: 31). Moreover, for Eadington and Smith (1995: 3), alternative tourism refers to 'forms of tourism that are consistent with natural, social, and community values'. In other words, alternative/niche tourism is small, personalized low-key tourism, though neither Carlisle nor Eadington and Smith clarify this with a threshold figure for when a niche is no longer a niche. For Wood (2000), niche tourism is a result of twentieth- and twenty-first-century globalization, a diversification away from the old S's (sun, sand and sea/sex) of international tourism. Niche tourism is also bound up in sociological notions of reflexive Modernity in that personal experiences are 'sequestrated': the 'trajectory of the self' (Giddens 1991: 82, 144) is increasingly rationalized according to specific leisure time activities and experiences. In other words, self-identity is now tied to leisure consumption rather than work production. The tourism industry has recognized this late-Modern shift and the contemporary 'disillusionment with mainstream or mass tourism' (Eadington and Smith 1995: 8) and responded accordingly by shifting from 'tourism' to a 'series of "tourisms"' (Parinello 1993: 239). The following is a case study of an attempt at niche tourism in Cuba, suggesting that this shift to niche tourism is complex and by no means straightforward or automatic.

Displeasure on Pleasure Island

DanceHolidays

'DanceHolidays' is a trading name of Carefree Travel International Ltd, a travel organization that has responded to the reflexive shifts in tourist consumer demand. It is a business corporation example of 'organic capitalism' (Miller 1997: 54) as opposed to 'pure capitalism', one that has expanded from the global to the local as opposed to the traditional capitalist model of expansion from the local to the global. Based in Spain, but operating for a British market, DanceHolidays (2003: 2) promote themselves as 'a small team of travel professionals and dance enthusiasts'. Out of the team of ten organiser/dancers, six work behind the scenes and four accompany holiday dancers on their 'intimate holidays' (DanceHolidays 2003: 1) as tour hosts. Individuality and niche tourism are stressed in their advertising brochure:

> Each holiday is a different blend of destination, dance, hotel and activities. Each departure date has special teachers or events associated with it. All our holidays celebrate the sheer joy and exuberance of learning to dance, music, the spectacle of dance and nights out, parties and soirees. (DanceHolidays 2003: 1)

DanceHolidays offers a range of different dance-style holidays (Tango, Salsa, Indian & Arabic, Flamenco, Ceroc and Jive, Line Dancing, and Modern & Latin Ballroom) and dance holiday destinations (Paris, Seville, Barcelona, Granada, Cuba, Canary Islands, Ibiza and Majorca, amongst others). All of the destinations have romantic and Latinate associations, and all of the many photographs are of couples dancing and striking dance poses on the beach or in a dance venue.

> Dance crosses frontiers and cultures and brings people together like almost nothing else. We extend a warm welcome to everyone from all around the world to join our multi-cultural family as we learn to dance together and grow to understand each other, and our host culture through dance. (DanceHolidays 2003: 2)

Behind this marketing rhetoric lie some suggestions that the dance holidays are a novel way of experiencing a place, and of using a hobby and passion to intensify vacation interactions. At the back of the brochure, DanceHolidays answer specific questions about the holidays and dance classes. In several answers, the travel company emphasizes the fact that 70 per cent of their 'clients' come on the holidays by themselves, thereby allaying fears that dance partners are needed for the holidays, whilst also appealing to the independent traveller, particularly the female. They reply to the first question, 'I'm coming on my own – will I find this a problem?', with the following:

> Absolutely not! You'll enjoy these holidays for a multitude of reasons … What all share however, is a thirst for adventure, a zest for life, and an attitude that knows life is for living – NOW! Because it's a Dance Holiday everyone shares a common interest so you'll have a whole host of dance partners in both the classes and on the lively evenings out. (DanceHolidays 2003: 32)

The voyeuristic, scopophilic (see Desmond, this volume, for contrast with dead bodies) aspect to tourism promotion is further captured with pictures of European women dancing on the beach with Cuban men, an image that challenges Urry's (1990) notion of the tourist's gaze as a normatively male gaze. It appears that niche tourism bucks mass tourism's advertising trends that Swain (1995: 249) argues typically stereotypes women as passive and available, and reinforces hierarchical divisions of labour. Furthermore, if there is a gender imbalance of males or females in the dance classes or on the dance holiday, the company will recruit local dancers for the tourists. This is their attempt – or contract with the predominantly male dance tourists – to reassure the wild imaginations of the dance tourists with the production of an experience that they desire, an experience that, as MacCannell (2001: 25) notes, generally exceeds that of Urry's 'gaze'. MacCannell is making a point about tourist agency: expectation and determinism can be found in tourism, for the tourist is often intent upon tracking down the semiotics of tourism sold to them back home. Or, as Beerli et al. (2007) connect, the destination and tourist experiences should have congruity with the advertising literature. This relationship is critical to tourist satisfaction and is one to which we can add the idea of the tourist's own self-image matching that of the tourist experience they are purchasing.

Whilst there are no explicit sexual references in the tourist advertising brochure, there was an implicit shared understanding between the promoters and the consumers that these traditional tourist times are for play, romance and enjoyment. The four- or ten-day dance holidays thus conform to the social scientific views that holiday times are ludic (Lett 1983), liminal (Turner 1979) and sacred (Leach 1979) high points in the tourists' working year. These understandings were confirmed by individual interviews with nearly all of the twenty participants on a DanceHolidays Ceroc/Jive holiday to Cuba for ten nights through the Easter period, and their collective behaviour as assessed by the author's overt anthropological participant observation throughout the package holiday. One tourist preferred not to be interviewed at all because it reminded him of work that he was trying to escape from, and another tourist volunteered to be interviewed so long as it was not tape-recorded. She preferred the informality of an evening conversation at the bar.

Mary, for example, is a 42-year-old recently divorced mother of three young children who has left them with her family whilst she has her holiday:

> Sun, sand, sea and … that's what I need right now. I want to get away from everything that's going on back home. Things have been real messy at present and I thought this would be fun. You don't need to go to Ceroc with a partner and you don't need a partner to come on these holidays. And I really don't want one at the moment!

Jason, a 32-year-old business lawyer, goes on several dancing holidays in the year. He too is a regular Ceroc dancer:

> Cuba should be interesting. I'm a socialist myself and I like what they're doing. I want to visit this part of 'the axis of evil' before it changes. I've been on lots of holidays dancing, and I've been to Russia and Poland before. This should be really good!

Cassie is a 29-year-old friend of one of the dance instructors who decided to come along at the last minute. She has only been doing Ceroc for three months, but takes private dance lessons. She is a receptionist at a large industrial goods outlet:

> I'm a bit nervous about the dancing really. I mean, I haven't been doing the Ceroc for very long now, but I know one of the instructors and they said I should come along. I saw Cuba on the television and it looks sunny and lovely this time of the year. If I come back with a tan and some holiday experiences – you know what I mean – I'll have something to show and tell my friends, eh!

All three informants are using the niche tourism package holiday as escapism from their everyday working world. They are buying a fantasy that has been pre-packaged and sold to them. Both Mary and Cassie, unlike Jason, are full of innuendo in their comments about their expected holiday. They expect to behave differently whilst away from home, and they expect the local men to behave differently to them as well. Jason has intellectual and political interests for visiting Cuba as well as his desire to enjoy the dancing. He is not interested in the sun or the sea aspects of the holiday. He is, perhaps, interested in getting to know the ladies on the trip but, as it transpired, he was too English for them. We might say then, after Gnoth (1997), that the tourists are buying a vacation for their ideal selves, bringing their real selves with them. Jason sees himself as a socialist and dancer and so books a dance holiday to Cuba. The difficulty comes when the perceived gap between ideal and real self is not narrowed by the envisaged vacation. As Gnoth (1997: 287) explains, cognitive and emotional satisfaction derive from the congruity of holiday expectations sold and holiday experiences lived and remembered. This was to become ever apparent as the package holiday progressed.

The brochure advertising carefully ties in with what appeals to the British tourists. It is tailor-made for a section of the dancing public. It both shapes and is shaped by the perceived consciousness of a U.K.-wide Ceroc tourist market. In the brochure, there were careful references in the holiday Information Pack (2003: 5) about bringing a set of strong contraceptives on holiday as opposed to buying them locally. There were also sections that discussed potential tourist–local interactions and understandings:

> Cuba is a place where people live for the moment, do not worry what tomorrow will bring, but dance for today and for their partner.

Jinetera (feminine) and *jinetero* (masculine) literally translate to the word 'jockey'. The words refer to those Cubans who ride on the back of or perhaps hustle foreigners. They sell anything from cigars to sex. Given the economic hardship in Cuba, the need to hustle tourists, including selling sex, is not perceived to be a particularly sleazy activity.

> Obviously the whole range of relationships between Cuban and foreign visitor are possible from casual friendship through to intense friendships, affairs, engagements and marriage. These may or may not involve jumping into bed together, and they may or may not be sincere. Whether they are sincere or not you may never know and you may not care. They all involve transfer of resources from foreigner to Cuban national in one way or another (paying for entrance to clubs, meals out, gifts big and small, or cash). None of this is frowned upon within the local culture. Having a fling in exchange for gifts and a good time is considered normal.

In sum, both tourism organizers and tourist participants felt that there was a sexual and romantic fantasy element in the packaging and structure of the vacation, not least because of its dancing orientation. Without stressing it further, the package advertising fostered and to some extent gave some licence to the tourists to engage with their exotic, erotic and fantastical sides (see also Skinner undated). Cuba would therefore appear to be the ideal tourist destination for a host of niche tourisms, with its informal and intimate appeal and structure: the stage was set, the players primed, and expectations 'aroused'.

Ceroc and Jive in Cuba

Ceroc is a franchised brand of modern jive dancing, a male-led partner dance that has successfully expanded throughout the United Kingdom such that there are currently a hundred branches and over three hundred thousand dancers (Skinner 2003b). With its simple hand movements and lack of footwork, this two-beat dance can be danced to a range of music – from pop to disco, blues to reggae. This 'McDonald's of dance', as one informant described it, is a popular choice of DanceHolidays that annually take groups of several hundred dancers on two-, three- and seven-day vacations to a number of Spanish destinations (Granada, Ibiza, Santa Susana, Barcelona and the Canary Islands). Following the success of their year-round Salsa vacations to Cuba, and the massive demand for Ceroc holidays, DanceHolidays took the strategic decision to expand their Ceroc holidays to Cuba. According to the DanceHolidays tour organizers interviewed, the intention was "to add a new Ceroc hub to the venue list before tourism to Cuba really takes off". This tourist destination also allows the company to draw a more affluent range of tourists, with prices ranging between £900 and £1,400, double the cost of many of their other holidays. These niche tourists are typically highly educated professional working people with both financial and cultural capital.

If, as Craik (1997: 135) notes, 'the dynamics of cultural production are about cultural differentiation and elitism', then DanceHolidays niche tourism is an opportunity for British social class groups to distance themselves from other classes whilst on holiday, to engage fully with a non-touristic culture and hence gain a seemingly authentic experience – a picture of an 'extra-ordinary' everyday life in the case of Castro's Cuba. This niche dance tourism thus provides for an embodied and sexualized tourism – a shift from the visual to the kinaesthetic.[2] Cuba is thus well suited as a niche tourism destination for British tourists as an island far off from the European mass market destinations, and an island where the islanders have a high standard of education and live by their socialist principles, factors which imply a commensurability between the niche tourists and the indigenous Cubans. It is ironic then that the democratizing potential of tourism should turn socialism into a selling point.

Cuba is a socialist Caribbean island that welcomes hard currency from tourism, one of the few viable foreign income generators. Often known by the epithet 'The Paris of the Antilles', Cuba has had an ambiguous tension between tourism and socialism – between 'relaxation and revolution' (Schwartz 1997: 164) – throughout the twentieth century: first as a 'pleasure island' for Americans escaping prohibition in the 1920s (eighty thousand per year) up until the Great

Depression of 1929; second as a post-Second World War destination in the 1950s under Batista until the success of the Cuban Revolution in 1959; and third as a foreign exchange earner from the 1980s under Castro. All three periods are characterized by an uneasy compromise with this necessary evil 'tourism', one that remodels the island on the tourists' terms (hotels and casinos in the 1920s, and Old Havana as a UNESCO World Heritage Site from 1982) and, again, ironically works as a catalyst for social change against the incumbent regime (Schwartz 1997: 180).

Though attracted to Cuba because of its socialism and its lack of touristic culture, Jason soon found himself publicly concerned about 'the state of the island and what tourism was doing to it'. He had not thought about his status as a capitalist tourist visiting the island because of his socialist sympathizings. He was also concerned about the social structure on the island and how it was being affected by tourism. It was not meeting his modest expectations:

> I hate all this prostitution and selling cigars. I bought a few from the shop instead of the street stuff. You don't know where they've been. And I can't believe the taxi-drivers, they're earning a month's salary for ten minutes work. It doesn't seem right. But all the people are on rations. I hadn't thought about it before but this place doesn't seem to be working at the moment.

After an organized group visit to a cigar factory in the centre of Havana, there were a diverse range of reactions to the cramped and hard working conditions of the workforce:

> 'What a job! At least they can smoke on the premises! Imagine being the cigar taster. I wonder if he gets a free cancer medical?'
>
> 'They're working I suppose. That's better than being out in the fields or on the streets. It's an honest wage and a living. Better than some.'
>
> 'God! That was awful. That was slave labour. We haven't come on at all in the last few centuries. I can't get over that.'

This suggests that expectations, reactions and the reality of tourist experiences are highly individual, relating to the personal history and outlook of the tourist, for all the collective and corporate tourism promotions. The common ground between the tourists was that they felt uncomfortable and out of 'their element' in Havana. Within several days, they had formed opinions that Cuba was changing and that Cuba had to change. Yet there was a poignancy about the nature of the change when the tourists reached Valadero, the coastal resort area where Cubans need a permit to live and work. They did not want to see Cuba turned back into an American playground. Their nostalgia for the past was for an imagined fantasy past sold in part to them by the tourist brochure and travel books they had consumed, and by their vivid imagination of a romantic glorious age that had seemingly existed on the island. Relying so heavily on semiotics to propel the tourist gaze, perhaps it is no wonder then that tourists will be disappointed by their experiences and find that the real never lives up to the ideal. Following on from the semiotician Jonathan Culler, John Frow (1991: 125) makes the point that there is a 'structural role of disappointment in the tourist experience' as the real is suffused with ideality. Holidays are primed to fail, in other words.

As de Holan and Phillips (1997: 781, 787, 788) note, Cuba is a low-cost tourist destination blessed with world-class 'sun and sand' but cursed with a lumbering state bureaucracy and low tourist numbers (326,000 per year in the mid-1990s, less than 3 per cent of the Caribbean market share but with an annual revenue of over $800 million) and low return tourist rates (<10 per cent vs. >40 per cent in Barbados). To these blessings, DanceHolidays add a third 'S': 'salsa'. DanceHolidays (2003: 10) market Cuba in their brochure in the following way:

> Magical Cuba, the land of salsa, rum, melodic music, exotic beaches, happy and easy-going people and a warm and sunny climate … You go salsaing during the day to venues which few tourists find and then partying until late in raunchy nightclubs … Experience salsa at its raunchiest – Return home with a salsa style so wild that you bring the dance floor to a complete standstill.

It was therefore an unusual and ambitious business choice to use the salsa holiday formula in Cuba to package a Ceroc holiday there, offering 'Cerocing and salsaing to the hottest salsa night spots' (2003: 24) in old Havana (4 nights) and in an all-inclusive resort in Valadero (6 nights). Though the tourist location is unusual for this dancing activity, the tourist marketing of the location fits into the vein of previous marketing of the pleasure island Cuba. This marketing strategy is consistent with Cuba's twentieth-century ambivalent flirtation with tourism, the tourist industry's long-term promotion of the 'sensual and mystical qualities of Afro-Cubans for purposes of profit … [and] Cuba as an erotic, exotic island devoted to their pleasure and entertainment' (Schwartz 1997: 87). This marketing also moulds tourist expectations.

Coy Expectations about Ceroc Dance Tourism on Cuba

As noted above, the pre-vacation interviews with a number of the informants revealed that they had in fact internalized much of the DanceHolidays advertising. When asked why they were going and what they were expecting from the vacation, replies such as 'Cuba is the land of salsa and dance and I want to dance there' were common. In the group of twenty, only two were a married couple, a doctor and his wife; all other tourists travelled as single professionals (predominantly business executives, IT workers and lawyers), though a number of tourists had regular – if casual – life partners back in the U.K.. Several tourists came on the holiday in groups of two or three as friends, and a number had accidentally met each other before on other DanceHolidays in Europe or had danced with each other at Ceroc venues in the U.K.. This meant that right from the outset there was a commonality about the group and that there were many points of contact in the conversation. Furthermore, in common with the author's last eight years of Ceroc research, the single tourist dancers on the vacation expressed the same sentiments with respect to relationships that were found back in the U.K., namely that they would be 'open to new relationships if they came along' but were happy with themselves and their casual dancing with others in the meantime. In other words, they were open to romance and casual sexual relations between each other if the conditions were right.

Jeremy is an elderly IT software worker who has visited Cuba a number of times. He has several young male friends whom he visits and 'parties with' each time he is on-island. He is not really a Ceroc dancer or there for the dancing:

> The Cubans are the friendliest people I know. Some of my male friends there really enjoy themselves. I've been to Cuba on Salsa holidays and that was really raunchy and fun. I'm not so sure about the Ceroc though, but I don't mind.

Isaac is another IT expert, a young computer programmer who works in Central Europe. He learnt Ceroc when he was on a contract in London. There, he geared his accommodation and non-working life around the Ceroc venues and dance times:

> This is great. I cannot wait to meet some new women and to learn some new moves! I have missed Ceroc so much. Some of my colleagues tried to put it on in Europe, but we were only doing it from memory. This is the real stuff, and to do it in Cuba!

Several of the tourists on the niche tourism package holiday had similar interests to Jeremy. Bill and Sarah were new to the Ceroc dancing and preferred the social scene that it offered them. They expected it to complement their holiday time, just as it does their newfound middle-age hobbies:

> 'This is great, it's gonna be a 'beer and dames' time. I can just feel it!'
> 'I hope this turns out to be a detox trip. I could really do with losing some weight. The dancing should help that. I'm not into salsa, all that wiggling, but who knows what will happen or who I could meet when up on the floor doing Ceroc. Oh, whisk me away, darling!'

The reasons for Francis's attendance on the holiday were unique, however. She liked neither salsa, nor Ceroc. Francis wanted to escape from a difficult personal life:

I don't want to dance. I don't want any men funny business. I just want to lie in the sun and have some good food and some good drink. This is a girly holiday for me.

For Francis, who is in her 40s, the vacation was a last minute escape route. She did not want to interact with other people but wanted to spend time with herself and to recuperate before returning home. The importance of the holiday was thus in terms of Francis asserting her independence and getting away from her family and home/work-life.

These tourist testimonies suggest a part-informed tourist vision of Cuba and the DanceHolidays holiday. Some of this is based upon the tourists' previous holiday and Ceroc dancing experiences. Apart from Francis, those attending the DanceHoliday have a lot of experience of the physicality of the dance world, of dancing close with a partner of the opposite sex. The satisfaction derived from this can offset the existential need for a sexual partner and allow the individual to concentrate and remain with themselves. Ironically, this means that the DanceHolidays tourists had a potentially more relaxed attitude to physical contact, but that that contact did not develop sexually despite the Ceroc dance occasions – like tourist destinations – being potential meeting places and spaces for intimacy and role play. This is significant when considering the Cuba tourist destination, a renowned Caribbean sex tourism destination.

Previous tourism research supports this point with the generality that for sex tourism 'the men go East and the Women go West' in that the men go to South East Asia (Cohen 1993; Hall 1992; Leheny 1995) and the women go to the Caribbean and South America (Pruitt and LaFont 1995; O'Connell Davidson 1996; de Albuquerque 1998; Herold, Garcia and DeMoya 2001). For all this, Cuba is still known predominantly as a sex tourism destination for men, a point which became evident upon the tour's arrival in Havana. There, the tourist men were hassled continually for business by *jinetaras*, though the worst anyone admitted to purchasing on the streets were mouldy old Cuban cigars. Nevertheless, the dancing evenings in Havana and Valadero did allow the tourists to experience each other and friendly Cuban dancers in a non-ordinary (dance-like) fashion. Thus this vacation in Cuba became associated with a 'territorialized hedonism' (Löfgren 1999) in two capacities or tropes: as 'sexualized' dance instruction and practice, and sex tourism destination.

The Reality of Ceroc Dance Tourism on Cuba

As part of the DanceHolidays package, the tourists were sold ten hours of Ceroc instruction by qualified Ceroc instructors, and were guaranteed an evening of Ceroc dancing plus salsa every night. In addition to these holiday package basics, there were optional excursions on offer such as group meals, a rum distillery and cigar factory visit in Havana, and pleasure-boat rides in Valadero. In Havana, the locally hired Cuban dancers – dancers who usually instructed the tourists on their salsa DanceHolidays to Cuba – offered three hours of basic salsa instruction as an additional package to the Ceroc. In this way, the salsa dance and salsa location as well as the Ceroc were commoditized and sold to the tourists. This is an 'involved' form of dance commoditization that is different from the traditional Cuban rumba dance performances described by Daniel (1995, 1996) which are passively consumed by tourists to Cuba and other exotic 'Latin' dance destinations. The active nature of the dancing between Ceroc tourists and salsa Cuban dance instructors did 'inadvertently stimulate creativity' (1996: 793) as the Cubans learned to vary and mix their dance tradition and to add Ceroc to their repertoire, dancing Ceroc with us and salsa amongst themselves in the evenings. Unfortunately, the tourists on this particular DanceHolidays vacation were unable to reciprocate dance-wise as they could not pick up and play with the salsa steps they saw or were shown. Nevertheless, the dancing engaged us tourists in an embodied tourism that we were partially comfortable with in an alien environment.

In fact, what became apparent amongst the tourists, the dance instructors (Cuban and British) and the tour organizers, was that the two dance forms and styles did not mix. Ceroc is very different from salsa: it has no particular footwork whereas salsa footwork is based around timed forward and backward steps; Ceroc is a two-beat dance whereas salsa works around four beats (4/4 timing in two measures); and Ceroc is composed around a number of short separate moves whereas salsa is more fluid and based around longer moves. This meant that the Cuban dancers struggled to dance to the Ceroc with the tourists and that no local Cubans in the salsa venues were able to dance with us at all. After the first night in Cuba, it became clear that it was necessary to hire local nightclubs for several hours so that the tourists' own music CDs could be played. During this time, the locals would watch bemused until the end of the tourists' rental time when salsa music returned to the loudspeakers and they could return to the dance floor. Dance expectations and imaginations of 'dancing with dusky Cuban women' were immediately moderated into Cerocers dancing with each other, and only dancing with Cubans when they were paid to dance with us.

The dynamic between tourists and locals was further complicated by the small size of the group, the gender differences, and the different tourist desires amongst the tourists – particularly the women. Schwartz (1997: 212) rightly concludes her history of tourism on Cuba with the comment that '[e]nforced isolation has enhanced the island's mystique'. A number of the tourist group had come on the tourist holiday to 'experience Cuba before it changes'. They were socialist sympathisers such as Jason who admired Cuba's stand against capitalism. With no sense of irony, these tourist consumers had booked this niche holiday with only a side-interest in the dancing. Unfortunately, because the group was so small in size and so male-dominated – unusual with the predominance of women at typical Ceroc nights back in the U.K. – when (female) tourists were absent from the group, away exploring Old Havana or parts of Valadero (Cuba's version of Miami Beach), their absence seriously disrupted the balance and size of the group. 'It is such a small group that it has no synergy of its own', explained the tour operator who was comparing this DanceHolidays Ceroc vacation with those in Spain that typically have several hundred participants, several of whose absence from the lessons or the excursions would not have been missed. Further to this, the small group of Cerocers had a wide range of expertise ranging from novice to expert that sometimes made it difficult to dance with each other, let alone teaching the group. Whilst the brochure encouraged all standards of Cerocers to holiday in Cuba, the follow-up sheets asked for estimates as to the dancer's ability. These personal estimates, however, did not correspond with the instructors' estimates. The result was that the group was difficult to teach as a whole, and several members of the group were difficult to dance with individually. The range of dance abilities did not match the organizer's expectations. The organizers were structuring the vacation along European large-scale lines, but for a small group of people and people who were – or saw themselves as – more upwardly mobile than the weekender or short-break dancers going to Ceroc holidays in Spain. Contra the European model, in a number of cases the Ceroc dancers on the Cuba package saw the dancing as secondary to their tourist experience.

Though there was little explicit romantic inter-activity amongst the members of the group, there was a lot of attention enjoyed by the white female tourists from some of the Cuban men. 'Flattery' and 'pushiness' are two seduction strategies used on female Western tourists visiting the Caribbean (Herold, Garcia and DeMoya 2001: 986, 988). These unexpected attentions and strategies from black, exotic and sexually charged men, as they were perceived, were preferred by several dancing tourist women over the British reserve of their fellow dancing tourist men. Likewise, several of the men attempted to enjoy the company of the Cuban women on the dance floor, taking liberties which they felt were allowed in the 'exotic and tropical' environment but would not have dared to take back home: they forced their tourist expectations. They played out the tourist role that they thought was expected from them according to the tourist brochure and information. These points were confirmed by follow-up research amongst the tourists and instructors back in their regular Ceroc venues in the U.K.. Back home, the male dancers interacted far more respectfully with their dance partners. It was clear then that the niche dancing holiday served both a social and a sexual purpose for many of the participants. Dance – a traditional means of escapism, mood change and socializing – was, for the purposes of the tourist vacation, coupled with an alien and less restrictive environment, that is, for the tourist.

Francis and Mary refused to go along to the dance classes in the mornings in Havana because of the interests of several of the men that they considered to be inappropriate. Ironically, they enjoyed the same kinds of interest from the Cuban men in the evenings, but that was considered more 'authentic' and the Cuban men's behaviour was expected and hence tolerated. Bill and Mary spent most of their days sunbathing by the pool or on the beach and their evenings in the bar, missing both lessons and dancing. Sarah, despite enjoying the Ceroc during the day, preferred going to Cuban bars by herself, also 'for a more authentic experience' in her evenings. Whilst these departures from the tour operator's expected tourist programme could have been accommodated in larger groups, in the small niche package holiday group to Cuba, it jeopardized the evenings' dancing for the rest of the group. Dancers were forced to dance with the same few people throughout the night. The topic of conversation thus turned to who was not joining the group for the evening, and to speculation as to what they were doing and who they were doing it with. This type of gossip is a typical group reaction. It sustains the group when feeling threatened.

Within the space of three to four days of travelling and dancing company with each other, animosities and inappropriate attentions had arisen. The group had fragmented into several sub-groups and everyone had been stereotyped and labelled with amusing nicknames that represented their behaviour or character whilst on the holiday: 'Twinkle-toes', 'Boring Man', 'Dance Tart', 'Mr Seducer', 'Anthro-man' (the ethnographer). By the end of the ten days, nearly all of the members of the group, including the organizers and instructors, were looking forward to their return to their everyday life. All of their leaving interviews were critical of the holiday, though not its organization or marketing – despite the unfulfilled expectations:

> It was awful. I'm not happy with it. There was nothing to do. I'm not coming back here again. I want a holiday in the sun without these people and without the dancing or hassle from the natives.

> The holiday was ok. DanceHolidays did their best, but there weren't enough people and Valadero was really tacky. I think I'd like to come back and explore the south of the island. But that would be on my own. Not on another dance package.

> The holiday was good. I enjoyed it, but I can see that others didn't. The Ceroc didn't really work here. I think I can afford holidays like this every other year. I want to go somewhere where it's not so poor though. Seeing all that here made me feel guilty.

Jason summed up many of the tourists' views when he spoke about tourism and its effects on Cuba:

> I hadn't really thought about it before. The tourism is what they want, but it's not necessarily good for the country and the people. I can see that the socialism is not working, but the capitalism and consumerism is going to make it just like America. And that could be worse for many Cubans.

The final view came from one of the DanceHolidays organizers who joined us on this pilot niche package holiday to see whether it 'lived up to expectations or not'.

129

They recognized the problems and difficulties associated with a small party Ceroc niche holiday. Despite this, the organization wanted to develop more exclusive upmarket Ceroc vacations to run alongside their mass market Ceroc holidays in Europe.

> We want to be here first. We can see Cuba as a hub of Ceroc operations alongside our European resorts. We need more people but that will come in time. This will become a mass tourism destination and we want to stake our niche here first.

Though cognisant of the problems associated with this particular first run of a Ceroc niche tourism package holiday, the organizers appeared to be confident that the numbers would build and that their tourism formula – the marketing and the structure of the events – would succeed.

Discussion

Participant observation of this entire niche tourism package holiday led to what I refer to as a 'total tourism event', the research of the tourist vacation experience from start to finish. This is a more holistic approach to studying tourism than carrying out surveys at some stage in the tourist process. Participating in – living – tourist experiences gives the researcher greater insight into the phenomenology of the experience, how it affects the tourists and how they affect it (cf. Bruner 1991, 2005; Cohen 1979, 1988), their role-playing and role changes through the tourist encounter (see Adler 1989). As Holy and Stuchlik (1983: 12) caution, there is a great difference between 'the verbal statements of the members of the society and their observed behaviour', between their notions and their actions. It is therefore necessary to observe first-hand actor situations and their contexts to have confidence in social science findings. Consistency in the tourist's behaviour and answers makes this participant observation research method more substantial than, say, the collection of data sets and mass questionnaires such as in the case of Dann's (1995) analytical report on an interview-based survey of 535 tourists to Barbados. Following the Ceroc participants through their niche tourism package holiday to Cuba, I was able to gain insight into the participants' expectations, their reactions to the vacation as it progressed, and their feedback at the end of the holiday. This insight is not only a detailed knowledge of the vacation from the actors' perspectives, but is also an accurate insight, one in which the researcher has a great deal of confidence in the findings.

The disappointment suffered by the participants in this trial Ceroc vacation to Cuba was palpable. In terms of consumer satisfaction, I have suggested, after Frow (1991), that the vacation never quite lives up to expectations. Perhaps the tourist experience is always a poor copy of the perceived original marketed in the brochures and bylines? Certainly 'real' Havana differs from Jason's 'idealized'

Havana; and likewise, the dancing and foreign companionship differ from Isaac, and Frances, Mary and Sarah's corporeal desires. Perhaps those with the most congruence between tourist/consumer expectation and experience were Jeremy who had been there many times before and thus knew what to expect and with whom, and Bill and Mary who travelled with few expectations but safe in a comfortable partnership with each other. In this fashion, the dance tourists let go whilst they are on holiday, experience new sensations and environments, but also retain some familiar habitual enactments as Ceroc dancers, as white tourists abroad practising self-surveillance and self-regulation off the dance floor as well as on the dance floor (cf. Gotfrit 1988). It was Ceroc in Cuba after all.

What each of the tourists did buy into on the Cuba trip was a *Verwerfung*, a status from the exclusive nature of the highly specialized and marketed dance holiday. We stayed in exclusive hotels, had local guides on hand, local dancers in hand, and Ceroc instructors leading our dancing and much of our socializing from start to finish. This accords with Carroll's (1980) thesis that tourism is often about positional competition, the fantasy of (upward) mobility and paid for privilege. We were attempting to live out and live up to images that had moulded our expectations. Those images and imaginations are the 'expectations-generating factor of a future encounter with a tourist service' (Del Bosque and San Martin 2008: 558; see also Introduction, this volume). They raise the expectations of the envisaged holiday and it is their fulfilment – or not as in this case – that leads to tourist satisfaction or dissatisfaction. The tourist self-actualizes their expectations in the holiday consumption.

However, as 'tentative (mental of neural) representations of future events or unfinished learning processes' (Gnoth 1997: 298), expectations are never exactly matched by reality. They belong to the imagination, and there is an increasing likelihood that the imagination comes to life in our postmodern consumer world (cf. Appadurai 1996), but it is always a shadow, silhouette or negation of the real, to invoke Sartre (1966). Beliefs about future performance expectations are rated as positive or negative disconfirmation according to consumer theorist Richard Oliver (1980): high tourist expectations can lead to negative disconfirmation. As noted above, the difference between the 'expected' and the 'experienced' remains critical. As Del Bosque and San Martin (2008: 554) phrase it: 'Individuals suffer a psychological conflict when they perceive discrepancies between performance and prior beliefs.' Jason, Isaac, Frances and Mary, the anthropologist, the DanceHolidays operator and others all experienced negative disconfirmation with the trial package holiday as tourism performance and execution failed to meet or live up to expectations. All of us were complicit in this failure, organizers as well as participants, each with our preconceptions (a key expectation variable).

Cuban 'culture' is appropriated as a commodity by tour companies such as DanceHolidays. Whilst there are problems with the packaging and consumption of the Ceroc niche tourism package holiday to Cuba, there is evidence of growing local and government control of tourism. Alaska is even seeing the growth of native-owned tourist industries that could possibly develop in Cuba under a post-Castro government (Nuttall 1997). At present, however, the tensions between the local government controls and external tourism organizations such as the package provider DanceHolidays are set to continue, perhaps even to grow with the potential increase in tourist numbers to the island. The danger is that Cuban culture becomes a stagnant artefact, deracinated; that the dances become static tourist representations disconnected from their context like West African limbo in hotel shows in Antigua (Pattullo 1996); and that, like the U.S. Virgin Islanders (Lewis 1972), Cubans become increasingly dependent on and resentful of tourism.

Clearly, the niche tourism sub-genre will continue to develop in Cuba. It is unlikely, though, to bring more foreign capital into Cuba than Cuba's existing mass tourism packages. Niche tourism is destined to remain a venture associated with small tourism operators whether exogenous or indigenous. Nevertheless, for both low-key niche and mass tourism markets the packaging and advertising of the tourist product is critical to its success and uptake. DanceHolidays react and attend to their questionnaire surveys given to tourists during their departure from Cuba. These, like the cursory interviews reported by Dann, were treated very casually by a number of the tourists who took the opportunity to complain about many aspects of the vacation; however, during follow-up after the vacation they relented upon their criticisms and comments that they would not go on such a holiday again. Though the consensus of opinion was that the holiday had failed, and that salsa was more appropriate as a niche venture to Cuba, and that larger numbers of tourists were needed, a number of the women such as Sarah and Cassie felt that they were returning from the vacation 're-energized' and 'tanned', and that they had enjoyed the 'attentions' of the local Cuban men. Jason returned in a state of shock at the poverty and effects of tourism and vowed not to vacation in 'non-metropole regions' again. And the tour organizers began preparing for the next – expanded – Ceroc package trip to Cuba, developing their advertising to Ceroc audiences by setting up marketing stalls at Ceroc venues, and by paying the Ceroc franchise to maintain a web-link to DanceHolidays and for allowing them to use the Ceroc brand name and logo. Since this pilot Ceroc package holiday, however, only salsa holidays have been led by DanceHolidays to Cuba.

Conclusion

Niche tourism is a relatively new development on Cuba. It is one that is loosening the government's controls on the tourism industry because it favours the low-key small operator, whether indigenous or exogenous. Though the DanceHolidays Ceroc niche tourism package holiday was well commoditized and marketed, it failed to meet the expectations of the tourists in terms of appropriacy and audience: it did not suit the salsa environment and 'it did not live up to' (Jason) the desires and fantasies of the visiting tourists. The vacation was financially successful for the DanceHolidays organizers and the Ceroc and salsa instructors only as a one-off pilot. It was not seen as a financially lucrative and satisfactory vacation initiative in the long-run alongside their salsa holidays. Fortunately, the failings of the vacation are only minor problems for DanceHolidays who have a large potential tourist population to draw upon. Furthermore, if DanceHolidays tourists do not 'find pleasure on "pleasure island"', they are still more than likely to join in on other European DanceHolidays niche tourism package holidays. This means that DanceHolidays does not have a large incentive to repackage the vacation once it has been tested and is up and running. Furthermore, it is so expensive that the same tourists are unlikely to return for the same package holiday. Nevertheless, DanceHolidays should be cautious that they do not superimpose their readings of local culture upon their tourists or ignore the tourists' points of view.

DanceHolidays continues to monitor and modify their vacations and the marketing of them. Recommendations for developing the dance tourism niche range from putting a minimum of tourist numbers on the package holiday, and rearranging activities to better suit the tourists (the Museum of the Revolution instead of the cigar factory for example), to developing their tourist dance vetting system. The last suggestion would make the tourist groups more exclusive and attractive to some dancers, and would create more cohesive dancing groups with the same ability. This can be done by working with the Ceroc dance instructors and local branches who would be in a better position to judge dancers' standards than the dancers themselves. A more discrete way of maintaining the cohesion of the groups would also be by more targeted marketing of dance tourists. This could have been done by advertising the Cuba dance tourism niche holidays at selected venues such as Ceroc competitions which attract the more experienced dancers, and by refining and honing the literature to attract the appropriate dance tourists and to give them realistic and sensible tourist expectations. Given that 'the niche' is here to stay, organizations other than DanceHolidays, the large as well as the small, would do well to turn their attentions to the tourists' new desires and demands, to providing new alternatives to the traditional mass holiday – which is, after all, an alternative lifestyle in itself. 'If expectations are appropriately communicated, tourists will be more satisfied, and consequently, more loyal after the experience' note Del Bosque and San Martin (2008: 567). It is not just the tourist that 'actualizes' the nature of expectation in holiday consumption: the tourism industry also plays a vital part in this satisfaction process, one which transitions through from expectation generation to vacation realization. If expectation lies in the shadows of our imagination, then the tourism industry would do well to follow the example of the tourist and to seek out the direct sun.

Notes

The author would like to thank DanceHolidays, the anonymized members of the package tour, Barnaly Pandé, Helena Wulff, Nelson Graburn, Dimitrios Theodossopoulos and James Carrier for their advice and encouragement, and to acknowledge that this research was supported by the University of Abertay Dundee.

1. In her involved study of rumba on Cuba, Daniel (1995: 21) refers to the immersed researcher as an 'observing participant' rather than traditional participant observer.
2. Moeran explains such a shift with an example from new directions in Japanese tourism culture: 'They want to experience not sights but action ... to participate with their own skins. ... Travel is contact [*tabi wa fureai*]' (Moeran 1983: 96 cited in Franklin and Crang 2001: 13).

References

Adler, J. 1989. 'Travel as Performed Art', *Journal of Sociology* 94(6): 1366–91.
Appadurai, A. 1996. *Modernity at Large: Cultural Dimensions of Globalization*. Minneapolis: University of Minnesota Press.
Beerli, A., G. Meneses and S. Gil. 2007. 'Self-Congruity and Destination Choice', *Annals of Tourism Research* 34(3): 571–87.
Beirman, D. 2002. 'Marketing of Tourism Destinations during a Prolonged Crisis: Israel and the Middle East', *Journal of Vacation Marketing* 8(2): 167–76.
Bruner, E. 1989a. 'Tourism, Creativity, and Authenticity', *Studies in Symbolic Interaction* 10: 109–14.
———. 1989b. 'On Cannibals, Tourists, and Ethnographers', *Cultural Anthropology* 4: 438–45.
———. 1991. 'The Transformation of Self in Tourism', *Annals of Tourism Research* 18(2): 238–50.
———. 2005. *Culture on Tour: Ethnographies of Travel*. Chicago: University of Chicago Press.
Burkart, A. and S. Medlik. 1981. *Tourism: Past, Present and Future*. London: Heinemann.
Butler, R. 1995. 'Alternative Tourism: The Thin End of the Wedge', in V. Smith and W. Eadington (eds), *Tourism Alternatives: Potentials and Problems in the Development of Tourism*. Chichester: John Wiley & Sons, pp. 31–46.
Carlisle, L. 2000. 'Niche or Mass Market? The Regional Context of Tourism in Palau', *The Contemporary Pacific* 12(2): 415–36.
Carroll, J. 1980. *Sceptical Sociology*. London: Routledge.
Casson, L. 1974. *Travel in the Ancient World*. London: Allen & Unwin Ltd.
Cohen, E. 1979. 'A Phenomenology of Tourist Experiences', *Sociology* 13(2): 179–201.
———. 1988. 'Traditions in Qualitative Sociology of Tourism', *Annals of Tourism Research* 15(1): 29–46.
———. 1993. 'Open-ended Prostitution as Skilful Game of Luck: Opportunity, Risk and Security among Tourist-oriented Prostitutes in a Bangkok *Soi*', in M. Hitchcock, V. King and M. Parnwell (eds), *Tourism in South-East Asia*. London: Routledge, pp. 155–78.
Craik, J. 1997. 'The Culture of Tourism', in C. Rojek and J. Urry (eds), *Touring Cultures: Transformations of Travel and Theory*. London: Routledge, pp. 113–36.
Crouch, D., L. Aronsson and L. Wahlström. 2001. 'Tourist Encounters', *Tourist Studies* 1(1): 253–70.
DanceHolidays. 2003. *Dance Around the World*. Travel Brochure. Sussex: Carefree Travel (International) Limited.
Daniel, Y. 1995. *Rhumba: Dance and Social Change in Contemporary Cuba*. Bloomington: Indiana University Press.

————. 1996. 'Tourism Dance Performances: Authenticity and Creativity', *Annals of Tourism Research* 23(4): 780–97.

Dann, G. 1995. 'Predisposition Toward Alternative Forms of Tourism Among Tourists Visiting Barbados: Some Preliminary Observations', in V. Smith and W. Eadington (eds), *Tourism Alternatives: Potentials and Problems in the Development of Tourism*. Chichester: John Wiley & Sons, pp. 158–79.

de Albuquerque, K. 1998. 'Sex, Beach Boys, and Female Tourists in the Caribbean', *Sexuality and Culture* 2: 87–111.

De Holan, P. and N. Phillips. 1997. 'Sun, Sand and Hard Currency: Tourism in Cuba', *Annals of Tourism Research* 24(4): 777–95.

Del Bosque, I. and H. San Martin. 2008. 'Tourist Satisfaction: A Cognitive-Affective Model', *Annals of Tourism Research* 35(2): 551–73.

Eadington, W. and V. Smith. 1995. 'Introduction: The Emergence of Alternative Forms of Tourism', in V. Smith and W. Eadington (eds), *Tourism Alternatives: Potentials and Problems in the Development of Tourism*. Chichester: John Wiley & Sons, pp. 1–12.

Franklin, A. and M. Crang. 2001. 'The Trouble with Tourism and Travel Theory?', *Tourist Studies* 1(1): 5–22.

Frow, J. 1991. 'Tourism and the Semiotics of Nostalgia', *October* 57: 123–51.

Giddens, A. 1991. *Modernity and Self-Identity: Self and Society in the Late Modern Age*. Stanford: Stanford University Press.

Gnoth, J. 1997. 'Tourism Motivation and Expectation Formation', *Annals of Tourism Research* 24(2): 283–304.

Gotfrit, L. 1988. 'Women Dancing Back: Disruption and the Politics of Pleasure', *Journal of Education* 170(3): 122–41.

Hall, C. 1992. 'Sex Tourism in Southeast Asia', in D. Harrison (ed.), *Tourism and the Less Developed Countries*. London: Belhaven Press, pp. 65–74.

Herold, E., R. Garcia and T. DeMoya. 2001. 'Female Tourists and Beach Boys: Romance or Sex Tourism', *Annals of Tourism Research* 28(4): 978–97.

Holy, L. and M. Stuchlik. 1983. *Actions, Norms and Representations: Foundations of Anthropological Enquiry*. Cambridge: Cambridge University Press.

Leach, E. 1979. 'Two Essays Concerning the Symbolic Representation of Time', in W. Lessa and E. Vogt (eds), *Reader in Comparative Religion: An Anthropological Approach*. New York: Harper Collins, pp. 221–28.

Leheny, D. 1995. 'A Political Economy of Asian Sex Tourism', *Annals of Tourism Research* 22(2): 367–84.

Lennon, J. and M. Foley. 2000. *Dark Tourism: The Attraction of Death and Disaster*. London: Continuum.

Lett, J. 1983. 'Ludic and Liminoid Aspects of Charter Yacht Tourism in the Caribbean', *Annals of Tourism Research* 10(1): 35–56.

Lewis, G. 1972. *The Virgin Islands: A Caribbean Lilliput*. Evanston, Illinois: Northwestern University Press.

Löfgren, O. 1999. *On Holiday: A History of Vacationing*. Berkeley: University of California Press.

MacCannell, D. 2001. 'Tourist Agency', *Tourist Studies* 1(1): 23–37.

McCrone, M., A. Morris and R. Kiely. 1995. *Scotland The Brand: The Making of Scottish Heritage*. Edinburgh: Edinburgh University Press.

Miller, D. 1997. *Capitalism: An Ethnographic Approach*. Oxford: Berg.

Moeran, B. 1983. 'The Language of Japanese Tourism', *Annals of Tourism Research* 10(1): 93–108.

Momsen, J. and J. Donaldson. 2001. *Cultivating Farm Stays in California*. California Community Topics 7. Davis, CA: UC Davis, California.

Morris, A. and J. Gladstone. 2001. 'Agricultural Heritage and the Social and Economic Regeneration of Farm Women', in A. Law, C. Di Domenico, J. Skinner and M. Smith (eds), *Boundaries and*

Identities: Nation, Politics and Culture. Dundee: University of Abertay Dundee Press, pp. 237–53.

Nuttall, M. 1997. '"Alternative" Tourists on a Canary Island', in S. Abram, J. Waldren and D. Macleod (eds), *Tourists and Tourism: Identifying with People and Places*. Oxford: Berg, pp. 223–38.

O'Connell Davidson, J. 1996. 'Sex Tourism in Cuba', *Race & Class* 38(1): 39–48.

Oliver, R. 1980. 'A Cognitive Model of the Antecedents and Consequences of Satisfaction Decisions', *Journal of Marketing Research* 17(4): 460–69.

———. 1997. *Satisfaction: A Behavioural Perspective on the Consumer*. New York, NY: McGraw-Hill.

Parinello, G. 1993. 'Motivation and Anticipation in Post-Industrial Tourism', *Annals of Tourism Research* 20(1): 233–49.

Pattullo, P. 1996. *Last Resorts: The Cost of Tourism in the Caribbean*. London: Cassell.

Perales, R. 2002. 'Rural Tourism in Spain'. *Annals of Tourism Research* 29(4): 1101–10.

Pruitt, D. and S. LaFont. 1995. 'For Love and Money: Romance Tourism in Jamaica', *Annals of Tourism Research* 22(2): 422–40.

Robertson, J. 2002. 'Anxieties of Imperial Decay: Three Journeys in India', in H. Gilbert and A. Johnston (eds), *In Transit: Travel, Text, Empire*. New York: Peter Lang Publishing Inc., pp. 103–24.

Robinson, M. and M. Novelli. 2008. 'Niche Tourism: An Introduction', in M. Novelli (ed.), *Niche Tourism: Contemporary Issues, Trends and Cases*. Oxford: Butterworth-Heinemann, pp. 1–11.

Sartre, J-P. 1966. *The Psychology of Imagination*. New York: The Citadel Press.

Schwartz, R. 1997. *Pleasure Island: Tourism and Temptation in Cuba*. London: University of Nebraska Press.

Seaton, A. 1996a. 'Reports: Hay on Wye, the Mouse that Roared: Book Towns and Rural Tourism', *Tourism Management* 17(5): 379–82.

———. 1996b. 'Guided by the Dark: from Thanatopsis to Thanotourism', *International Journal of Heritage Studies* 2(4): 234–44.

Skinner, J. 2003a. 'Voyeurs, Voyagers and Disaster Tourism from Mount Chance, Montserrat', in D. Macleod (ed.), *Niche Tourism and Anthropology*. Glasgow: University of Glasgow Press, pp. 129–44.

———. 2003b. 'At the Busk and after Dusk: Ceroc and the Construction of Dance Times and Places', *Focaal: European Journal of Anthropology* 42: 117–27.

———. undated. 'Sex, Temperament and Transgression on the Dance Floor', unpublished paper.

Smith, V. and W. Eadington (eds). 1995. *Tourism Alternatives: Potentials and Problems in the Development of Tourism*. Chichester: John Wiley & Sons.

Swain, M. 1995. 'Gender in Tourism', *Annals of Tourism Research* 22(2): 247–66.

Turner, L. and L. Ashe. 1975. *The Golden Hordes: International Tourism and the Pleasure Periphery*. London: Constable.

Turner, V. 1979. 'Betwixt and Between: The Liminal Period in "Rites De Passage"', in W. Lessa and E. Vogt (eds), *Reader in Comparative Religion: An Anthropological Approach*. New York: Harper Collins Publishers, pp. 234–42.

Urry, J. 1990. *The Tourist Gaze*. London: Sage.

Walton, J. 1982. 'Residential Amenity, Respectable Morality and the Rise of the Entertainment Industry: The Case of Blackpool, 1860–1914', in B. Waites, T. Bennett and G. Marton (eds), *Popular Culture: Past and Present*. London: Croom Helm, pp. 133–45.

———. 1983. *The English Seaside Resort: A Social History 1750–1914*. Leicester: Leicester University Press.

Weaver, D. 1995. 'Alternative Tourism in Montserrat', *Tourism Management* 16(8): 593–604.

Wood, R. 2000. 'Caribbean Cruise Tourism: Globalization at Sea', *Annals of Tourism Research* 27(2): 345–70.

Chapter 8
THE COACH FELLAS: TOURISM PERFORMANCE AND EXPECTATION IN IRELAND

Kelli Ann Malone

Since 2001, I have studied tourism at several archaeological sites in Ireland, among them the Hill of Tara, the Bru na Boinne, Loughcrew, Emain Macha, and Rathcroghan. A common compelling factor among visitors to these sites, especially amongst those claiming Irish descent, was to somehow 'touch' their past, to commune with ancestral spaces, or to otherwise satisfy a felt need to experience and understand themselves. Almost without exception there were few visitors among those whom I observed who had any real knowledge of the sites beyond stories of druids, human sacrifice, leprechauns, fairy mounds, and kings (of whom many were direct descendants). Yet for all this, there exists a palpable assumed familiarity and relationship with the landscape of Ireland, an expectation of immediate recognition and invitation without hesitation to engage with it.

The experience of and expectation of Ireland and its past can, at times, overwhelm the visitor. On many occasions, as I observed and took part in more than twenty-five coach tours from 2005–2008, the difficulty in reconciling an Ireland of the imagination and an Ireland as lived challenged and perplexed many tour participants. First-time visitors (and I will qualify this by saying the majority of participants on the tours I observed were English-speaking from America, Canada, New Zealand, the U.K., and Australia) often arrived in Ireland with little preparation for the modern and urban lifestyle which embraces Ireland in the twenty-first century. The ancient sites, especially the megaliths, burial mounds and earthworks in Ireland often become over-mythologized in the touristic imagination, thus becoming far more than sites of archaeological importance –

they become symbolic conduits to a created past, a lifeline and a lifeblood for many visitors. The process of re-creation conflates them in the imagination of the visitor, collapsing the vast period of time since their construction, making them part of a memory sourced from a collection of stories, visual prompts, and shadowy remembrances (Cooney 1996; Bender 2001; Urry 2002). Though the opportunity to commune with the archaeological past is available worldwide, it is in Ireland that many visitors expect to find their consanguineal origins in the physical landscape (Costa 2004, 2009). This desire to join and commune somehow with Ireland is not limited to ancient sites and monuments; it is expected everywhere and with everyone.

Coach Tourism and the Experience of Ireland

These sought after experiences are commonplace among long-haul coach tourists in Ireland who represent close to half a million of Ireland's tourist numbers each year (somewhere near 10 per cent of the total of all tourism numbers including weekend and city break participants). Coach tourism takes place twelve months a year in Ireland but the busy season begins in May and reaches its peak in July and August. The slowest periods are from November to February, though new markets are continually being developed making off-season and shoulder-season coach travel more attractive to participants (see www.failteireland.com and www.tourismireland.com).

Unlike fly and drive opportunities, or independent travel in Ireland, coach tourism offers a full-service experience of the country and its culture; it can offer standard, packaged introductions to a country, but can also provide bespoke travel based on a group's interests (such as archaeology or genealogy). Travel, site visits, luggage transfers, most meals, and information will be taken care of by a series of stakeholders in a hierarchy of participation. Those furthest removed from the experience itself, the tour operator or travel agent, often do the least and benefit the most. The coach operator who owns and organizes the coaches is equally removed from the actual participants (the exception being the rare cases when an owner is pressed into service as a driver). The coach operator gleans high returns on the hiring of his coaches, drivers, guides, and driver-guides; for example, the average charge per day for a coach is currently €400, while the driver-guide usually receives minimum wage up to €100 per day. It must be understood that the coach operator has invested large sums of money in his fleet and the associated services needed to keep it running at an optimum level. The stakeholders responsible for the most work during a tour are also those who are in direct contact with the tour participants: the drivers, guides and driver-guides (the *Coach Fellas* mentioned in the title of this chapter). They are also the members of the service hierarchy who benefit the least financially, often receiving minimum wage plus tips for hours spent driving, organizing, resolving problems, and answering endless questions (in Ireland the 2008 minimum wage was €8.65 per hour and tips fluctuate but are recommended at about €4 per person per day, an amount only rarely received). For the purposes of this chapter, I will focus upon tourist expectations and the coach driver-guide who must attempt to provide an experience that will best accommodate those expectations.

Coach driver-guides are multi-purpose participants in Irish tourism. They meet and greet; do airport transfers; organize luggage and bags (often loading, unloading and delivering to rooms all over hotels); schedule meals, entertainment, and shopping stops; deliver information on Ireland and the tour; transport passengers to sites and sights; explain the difference between gorse and rape-seed; coordinate arrivals and departures with hotels; arrange rooms at hotels (or other accommodation); troubleshoot client difficulties; reschedule whatever may need to be changed; communicate with passengers, coach operators, hotel personnel, travel agents, tour operators, and site managers daily; and they are continually planning ahead – often weeks ahead – in order to schedule visits and hotels for upcoming tours. For a coach tourist, the driver-guide is the first and most important point of contact with the destination of Ireland. He must meet or exceed their expectations of what is understood to be genuine Irish-ness. And he must accomplish all of his duties seamlessly and without visible effort. It should be noted here that over the course of my research all of the driver-guides I met were male and none of them knew of any women who routinely worked as driver-guides in the Republic of Ireland. I would suggest that the propensity for men to be drivers and driver-guides has to do with the job being traditionally a man's position, and with the amount of physical labour involved in the task. On an average tour, roughly forty suitcases will need to be transferred in and out of the coach, often on a daily basis; with each suitcase an average of 50 lbs (22 kilos), drivers must lift more than 4,000 lbs on a given day. The 'coach fellas', a term I heard used among the drivers and driver-guides and others associated with the industry, is an informal reference to the group of men who drive the tour coaches.

The coach driver-guide is responsible for presenting Ireland to the participants on the tour. Much the way Edward Bruner suggested visitors to historical sites must be accommodated based on expectation (1994), the driver-guide must be adept at teasing out the general understanding his passengers have of Ireland in the very early stages of the tour. Are they in Ireland primarily to visit 'typical' sites such as Newgrange, Glendalough, Waterford Crystal, Blarney Castle and the Ring of Kerry? Are they a church group led by a priest visiting Knock Shrine, Galway Cathedral, Clonmacnoise, St Patrick's Cathedral, and having mass every day at 3 P.M.? Is it a group of friends and acquaintances who are mostly interested in pubs and late nights? Are the majority seeking roots or some other family connections? Once he has established their principal expectations he can then begin to weave together his oral presentation of Ireland. A few driver-guides related instances when determining clients' expectations went awry, making for difficult days on tour. These difficulties tested their ability to communicate with their clients as well as their clients' patience and openness to new and unexpected experiences. General tours get a fairly well rehearsed and scripted presentation of Ireland with extensive amounts of local and personal knowledge used to emphasize what the driver-guide understands as important or interesting. Specialized groups (such as those on a monastic tour) will hear specialized presentations tailored to their wants and needs. In many cases what the client wants to know is not contained in standard tourism literature, but must be retrieved from the driver-guide's own local knowledge. For example, while observing one tour in early 2008, the coach I was on was travelling from Dublin to Westport along the N4/N5. When going through the Midlands we passed several signs for 'coarse fishing' and one of the passengers asked the driver-guide to explain it. It happened that he was an experienced coarse fisherman and he proceeded to tell everyone about the sport, his memories of fishing as a boy, and the difference between coarse fishing and other forms of fishing. This ability to exchange information 'on the fly' to unusual questions is part of what makes a coach holiday in Ireland a special experience in the minds of passengers. It may be the case that many coach tourists in Ireland have few expectations beyond an enjoyable visit to a foreign country. Moments such as the session on coarse fishing can make the difference between a memorable holiday and one that is easily forgotten.

People visit Ireland for any number of reasons, but their reasons for visiting are not the sum total of their actual experience. Experience for the tourist far exceeds why they want to go to a particular place. It includes factors as mundane as the weather, the screaming child in the seat next to them on the plane, or the serendipitous chat with an old friend at Bewley's Cafe on Grafton Street in Dublin. It includes the unexpected, unprepared for experiences, as well as the repetitive ones like the climb onto the tour bus and the Irish fry-up at breakfast. Some tourists seek out new experiences while on tour; others seek out something that feels like a familiar living memory; others may have no notion of what they seek but when they find it, they will know it.

During the course of my research on coach tourism, I asked visitors their reasons for choosing Ireland as a destination. Many suggested they were pursuing memories that could be created by the physical and emotional journey of travelling here; the unique and out of the ordinary occasion of being in Ireland (Cohen 1994; Lowenthal 1985, 1998). The liminality of Ireland in relation to the coach tourist is central to understanding this as a transcendent experience, one that changes a person's life (Graburn 2004; MacCannell 1976; Turner 1985a, 1985b; van Gennep 1961). The tourists are physically removed from home, by their own choice, and placed into a culture that is at once familiar, perhaps due to a sought-after descent relationship or family tie, and foreign – a time, a people and a place that exists outside of the familiar. Time is measured differently – they are on a wholly alien schedule, governed by someone else, and they must comply. They may be on a coach with people they do not know. They may be sleeping in a different part of the country every night. The place and the people are different, new, exotic and temporary. In a literal sense, for the tourist, the destination exists only while they are physically present in it. Once they get back on the coach and are moving on to their next destination, they are suspended in a state of anticipation, the previous site now a memory and a topic of discussion (Hiss 1990; MacCannell 1976; Schama 1995). Their destination-world proceeds as a cinematic experience, unfolding in front of and around them (Urry 1990, 2002, 2004). One tourist remarked that it was 'like it was happening to someone else' and that he 'was watching what was happening from a grandstand' (Personal communication 16 June 2006). Much like a traumatic experience, the tourist experience can feel somewhat unreal.

From an anthropological standpoint, the actual felt experience of the tourist has not been extensively examined. Instead, tourism and tourists are objects that perform and occur, and their experiences are products to be consumed (Baranowski and Furlough 2004). How tourists feel about their own touristic adventures and non-adventures has been easily speculated upon and viewed from above by those who would study them rather than participate with them (cf. Jorgensen 2003). The experience has been called 'transformative', a 'mediated activity', 'harmful', or 'inauthentic' (Bruner 1994, 2001, 2004; Graburn 1989, 2004; MacCannell 1992, 1999; Nash 1989, 1996). Only occasionally have the tourists themselves been asked about their experiences, or asked to consider what these experiences may mean (Bruner 2001, 2004; Pi-Sunyer 1989; Prentice and Andersen 2000). Anthropologists also rarely act as participants themselves, depending more on observation from afar, post-tour discussion, document analyses, eavesdropping, or their own often jaded opinions of the tourist and the tourism industry. Exceptions to this include Edward Bruner and Barbara Kirshenblatt-Gimblett who have both served as tour directors and guides on several occasions (Bruner 2001; Kirshenblatt-Gimblett 1998).

The tourist experience in Ireland begins long before the actual arrival of the tourists. In many cases, the tourist experience begins with family memories, exotic fabrications of place, movie trailers, or literary references (Baudrillard 1988; Costa 2007; Cusack 1998; Foley and Fahy 2004; Graburn 2004; Kiberd 1995; Kincheloe 1999; Lowenthal 1985, 1998; McCarthy 2005; Negra 2001a, 2001b; O'Connor 1993; O'Hagan 2004; Prentice and Andersen 2000). The power of suggestion in the realm of the touristic experience cannot be undervalued (O'Connor 1993; Nash 1993). Richard Prentice and Vivien Andersen have called this an 'evocation' and recognize it as a sensory process that begins through developing a familiarity with a destination through image, or, in some cases, imagination (2000). 'For persons who have not visited a destination, image can be regarded as a pre-taste of a destination, leading to expectations about it' (Prentice and Andersen 2000: 492). They also suggest that potential visitors to destinations are attracted through marketing schemes that include 'generic dimensions' that are easily recognizable across cultures such as dance, art, music or literature (2000: 494). They indicate that manipulation of the imagery in pre-trip materials in these cases is utilized to evoke emotional responses to a destination brand. In Ireland, the imagery constantly evokes the brand triumvirate of 'people, pace and place' (Costa 2007; Foley and Fahy 2004; ITIC 2000; Urry 2004; Volkman and Guydosh 2001).

Tourists from America who visit Ireland overwhelmingly claim some familiarity with the country, whether it be due to family relationships or descent which may be several generations past. As David Lowenthal has suggested, many may also carry images of Ireland that are not their own (1985). Prentice and Andersen support Lowenthal's writing:

> Non-visitors may hold complex images of destinations, gained from study, or personal contacts with tourists or nationals. Family contacts in particular within a destination may lead not only to an increased propensity to visit, but may also lead to complex images being held by family members who have never visited it. At its most extreme, the destination may be in essence 'lived' in another place. (2000: 495)

Michael Cronin uses the Irish Tourism Board publication *Ireland of the Welcomes* as an example of a preparatory device many consumers of Ireland have utilized in establishing these destination images (2003). A magazine in circulation since the 1950s, *Ireland of the Welcomes* both represents Ireland to the non-visitor as a glossy holiday – 'a nomadic encounter with the culture, mediated through print and illustration' (Rojek and Urry 1997: 1–19, cited in Cronin 2003: 181) – and serves a rhetorical function based on imagined ideas of who the visitor to Ireland is and what they might expect. These images of expectation, or 'the "framing" of tourist sites through images' (Baranowski and Furlough 2004: 9), as well as the actions of expectation, or activities of expectation, are central to pre-forming the tourist experience (MacCannell 1976; Urry 1990, 2002, 2004). This is what van Gennep (1961) and Turner (1985b) would refer to as the pre-liminal or separation phase of experience where the participant is beginning the process of leaving the familiar but has not yet transitioned into the fully transformative stage of the liminal experience.

Authenticity

While an authentic experience may be important to the visitor, that authentic experience is pre-conceived and highly anticipated. For many scholars it too lies at the heart of the tourism experience (Bruner 1994; Corkern 2004; MacCannell 1976; McManus 1997). It is waiting to happen. It is based to a high degree on imagery and expectation, rather than on something that may actually exist or have any possibility of happening (Urry 1990, 2002). This is very true of visitors to Ireland who anticipate their visit with powerful emotions and again, that notion of connectedness or familiarity so common among them. An 'authentic' experience in Ireland must include Guinness Stout, hours spent in pubs, a visit to Newgrange or Cobh or Trinity College to see the Book of Kells. And it must meet to some degree the romantic notion of the island of Ireland: the ethereal, stuck in the distant past, land of lads and lasses, that is timeless, has forty shades of green, is slightly regressive, and is an altogether 'airy-fairy realm' (Witoszek 2002: 347). But, this is the anticipated, the hoped-for Ireland. The real Ireland (not necessarily the same as the authentic Ireland in this sense) (cf. Bruner 1994; Lowenthal 1985, 1998; MacCannell 1976; Robinson 1999) may never even be recognized or acknowledged by some visitors who may float (or be driven?) through their visit in a dreamlike trance with their feet never actually touching the ground. The real Ireland may be a surprise; it may disappoint; it may be brushed off as 'not Irish'. In order for the tourist experience in Ireland to be positive, nevertheless, it must come very close to meeting the pre-experience expectations as van Gennep (1961) and Turner (1985, 1986) and others (cf. Bruner 1994, 2001, 2004; Rojek 1993, 1997) have suggested. How authentic that experience may be largely depends on how well the visit translates into an acceptable ideal for the individuals who participate in the touristic endeavour.

Attractions

Tourist destinations must also have attractions or 'demand generators' (McKercher and du Cros 2002). Attractions are assets and products, they are part of the process of commodity production and exchange in the world of tourism. Based on the work of Mill and Morrison (1985), McKercher and du Cros define a three-stage hierarchy of attractions: primary attractions are so important to most destinations that they play a critical role in shaping their image and influencing visitation; secondary attractions may be locally significant tourist attractions that complement the tourism experience; and tertiary attractions are largely convenience-based or occur by happenstance (2002: 109–10). They suggest that the greater the distance a consumer has to travel to a site, the more spectacular or unique it has to be (2002: 110). They also indicate that 'the more dominant the attraction is, the greater the sense of obligation to visit' (2002: 31). Attractions often attain this level of significance because of their symbolic importance to a nation or culture, such as the Arlington Cemetery or the General Post Office, or through their natural beauty such as Victoria Falls or the Giant's Causeway, or through their historic importance such as Gettysburg or the Hill of Tara.

Whatever their status, tourists actively engage with the attraction. They can also engage in what appears to be an aloof, disconnected manner, but the purpose of 'being' a tourist is to engage with sites and attractions on some level. According to Adrian Franklin, this engagement is because, '[t]ourists have an intimate and complex relationship *with* tourist sites, heritage buildings, museum artefacts, art gallery objects, souvenirs and postcards, cameras and videos, foods and drinks, tickets and passports, planes and trains' (and I would add coaches) (2003: 101). He goes on to suggest that in many cases this involves a process of 'interpellation', where an object (which could include sites, centres, works of art in museums, as well as kitsch), 'speaks' to an individual in a deeply meaningful way, binding them not only to a moment in time, but to a place, an event or a community that has also experienced a similar sense of connection (2003: 132). The collection of things, whether they be souvenirs, postcards, pebbles, dried flowers, or photographs, extends this interpellative experience into the post-event, back to the lived world and beyond the liminal space of the touristic experience (MacCannell 1976; Turner 1985; van Gennep 1961).

Over and above the abundance of tangible attractions so well known in Ireland, are the intangible attractions of memory, myths, spirituality and reputation. These can also be understood as primary attractions and may be equally appealing to the consumer of Ireland. Visitors may go to Newgrange, the Skelligs, the Burren or the Ring of Kerry because 'they are there', but, according to many visitors I interviewed, they are 'drawn' or 'compelled' to visit. In the course of planning a month-long study trip to Ireland with university students from the United States, I asked the students to choose a variety of places they would like to go to, and to write down the reasons why they wanted to go there. The students were, for the most part, middle-class attendees of a small, private university in their second, third or final years; most had never experienced international travel, but all claimed to have a strong interest in Ireland and its cultural landscapes. The majority of students chose places they described as having spiritual value, whether these values were Christian, Celtic or prehistoric. When asked why they had decided to accompany me to Ireland when other field-school options were available at a much more affordable price, students overwhelmingly suggested that Ireland was a special place, full of meaning and history, a place they wanted to partake of. Many felt it would be a life-changing and renewing experience. One student wrote:

> Just the thought of climbing up to the tombs at Loughcrew and running my fingers along the rock art makes me want to cry with joy. I can't wait to shed this old skin of mine and commune with my ancient self. For the first time in 15 years of school I'm excited about learning, about *being*. (Renee, 20, 3rd year Anthropology major)

Though clearly tinged with what Rojek would call 'the cult of nostalgia' (1993) and a bit of bottled Celtic mysticism, the romance of Ireland, the intangible qualities are as important to this student's decision-making as the tangible ones. There is a longing in the writing, a desire to feel the culture and the place, to affect change – not to Ireland, but to or within herself. It is, as Franklin would say, 'the pleasure of possessing something in the imagination' (2003: 180). Nina Witoszek calls this the 'prolonged agony of Romantic Ireland', the intangible and ethereal magnetism that attracts so many to its shores, a 'fatal attraction of the Irish mystique' (2002: 345). Visitors want to experience this, they want to feel touched somehow by a magic they are unable to articulate. Though the physical experience of Ireland may be fleeting, the psychic experience will hopefully linger long after they have returned to their mundane lived worlds.

The Coach as Border and Boundary

Most of the coach tourists I observed over the course of three years principally interacted with other tourists on their tour and quite often attached themselves to their guide, driver-guide and, to a lesser degree, their driver. They were comfortable with this in most situations and made few explicit efforts to change their position as passive participants while on their tour. As Kaul suggests, groups 'experience the group, not locality', because the group provides a protective shell – a barrier – between the individual and the locale (2004: 31). The notion of being 'on tour' denotes a high degree of passivity; people on tour are literally sightseeing, they are not actively learning, investing in the culture, or planning to move to the region.

I would suggest that few tourists have the luxury of actually being actively involved during their holiday or being deeply engaged with the people and places at their destination. There simply is not enough time. A week or two in a different place, especially when travelling through and across a destination as people do in Ireland, does not allow more than a tangential participation in the culture, no matter how determined the tourist may be to do this. Travellers, trippers, and all variety of visitor, even high-brow ones, are not fully and actively engaged with the cultures they visit – they are just passing through. This is due, in part, to the movement of the tour; that the actual site of tourism in the case of the coach tour, is not in a 'fixed geographic space' (Kaul 2004: 34).

Wulff (2007) and many other anthropogists (Marcus 1998; Clifford 1997; Hannerz 1998, 2003) have discussed the methodolgical challenges of studying modern cultures in general because of the shifting nature of modern life and the ways in which the practice of anthropology has had to change in order to keep pace with it. They suggest that multi-local and mobile fieldwork (or 'yo-yo' fieldwork as suggested by Wulff 2007), such as the fieldwork I undertook in my longitudinal study of coach tourism, is useful in answering 'the research questions that come out of modern social life where so much is in motion' (Wulff 2007: 139). This study of coach tourism not only faces the challenge of modern anthropological methodologies (time, space, multi-locality), it adds a dimension of the literally moving fieldsite which transports subjects from destination to destination.

This places the coach tourist in a position of viewing the landscape and people of Ireland from afar. Whilst in the coach they are removed from active engagement with the culture; they are like visitors to a zoo: they can 'see' the inhabitants and their environment, but they cannot touch them; they can only watch them as they glide by the coach windows. Likewise, the coach (and one could say the identity of 'coach tourist') can act as a boundary between visitor and visited. Both are completely aware of the temporary nature of the other, and though the experience of meeting each other may be enlightening, fun or exciting, 'knowing' the other is simply not possible; within a matter of hours they will part and the probability of ever meeting again is incredibly small. Tove Oliver has discussed the organized tour route in terms of 'the destination bubble' where tourists exist as separate from their host cultures both physically and culturally (2000, 2004a, 2004b). She also suggests that pre-trip preparation (both through research and through the transmission of memory) is highly influential in tourists' abilities to interact with these cultures of 'imagination' (2004a, 2004b).

Along with the difficulty of actually being engaged with a destination during a coach holiday is the circumscribed route of visitation and limited selection of sites available to the coach tourist. When viewing tour literature during pre-trip planning, potential visitors to Ireland may be confronted with itineraries and descriptions of places in tour marketing literature such as Killarney, Blarney Castle, 'The West' or the Antrim Coast that are used repeatedly by dozens of tour operators. Even if the potential visitor had no real agenda prior to studying tour literature, he can develop a desire to visit and consume particular sites due to their recurring nature. In much the way fast food advertisements can make one hungry, these sites and places become part of an 'orthodoxy of musts': sites that must be seen, visited and recorded to demonstrate visitors' presence in a highly popular area others may only dream of (Costa 2001, 2004, 2007, 2009). Among the most popularized sites in the Irish orthodoxy of musts are ancient sites such as Newgrange, castles such as Trim and Ross Castle, and monastic sites like Clonmacnoise, Glendalough or Monasterboice. Regions are also particularly touted such as the Ring of Kerry or Connemara. Tourists flock to these sites and areas that are typically included on coach tours and which construct a 'viewbook' of Ireland that reflects the catalogue of what is easily and commonly scheduled.

Understanding the Heritage Landscape

David Brett suggests that in order for us to better understand the relationship between tourism and heritage we should reconcile 'the heritage' as an engagement of 'then' with 'now' (1996). He also notes that the language of heritage tourism marketing 'is being transferred from travel in space to travel in time' (1996: 14). Further he proposes that the modern 'preoccupation with the past is created out of the experience of continual change' (1996: 15), reflecting similar comments by MacCannell (1976, 1992), Baudrillard (1988) and Eco (1986), among others. Are coach tourists similarly preoccupied with the past and the passage of time?

In order to contextualize the relationship between the coach tourist, the past and heritage in Ireland, the pace and continual sensory barrage of touring, stopping, moving and experiencing must be taken account of. Tourists on tour are limited to what the tour itself offers: if you want to see Cork but the coach tour you are on does not go there, you will not be seeing Cork this time around. Likewise, when given leeway, tourists' choices may appear wasted when a variety of opportunities are available. For example, on a day-tour to Inishmore in the Aran Islands, a group of American tourists from the southern United States were taken out to the great stone fort of Dun Aenghus. The coach driver-guide had explained the island's most popular and famous site on the coach, and then on the shuttle to the site the shuttle driver reiterated his explanation. The explanations were well-presented, the tourists seemed interested, and many asked questions as they approached the site. However, once they were dropped on the road leading to the fort, many chose to remain in the shops near the visitor centre buying trinkets, trying on 'genuine Aran sweaters', and eating ice cream. They seemed satisfied to see the fort from afar (some clicked a few photographs and hurried into the shops, barely glancing at it again). The few who did walk out to the fort were pleased that they had made the effort and felt that it was an exciting and interesting place, something they would remember and tell others about when they returned to the United States. Afterwards at lunch, those who went to the fort busily showed their photos to those who chose to shop, while those who shopped busily showed their purchases to the fort visitors. Both tourist groups seemed satisfied with their tourist experience, yet both seemed also to feel they had missed out on something, vowing to either 'hit the shops' at the next stop or to 'see the next bit' at the next site. The time constraints of the coach tour, rather than a pre-occupation with time writ large, and what is on offer while on tour, seem to be the pivotal factors in the decision-making of the coach tourist.

The Return

At some point the tourist will emerge from his or her liminal space and return home laden with goods and memories of their trip (Graburn 1989, 2004; Leach 1961; Turner and Turner 1978; Turner 1985). They may not be conscious of it, but they are changed by their experience. They have 'seen and done'. They have slept in strange beds, eaten strange food, spent time in a strange place. They have come back and begun their lives again full of new thoughts and prepared to invite others to share in their memories. How good or bad those memories are depends to a large extent on their driver-guide. Was he friendly? Did he represent the expected Irish personae? Did he appear to accommodate their needs? Did things go smoothly? Did his local knowledge support their assumptions? Was he handsome? Witty? Well turned-out? The positive memories of Ireland that return with the visitor are often linked to positive interactions with the driver-guide.

Likewise, negative memories can be linked to negative interactions with the driver-guide. Occasionally, a bad trip (usually having to do with the weather or less than salubrious accommodation) will be offset by the positive relationship cultivated by the guide with his clients. What matters to the stakeholders in the tourism industry in Ireland is that the positive experience be relayed by word of mouth to other potential visitors in an ever-expanding circle of tourism development; it is the returning visitor and the potential visitor who will continue to breed the expectation that is Ireland: something and somewhere that is at once reality and hoped for fantasy.

All tourists share their experiences with others once they return home. Most will also share their experiences with those who remain at home during the tour through calls home, postcards sent, and emails detailing each and every moment. There must be some 'proof' of travel, some acknowledgement that the liminal space was inhabited, some indication that Ireland has been seen and done and that this personal experience was unlike any other. Souvenirs, postcards, photographs, and other portable items will be collected and passed around between the travellers and those who remained at home, and stories related to each will be reported. The point is to garner admiration from the homebody (who could be anyone who was not along for the trip including family, friends, workmates). Stories about the trip will be repeated to everyone who will listen, even if the trip is only mentioned in passing to strangers and acquaintances. The reportage may range from tones of excitement to bored-with-the-world renditions of the tour. People are glad to be home in their own beds and among familiar surroundings, but they also 'miss' the place they have been to. Upon return, tourists will also display their experience in a myriad of ways: photo montages on websites, blogs, articles of clothing that proclaim 'being' in Ireland (Ireland or Guinness T-shirts for example, or 'fisherman-knit' sweaters), framed photographs will be placed in prominent positions in 'public' areas such as sitting rooms or offices (Gordon 2004; Hitchcock and Teague 2000; Kim and Littrell 2001; Littrell et al. 1994). These souvenirs serve not only as symbols of worldliness, but as reminders of a life-event for those who participated. The displays may encourage feelings of longing, annoyance or jealousy among those who did not participate (Asplet and Cooper 2000; Kim and Littrell 2001). They do not share the first-person memories and experiences; they can only live vicariously through the traveller. For the tourism industry, it is in this moment that a potential customer is made and the seed of travel planning is planted.

The coach-driver guide who inhabited what Bruner would refer to as a 'borderzone' (a place that exists liminally outside of most experiences of the visitor) (2004) takes up his place in the returned-tourist's imagination. The single pint he may have shared on an evening in a pub may transform into a wild night of drinking and storytelling back home. A quiet conversation with him may be repeated as a tale of a budding best-friend or a come-on from a potential lover. An in-transit discussion becomes an argument where displays of 'real Irish temper' flared. He may, likewise, disappear from the participant's memory or at least those memories shared with others. His presence during the tour, and his clients' dependence on him, are now reduced and washed away once the tour has ended – returning control, power and independence to the traveller, now safely returned to home soil.

The tourist at home is a changed person. His or her status will change in both their minds and in the minds of others. This is van Gennep's post-liminal or re-incorporation stage of the tourist's journey (1961). They hold memories others do not have, and have experienced life in unique ways, ways that can only be shared through visual and oral second-hand means. Gift giving done upon return revolves around memento exchange (Franklin and Crang 2001; Gordon 2004; Hitchcock and Teague 2000; Littrell et al. 1994). Tales are told of the places where they were purchased, such as the Cliffs of Moher or Blarney Woolen Mills, and the context of the gift-giver's presence in the place. Whether the gift is appreciated or not is not the primary consideration: that the giver can prove through this presentation that they have been somewhere and done something is what is all important. Further, it impresses that they were thinking of the recipient whilst away. There is no reciprocation expected in this exchange. At the moment the exchange of information or presentation of the gift takes place, the giver's status elevates, even if just temporarily, by virtue of their gift, their photos and the narrative of their exploits.

Expectation

With the advent of the Internet, many first time visitors to Ireland can be mentally well prepared for their holiday. Virtual brochures displayed on the various websites include a wide array of photographs of scenic Ireland and modern cityscapes. Stressing either relaxation and 'getting away from it all' or the glitz and glam of urban life, the websites promise visitors that they will experience something unique and incomparable, something they will treasure and remember for a lifetime. In the case of this chapter, the coach tourist will have the added benefit of sitting back and letting Ireland happen to them without having to go out of their way to find it. It is this passivity of the coach tour participant that often lulls them into a state of unpreparedness when faced with an Ireland not found in the brochure. Gangland slayings in Dublin, oil spills in Boyle, traffic jams in Corofin (caused by automobiles and not by sheep or cattle) are not expected by the visitor and are certainly not mentioned in the brochures. The rural touristic idyll (Cusack 1998) can often be disrupted by something as common as waiting in a queue in the wind and the rain for a ferry to cross to the Aran Islands. Though told by tour guides and tour companies that rain is common, the fact that it does rain in Ireland while a holiday is in progress can be the deciding factor in whether or not to return to Ireland in the future.

In the new millennium, the rural idyll is hidden from view in areas of the island that rarely cater to visitors. Today's visitors, often expecting an Ireland of the past, are frequently disappointed with what they get. At the same time, they demand modern facilities such as en suite rooms in out of the way bed and breakfast accommodations, and hotel-quality service from the families that run them. Complaints regarding the facilities are rarely directed towards the accommodators themselves, but towards the guides and drivers who then must try to repair any damage while the tour is in progress. Once the tour is over and tourists have returned home, letters and emails of complaint will then include the success or failure of the guide or driver-guide to remedy the situation. These letters, inevitably, are directed to the tour operators who may decide to discontinue using a guide or driver based on letters of complaint by clients who have expectations that are at odds with reality.

It is this paradox of expectation of today's tourist – the rural idyll, the backward, suspicious country farmer, the countryside of thatched cottages, modern facilities, and being catered to by their guides, drivers and hosts – that moulds the end result of the coach tourism experience. Coach drivers, driver-guides, and tour guides associated with coach tours must bend over backwards to provide their charges with a positive experience of Ireland even when things are beyond their control (such as rough seas on ferry crossings). In the world of coach tourism, clients frequently demand that their hosts take part in cheerful chatter, remember their names, have endless knowledge of local, regional and national sites and sights, be approachable at all hours, and enjoy what they do – even when they themselves may behave in ways that would be unacceptable in other contexts.

Conclusion

> To communicate a coherent narrative, we must not only reshape the old but create a new past. (Lowenthal 1985: 209)

Among visitors to Ireland, memories are often highly mythologized and selective. Descendants of Irish émigrés often have a singular goal of returning to the old country to visit their family homestead. Though generations removed from Irish soil, it nonetheless is a major reason for visiting the island. It is vitally important for many tourists to Ireland, especially those engaged in family searches, to reminisce or remember even if those memories belong to someone else in their family such as a parent or grandparent. David Lowenthal suggests that 'many events we think we recall from our own experience were in fact told to us and then become an indistinguishable part of our memory' (1985: 196). Heritage can also include the inheritance of memory and recollection. In some cases the memory can be self-generated, based upon very ancient or fantastic views and illustrations of Ireland (Lowenthal 1985). In interviews with tourists intent on locating homesteads, church records, burial sites, or some other snippet of family, most would become misty-eyed and nostalgic when recollecting the stories told to them by older generations of the Ireland left behind long ago. For them, the pre-industrial landscape of Ireland is still foremost in their collective memory – it is a countryside devoid of urbanization and modern life. There are few cars; cows are still milked by hand; and country people remain innocent of the evils of technology and modernization: they are veiled in the mists of the island. When viewed from the cinematic windows of a coach, the realities of the modern rural landscape are often camouflaged by the countryside itself. Though often surprised by the degree of contact the rural Irish have with the modern world, many of the same tourists found someone or something to 'blame' for this. Several, indeed, remarked that it was a pity that the old ways were dying or dead, or suggested that the Irish government should do more to preserve the old way of life. Many felt that America, Dublin, television, or 'the Troubles' were responsible, but when pressed to explain their reasoning, most could not respond with a substantive answer. The Ireland that remains frozen in memories generations old is the only Ireland that is allowed to exist for these visitors. And yet, when they located a corner of the modern state that nearly met with their expectations, visitors often contended that they had gone off the beaten path, to a place where tourists never go – a place that had not evolved. When reminded that they too were tourists, the response inevitably was one of exasperation – they were descendants of someone who had once lived in Ireland and so they had a 'right' to be there.

References

Asplet, M. and M. Cooper. 2000. 'Cultural Designs in New Zealand Souvenir Clothing: The Question of Authenticity', *Tourism Management* 21(3): 307–12.

Baranowski, S. and E. Furlough (eds). 2004. *Being Elsewhere: Tourism, Consumer Culture, and Identity in Modern Europe and North America*. Ann Arbor: University of Michigan.

———. 2004. 'Introduction', in S. Baranowski and E. Furlough (eds), *Being Elsewhere: Tourism, Consumer Culture, and Identity in Modern Europe and North America*. Ann Arbor: University of Michigan, pp. 1–31.

Baudrillard, J. 1988. *America*. London: Verso.

Bender, B. 2001. 'Introduction', in B. Bender and M. Winer (eds), *Contested Landscapes: Movement, Exile and Place*. Oxford: Berg, pp. 1–18.

Bender, B. and M. Winer (eds). 2001. *Contested Landscapes: Movement, Exile and Place*. Oxford: Berg.

Brett, D. 1996. *The Construction of Heritage*. Cork: Cork University.

Bruner, E.M. 1994. 'Abraham Lincoln as Authentic Reproduction: A Critique of Postmodernism', *American Anthropologist* 96(2): 397–415.

———. 2001. 'The Maasai and the Lion King: Authenticity, Nationalism, and Globalization in African Tourism', *American Ethnologist* 28(4): 881–908.

———. 2004. 'Tourism in the Balinese Borderzone', in S. Gmelch (ed.), *Tourists and Tourism: A Reader*. Long Grove, IL: Waveland Press, Inc., pp. 219–38.

Clifford, J. 1997. *Routes: Travel and Translation in the Late Twentieth Century.* Cambridge: Harvard University Press.

Cohen, A. 1994. *Self Consciousness: An Alternative Anthropology of Identity.* London: Routledge.

Cooney, G. 1996. 'Building the Future on the Past: Archaeology and the Construction of National Identity in Ireland', in M. Díaz-Andreu and T. Champion (eds), *Nationalism and Archaeology in Europe.* Boulder: Westview, pp. 146–53.

Corkern, W. 2004. 'Heritage Tourism', *American Studies International* 42: 2–3.

Costa, K. 2001. *The Brokered Image: Material Culture and Identity in the Stubaital.* Lanham, MD: University Press of America.

———. 2004. 'Conflating Past and Present: Marketing Archaeological Heritage in Ireland', in Y. Rowan and U. Baram (eds), *Marketing Heritage: Archaeology and the Consumption of the Past.* Walnut Creek, CA: AltaMira Press, pp. 69–92.

———. 2007. 'Globalizing Heritage: Marketing the Built Environment in Ireland', in U. Kockel and M. Nic Craith (eds), *Cultural Heritages as Reflexive Traditions.* Basingstoke, Hampshire: Palgrave Macmillan, pp. 171–82.

———. 2009. *The Coach Fellas: Heritage and Tourism in Ireland.* Walnut Creek, CA: Left Coast.

Cronin, M. 2003. 'Next to Being There: Ireland of the Welcomes and Tourism of the Word', in M. Cronin and B. O'Connor (eds), *Irish Tourism: Image, Culture and Identity.* Clevedon: Channel View, pp. 179–95.

Crouch, G., R. Perdue and H. Timmermans (eds). 2004. *Consumer Psychology of Tourism, Hospitality and Leisure.* Oxfordshire: CABI.

Cusack, T. 1998. 'Migrant Travellers and Touristic Idylls: The Paintings of Jack B. Yeats and Post-colonial Identities', *Art History* 21(2): 201–18.

Díaz-Andreu, M. and T. Champion (eds). 1996. *Nationalism and Archaeology in Europe.* Boulder: Westview.

Eco, U. 1986. *Travels in Hyperreality,* trans. W. Weaver. New York: Harcourt Brace Jovanovich.

Foley, A. and J. Fahy. 2004. 'Incongruity between Expression and Experience: The Role of Imagery in Supporting the Positioning of a Tourism Destination Brand', *Brand Management* 11(3): 209–17.

Franklin, A. 2003. *Tourism: An Introduction.* London: Sage.

Franklin, A. and M. Crang. 2001. 'The Trouble with Tourism and Travel Theory', *Tourist Studies* 1(1): 5–22.

Gmelch, S. (ed.). 2004. *Tourists and Tourism: A Reader.* Long Grove, IL: Waveland Press, Inc.

Gordon, B. 2004. 'The Souvenir: Messenger of the Extraordinary', *The Journal of Popular Culture* 20(3): 135–46.

Graburn, N.H.H. 1989. 'Tourism: The Sacred Journey', in V. Smith (ed.), *Hosts and Guests: An Anthropology of Tourism.* Philadelphia: University of Pennsylvania, pp. 21–36.

———. 2004. 'Secular Ritual: A General Theory of Tourism', in S. Gmelch (ed.), *Tourists and Tourism: A Reader.* Long Grove, IL: Waveland Press, Inc., pp. 23–34.

Hannerz, U. 1998. 'Other Transnationals: Perspectives Gained from Studying Sideways', *Paideuma* 44: 109–23.

———. 2003. 'Being There ... and There ... and There! Reflections on Multi-site Ethnography', *Ethnography* 4: 229–44.

Hiss, T. 1990. *The Experience of Place: A New Way of Looking at and Dealing with our Radically Changing Cities and Countryside.* New York: Vintage.

Hitchcock, M. and K. Teague. 2000. *Souvenirs: The Material Culture of Tourism.* Aldershot: Ashgate.

ITIC (Irish Tourism Industry Confederation). 2000. *The People and Place Programme Report.* Dublin: Tansey, Webster and Associates.

Kaul, A. 2004. 'The Anthropologist as Barman and Tour-guide: Reflections on Fieldwork in a Touristed Destination', *Durham Anthropology Journal* 12(1): 22–36.

Kiberd, D. 1995. *Inventing Ireland: The Literature of the Modern Nation.* London: Jonathan Cape.

Kim, S. and M.A. Littrell. 2001. 'Souvenir Buying and Intentions for Self versus Others', *Annals of Tourism Research* 28(3): 638–57.

Kincheloe, P.J. 1999. 'Two Visions of Fairyland: Ireland and the Monumental Discourse of the Nineteenth Century American Tourist', *Irish Studies Review* 7(1): 41–51.

Kirshenblatt-Gimblett, B. 1998. *Destination Culture: Tourism, Museums, and Heritage.* Berkeley and Los Angeles: University of California.

Kockel, U. and M. Nic Craith (eds). 2007. *Cultural Heritages as Reflexive Traditions.* Basingstoke, Hampshire: Palgrave Macmillan.

Leach, E. 1961. *Rethinking Anthropology.* London: Robert Cunningham and Son.

Littrell, M.A., S. Baizerman, R. Kean, S. Gahring, S. Niemeyer, R. Reilly and J. Stout. 1994. 'Souvenirs and Tourism Styles', *Journal of Tourism Research* 3(1): 3–11.

Lowenthal, D. 1985. *The Past is a Foreign Country.* Cambridge: Cambridge University.

——— 1998. *The Heritage Crusade and the Spoils of History.* Cambridge: Cambridge University.

MacCannell, D. (1976). *The Tourist: A New Theory of the Leisure Class.* Berkeley: University of California.

———. 1992. *Empty Meeting Grounds: The Tourist Papers.* London: Routledge.

Marcus, G. 1998. *Ethnography Through Thick and Thin.* Princeton: Princeton University.

McCarthy, M. 2005. 'Historico-geographical Explorations of Ireland's Heritages: Towards a Critical Understanding of the Nature of Memory and Identity', in M. McCarthy (ed.), *Ireland's Heritages: Critical Perspectives of Memory and Identity.* Aldershot: Ashgate, pp. 3–51.

McKercher, B. and H. du Cros. 2002. *Cultural Tourism: The Partnership between Tourism and Cultural Heritage Management.* New York: Haworth Hospitality Press.

McManus, R. 1997. 'Heritage and Tourism in Ireland – an Unholy Alliance?', *Irish Geography* 30(2): 90–98.

Mill, R. and A. Morrison. 1985. *The Tourism System: An Introductory Text.* Englewood Cliffs: NJ: Prentice-Hall.

Nash, C. 1993. '"Embodying the Nation": The West of Ireland Landscape and Irish Identity', in B. O'Connor and M. Cronin (eds), *Tourism in Ireland: A Critical Analysis.* Cork: Cork University, pp. 86–112.

Nash, D. 1989. 'Tourism as a Form of Imperialism', in V. Smith (ed.), *Hosts and Guests: The Anthropology of Tourism.* Philadelphia: University of Pennsylvania, pp. 37–52.

———. 1996. *Anthropology of Tourism.* Oxford: Pergamon.

Negra, D. 2001a. 'The New Primitives: Irishness in Recent U.S. Television', *Irish Studies Review* 9(2): 229–39.

———. 2001b. 'Consuming Ireland: Lucky Charms Cereal, Irish Spring Soap, and 1-800-Shamrock', *Cultural Studies* 15(1): 76–97.

O'Connor, B. 1993. 'Myths and Mirrors: Tourist Images and National Identity', in B. O'Connor and M. Cronin (eds), *Tourism in Ireland: A Critical Analysis.* Cork: Cork University, pp. 68–85.

O'Hagan, S. 2004. 'Bangers and Machinations: From Riverdance to the Famine – the Disneyfication of Ireland's Heritage Continues Apace', *The Observer Review,* p. 5.

Oliver, T. 2000. 'Consuming Culture: The Case of the Cultural Tour Route', *Tourism Analysis* 5: 177–82.

———. 2004a. 'The Cultural Tour Route: A Journey of the Imagination?', *Tourism Analysis* 8(2–4): 259–71.

———. 2004b. 'Journeys of the Imagination? The Cultural Tour Route', in G. Crouch, R. Perdue and H. Timmermans (eds), *Consumer Psychology of Tourism, Hospitality and Leisure.* Oxfordshire: CABI, pp. 319–31.

Pi-Sunyer, O. 1989. 'Changing Perspectives of Tourism and Tourists in a Catalan Resort Town' in V.L. Smith, *Hosts and Guests: The Anthropology of Tourism* (2nd edn). Philadelphia: University of Pennsylvania, pp. 187–99.

Prentice, R. and V. Andersen. 2000. 'Evoking Ireland: Modeling Tourist Propensity', *Annals of Tourism Research* 27(2): 490–516.

Robinson, M. 1999. 'Is Cultural Tourism on the Right Track?', *UNESCO Courier* 22–23.

Rojek, C. 1993. *Ways of Escape*. London: Routledge.

Rojek, C. and J. Urry. 1997. 'Transformations of Travel and Theory', in C. Rojek and J. Urry (eds), *Touring Cultures: Transformations of Travel and Theory*. London: Routledge, pp. 1–19.

Rowan, Y. and U. Baram (eds). 2004. *Marketing Heritage: Archaeology and the Consumption of the Past*. Walnut Creek, CA: AltaMira Press.

Schama, S. 1994. *Landscape and Memory*. New York: Vintage.

Smith, V.L. (ed.). 1989. *Hosts and Guests: An Anthropology of Tourism*. Philadelphia: University of Pennsylvania.

Turner, V.W. 1985a. 'The Anthropology of Performance', in E. Turner (ed.), *On the Edge of the Bush: Anthropology as Experience*. Tucson: University of Arizona, pp. 177–204.

———. 1985b. 'Images of Anti-temporality: an Essay in the Anthropology of Tourism', in E. Turner (ed.), *On the Edge of the Bush: Anthropology as Experience*. Tuscon: University of Arizona, pp. 277–346.

Turner, V.W. and E. Turner. 1978. *Image and Pilgrimage in Christian Culture: Anthropological Perspectives*. New York: Columbia University Press.

Urry, J. 1990. *The Tourist Gaze: Leisure and Travel in Contemporary Societies*. London: Sage.

———. 2002. *The Tourist Gaze*. London: Sage.

———. 2004. 'Tourism, Europe and Identity', in S. Gmelch (ed.), *Tourists and Tourism: A Reader*. Long Grove, IL: Waveland Press, Inc., pp. 433–41.

van Gennep, A. 1961. *The Rites of Passage* (trans. M. Vizedom and G. Caffee). Chicago: University of Chicago.

Volkman, K.E. and R. Guydosh. 2001. 'Tourism in Ireland: Observations on the Impact of European Union Funding and Marketing Strategies', Paper presented at the ASAC meetings 2001.

Witoszek, N. 2002. 'All that is Airy Solidifies: the Prolonged Agony of Romantic Ireland', *Textual Practice* 16(2): 345–63.

Wulff, H. 2007. *Dancing at the Crossroads: Memory and Mobility in Ireland*. Oxford: Berghahn Books.

Chapter 9
GOING ON HOLIDAY TO IMAGINE WAR: THE WESTERN FRONT BATTLEFIELDS AS SITES OF COMMEMORATION AND CONTESTATION

Jennifer Iles

Introduction

The First World War of 1914–1918 is now slipping beyond the realm of lived experience, yet it continues to wield a profound impact on the British imagination. The Western Front in Belgium and France, which was the decisive theatre of operations for the Allied troops, has created its own iconic representation and mythology and has secured a firm place in modern memory (Williams 1994: 19). Ninety years after the last shots were fired, Britain's 'Great War' continues to provoke historical controversy and debate, and as Heathorn contends, its legacy still matters to 'British society at large' (Heathorn 2005: 1103). In many respects, Ferguson points out, the war actually remains contemporary and 'unlike more recent conflicts (the Korean, for example), it is still newsworthy' (Ferguson 1998: xxxiii). Despite some lapses since the Armistice was declared in November 1918, Binyon's promise that 'We will remember them', which he made in his poem *For the Fallen* written in 1914, has largely been honoured. Although popular interest in the conflict remained dormant during the 1950s and early 1960s, the approach of the fiftieth anniversary of the outbreak of hostilities prompted a spate of new books about the war.[1] These publications, together with the broadcasting of the BBC's groundbreaking television series, *The Great War,* in 1964, reinvigorated public awareness of the Western Front battlefields and memorials (Simkins 1999: 30) and since the mid-1970s the Somme and Ypres Salient areas of the Front lines have been popular destinations for British visitors and continue to grow as tourist attractions (Saunders 2001: 45). As Saunders observes, the region is now part of an integrated tourist circuit and its former battlefields, memorials, military cemeteries and museums are visited by thousands of people throughout the year (Saunders 2001: 45).

The Front consisted of a line of earthworks or trenches that stretched for approximately 450 miles from the Belgian Channel ports to the Swiss frontier. Yet the landscape that tourists now flock to reveals little of the momentous nature of the campaigns fought out across its terrain. Much of the battle-scarred Front lines have long since vanished under crop cultivation and urban development. The military historian, Stedman, notes, 'it is difficult to visualise what those involved went through – but we must try' (Stedman and Skelding 1999: 92). Often for first time visitors, their tour can be a frustrating experience, particularly around the former Ypres Salient in Belgium, where, because of the semi-circular nature of the Front lines, the battlefields can be confusing to follow. Even for those visitors who arrived shortly after the Armistice the destruction along the battle lines was so complete that there was very little for them to see. Four years of fighting over the same areas of ground left a devastated torn-up landscape described by the poet Wilfred Owen as 'the topography of Golgotha'.[2] Whole villages vanished, reduced to 'handfuls of smoke-grimed dust' (Oxenham 1918: 34) and in places entire sections of topsoil disappeared, exposing the limestone substratum underneath. The historian Lloyd comments that the landscape which first attracted travellers to the battlefields was largely an imaginary one. It was not the actual sights that were of primary importance but their associations and meanings such as feelings of excitement and horror (Lloyd 1998: 112–14). A guidebook of the Marne battlefields published in 1919 advised its readers: 'Seeing is not enough, one must understand ... a stretch of country which might seem dull and uninteresting to the unenlightened eye, becomes transformed at the thought of the battles which have raged there' (Illustrated Michelin Guides to the Battlefields, 1919: n.p.).

And today, again, the draw for tourists seems to be not so much a desire to sightsee but rather a wish to identify and empathize with its symbolic commemorative spaces in order to gain a greater feeling for the lives and experiences of an earlier generation tested by brutal and violent military combat (McPhail 2005: 16). For British visitors, the Western Front remains a sacred place which embodies the memory of the men who were physically and symbolically woven into the battlefield landscape (Saunders 2004: 9). While Verdun remains the focus of French memory of the war and the Trench of Death at Dixmuide[3] is deeply symbolic for the Belgians, the Somme in France and Passchendaele near Ypres in Belgium are key sites in British memory. Winston Churchill's proposal in 1919 that the town of Ypres should remain frozen in its wartime state of ruin as a permanent memorial to the dead because 'a more sacred place for the British race does not exist in the world' (cited in Longworth 1985: 75) reflected the popular British view that the former battlefield sites had become holy ground. A comment made more recently in August 2008 in the visitors' book of a Commonwealth War Graves Commission (CWGC) military cemetery on the Somme which simply states, 'The Holy Land of our people', indicates that for some this belief still retains its significance.[4]

Paradoxically, however, as Franklin notes following the publication of Urry's *The Tourist Gaze: Leisure and Travel in Contemporary Societies* in 1990, many researchers have explained tourist behaviour as an activity that is primarily carried out through the medium of vision or the gaze (Franklin 2003: 83; see also Macnaghten and Urry 1998; Rojek 1995; Crawshaw and Urry 1997). Yet, while research continues to build on Urry's notion of the gaze, new directions acknowledge that tourism is a multidimensional and complex practice and that the tourist is more than a disembodied sightseer. Increasing attention is now being paid to the embodied and performative nature of tourist activities (Franklin 2003: 83; see also Bowman 2005; Coleman and Crang 2002; Crouch and Lübbren 2003; Edensor 1998, 2000, 2001; Franklin and Crang 2001; Kirshenblatt-Gimblett 1998; Iles 2006, 2008; Tucker 1997).[5] This approach recognizes that people on holiday continue to mediate and make sense of the world through their bodies, through social interaction, feelings, imagining and 'doing' (Crouch 2002: 209). Whilst it is true that tourists travel to the Western Front armed with their cameras, keen to record its images, many of them will also expect to 'experience' it rather than merely to 'see'. The former manager of Talbot House Museum in Poperinge, near Ypres, for example, commented on the experiential quality of the area that tourists find attractive:

> Young and old visit those battle sites, either here or on the Somme area. This shows that people want to know. Something happened here beyond description, beyond comprehension. ... I think you can learn a lot from when you visit those battlefields. Not only about the battles but also about the pain and the dramas. It's when a headstone gets a face, or a battle site has a history, that it makes someone think. (J. Ryckabosche, communication, April 1999)

Touring the battlefield landscape requires a multi-sensual awareness and, as the geographer Relph recognizes, a sense of 'empathetic insideness' or a 'willingness to be emotionally open to the significance of a place, to feel it, to know and respect its symbols' (Relph 1976: 54). In order to engage meaningfully and empathize with its commemorative spaces and to decipher and decode its landscape of war (Gough 2001: 231), I propose in this chapter that in combination with the gaze, the most powerful engagements practised by tourists visiting the Western Front, whether travelling alone or on a commercial coach tour, are with and through their imaginations and emotions. Although the embodied components of bodily movement and sociality also play a central role in the experience of battlefield visitors, imagination and emotion are the triggers that allow them to construct an empathic and historical connection to the present-day landscape that, notwithstanding the presence of the military cemeteries and memorials, can today only hint of the horror and turmoil that took place during the conflict.

But while this landscape is regarded as sacred by tourists it is also a contested one. The activities of the growing numbers of visitors attracted to its former battlefields, its evocative military cemeteries and its impressive memorials and memorial parks, can sometimes conflict with the demands of modern-day life and economic considerations of local communities. As Bremer contends, meaningful places are inherently social in nature and are vulnerable to contestation by different groups of people (Bremer 2006: 27). This study then will also examine some of the tensions that have arisen between tourists and the local population who are at odds regarding the ownership and space of the multi-layered battlefield landscape.

A Corner of a Foreign Field

The battlefields attract people with all kinds of interests and pursuits: historians and military enthusiasts; people who have been stirred by the work of the 'trench poets' Wilfred Owen, Siegfried Sassoon and Edmund Blunden; and due to the requirements of the national curriculum in Britain, thousands of schoolchildren have also made the journey there. For others, the region represents an important part of their family history and they want to trace the movements or resting place of a past relative. Stedman has said of its lasting appeal that, 'this is where so many of our roots lie. From India, New Zealand, Australia, Canada and Britain, a whole generation passed through this place' (Stedman and Skelding 1999: 74). The foreign countryside of the Western Front has effectively become established in what Anderson (1991) has called the 'imagined community' of English, and by extension, British and Empire nationhood. Today, there remains an almost tangible sense of British appropriation and ownership over the areas where the Allied armies were stationed and fought. Writing about his experiences in battle, Mottram remarked that there were so many soldiers in some areas of the Front that they 'far exceeded the local inhabitants' (Mottram 1936: 2). For him, the battlefields had become 'a part of Britain, to be defended' (Mottram 1936: 72). This sense of ownership is movingly conveyed by a sign erected at a military cemetery on the Somme shortly after the war which reads: 'The Devonshires held this trench; the Devonshires hold it still.'

Still woven into the historic and spatial composition of the former battlefields are traces of the soldiers' vernacular landscape. The wartime names soldiers gave to particular places and areas remain in common usage, ensuring an enduring British presence in the region. In addition to the hundreds of CWGC signs which point to military cemeteries bearing names such as 'Thistle Dump', 'Dartmoor' and 'Caterpillar Valley', English names for places and land features are habitually used in tourist guides and history books. Tour guides will routinely point out High Wood on the Somme and take their clients to visit the Sausage and Mash valleys which lie on either side of the Lochnagar Crater. At Ypres, a typical tour will take in Clapham Junction, Hellfire Corner and Sanctuary Wood.

In addition to place names, the individual names of the dead have also been set on the landscape. Thousands of names, on headstones in cemeteries, on monuments to the missing, thread their way down the contours of the Front. As Laqueur notes, 'the pyramids pale by comparison with the sheer scale of British commemorative imposition on the landscape – let alone the German, French, Belgian [and] Portuguese' (Laqueur 1994: 155). The cemeteries, or 'silent cities' as they are sometimes called, contain the bones of whole communities. With their serried rows of headstones, tourists are soon alerted to the terrible human losses of the conflict. Clearly inscribed on the white Portland stone are the ages of death of the men buried beneath – aged nineteen, aged twenty-three, aged twenty-one. Only occasionally will the visitor pass a headstone that records the death of a soldier who was over the age of forty. Although the growing distance in years may have resulted in a dilution of the sense of stark tragedy and loss so keenly felt during the interwar years, people may still find themselves to be deeply touched by the emotional impact of the cemeteries and memorials. The historian McPhail, in her work *The Long Silence* (1999), acknowledges that however dispassionate we wish to be, and despite the considerable span of time that has elapsed since the Armistice in 1918, it is not difficult to apply the soldiers' circumstances 'to ourselves, our own families and communities' (McPhail 1999: 8). A tourist from Cheshire who was making his first journey to the Western Front said during a visit to Guillemont Road Cemetery on the Somme, 'It's a long way to the Somme, but now I'm here I feel I'm standing before my brothers' (C. Murray, communication, May 2009).

For those making a visit to a particular grave, the undertaking is of 'immense emotional meaning' and, as one tour guide acknowledges, some are achieving the ambition of a lifetime (P. Storie-Pugh, communication, August 2000). Similarly another guide also observes that many of his clients are fulfilling promises they made to themselves:

> To these people the grave visit is the be all and end all of them coming. Often they will miss another bit out of the tour to allow them to visit the grave or will not bother with the rest of the tour once they've done their bit. They have achieved their mission. ... They are always acutely aware that they will be the first members of the family to have been able to come and pay their respects. (V. Piuk, correspondence, June 2000)

The entries in the visitor books of the military cemeteries are replete with messages from people who have realized their personal goals. A comment made at the Vadencourt British Cemetery on the Somme is typical: 'The first one to visit you Granddad – you gave so much for your generation.' Another makes a pledge to return in the future: 'Visiting my great grandfather and I will bring my children one day so we will all know the sacrifice they made.'

Many of the people who travel to the Western Front are repeat visitors, attracted to its highly evocative dimensions, or, in the words of the soldier-poet Edmund Blunden, its 'peculiar grace'.[6] Some feel such a deep attachment to the area that it has become a kind of nostalgic 'home from home' and their trips enable them to physically enact a sense of historical connection with a place associated with an imagined collective past, untarnished by the values of contemporary society. Like MacCannell's tourists, they want to believe that 'somewhere, only not right here, not right now, perhaps just over there someplace, in another country, in another lifestyle … there is *genuine* society' (MacCannell 1976: 155, author's emphasis). Entranced by the promise of the past, they long 'to live in times superior to today' (Lowenthal 1985: 21). As Lowenthal suggests, a romantic view of the past can be a burden in the sense that it can fuel a negative and dispiriting rejection of the present (Lowenthal 1985: 13). The seemingly simpler values that the soldiers held, the belief that most of them fought unquestioningly for the cause of freedom and peace, that service to one's country was more important than individual self, and the sense that today we seem to be existing in some kind of spiritual and moral vacuum, are common views mentioned by the tourists I have conversed with on my field trips. A tour guide told me that visiting foreign battlefields is perhaps one way in which tourists can attempt to recapture the 'more noble ideals that existed then'. In view of the fact that the Great War is still regarded by many as a catastrophic and bloody conflict that brought about the destruction of the nation's youth, these sentiments may seem perplexing. And yet a veteran of the Korean War who was in Ypres for an Armistice Day ceremony said that, 'the First World War is more moving to me than my own war. … I have great respect for those young men and their ideals and hopes'.

An interest in family history appears to be the initial impetus for many repeat visitors when they first made the decision to tour the Western Front. As Samuel comments, today we live in an expanding historical culture in which history as a mass activity has probably never had so many followers (Samuel 1994: 25). With the distance in years since the Armistice was declared, the level of family connection has widened considerably and the majority of people presently looking into their family history will inevitably find a relative who saw active service in the Great War. By retracing their ancestors' movements across the battlefield terrain, visitors are given the opportunity to reinforce their sense of family pride and acquire some kind of affirmation of their own self-identity. A repeat tourist said that as both sides of his family had relatives who served in the war, he felt that he 'grew up with the Western Front'. Although he made his first visit there late in middle age, once he discovered the place where one of his uncles was killed, 'that was it, I never looked back' (A. Potton, communication, March 2003). In his account of his journeys to the battlefields, entitled *Riding the Somme* (n.d.), he wrote:

> This had been my sixth visit to the Somme, and that alone bewilders some of my acquaintances. ... They think that there is something morbidly sentimental in returning to what was then such a cauldron of death and destruction and what is now such a memorial. Sentiment, yes: sentimentality, no. (Potton n.d.: 16)

The Western Front has become a place where subjective narratives can be located and brought back to life, somewhere, as Shepheard suggests, 'you [can] take your own stories to' (Shepheard 1997: 216). Yet in the multi-layered landscape of the former battlefields not everyone's history can find its proper place (Clifford 1997: 338). McPhail is critical of the way in which some repeat visitors tend to focus only on the narratives and memory of their own social identities and losses, and she urges visitors to 'press on past this barrier of the imagination' and look beyond the fading lines of the trenches to consider the terrible sufferings and privations of the civilian population under occupation (McPhail 1999: 3). She also indicates in her report to L'Historial de la Grande Guerre (2001) in Peronne that it is all too easy for visitors to become nostalgic and sentimental about the events that occurred on the Western Front because Britain did not suffer the direct consequences of brutal warfare. While visitors may be knowledgeable about particular battles and the heroism and sacrifices made by the Allied forces, they are too locked in their own reflective gaze to be able to comprehend the bigger picture of the consequences of war. For McPhail, visits to the battlefields enable some visitors to feed their emotional thirst for the drama of war without having to endure the drawbacks of its realities, namely the violence, carnage, mud and lice (McPhail 2001: 9). On occasion, I have also encountered an overlay of dubious sentimentality in the motives of a few visitors whose interest in the past seems to have become obsessive. Their performance appears to be not so much honouring the soldiers as trying to recapture and appropriate their forefather's heroism or suffering for themselves. The commemorative landscape of the battlefields is certainly conducive for British visitors to reaffirm their heritage and feel pride in the specific contribution of their ancestors. However, as McPhail observes, it seems easier to revisit the war and become nostalgic about particular actions and events when the fighting was located in another country (McPhail 2005: 15). Although the anthropologist Smith maintains that battlefield tourism is honorific rather than maudlin in intent, there is an element of sentimentality and romanticization that some tourists are able to exploit (Smith 1996: 263).

The Western Front as Contested Territory

For British visitors, the landscape of the Western Front remains redolent with historical association and perceptions of nationality which generate emotions, memory and imagination. Embedded in its earth are personal biographies, social identities and memories of previous movement (Tilley 2004: 26). Yet the battlefield terrain is not a static, fossilized background to military engagement, nor is it simply a setting for commemorative monumentality (Saunders 2004: 7). It is lived in, mediated, worked on and altered, and for the local inhabitants it is their everyday working environment (Tilley 1994: 26). Tourists, however, in the performance of their historical interests and commemorative activities, can sometimes overlook this. As Bender asserts, landscapes are political, dynamic, re-worked, appropriated and contested spaces (Bender 1993: 2–3) and in the complex, multi-layered nature of the former battle zones, tensions can be triggered between the different groups who engage with it.

While the steady flow of holidaymakers makes an important contribution to the local economy, one contentious point between tourists and locals concerns visitor trespass over privately owned land. Urry explains that in Britain today it is commonly thought that landscapes should be communally owned, or as Wordsworth remarked, a 'sort of national property' (Urry 2000: 138). Enshrined in the popular imagination, as Gough points out, is a freedom to roam, even though rights-of-way in Britain are more restricted than in many European countries (Gough 2007: 700). As a consequence, some battlefield tourists may exercise their perceived rights to walk over privately owned fields and woodlands, searching for the location of a particular battle or military action. Many tourist guidebooks remind readers to be aware that the landscape they are travelling through is a working one and it is not 'open access' land based on the National Trust model. Stedman warns, for example, 'it is all too easy to let our two interests clash. ... The farmers will not welcome the sight of your tramping the fields with little regard to crops and seeds. Please ask before you enter' (Stedman 1995: 14).

At times, even in those areas which have been acquired by Britain and its allies 'in perpetuity', namely the military cemeteries and memorial parks, tensions can arise between tourists and locals. There are varying degrees of access to these sites. In some cases, a cemetery *chemin*, or path, belongs to the Commission, but in others it does not and the Commission only has a right of way rather than a legal right to a permanent path. Even where *chemins* do belong to the Commission, however, some farmers regularly plough them up leaving tourists and the Commission gardeners to 'beat a path through the crop'. The former Director of the CWGC in France, Mike Johnson, explains that as the old farmers die off and hand their properties on to the younger members of the family who have no memory of either of the two world wars and 'who don't have the same feel for it', conflicts are increasingly occurring (M. Johnson, communication, April 1999). However, as Johnson points out, many of the cemetery sites are set within a day-to-day working rural landscape owned by farmers who are often under considerable financial pressure to make use of every square inch of their land. Although the majority of them are quite tolerant and helpful, some are not. The Commission keeps 'relatively quiet about that' and tries its best to play down conflicts because 'creating a fuss doesn't get you anywhere'. Yet despite its conciliatory, low-key stance, a few heated 'run-ins' have taken place on occasions. A farmer who owns property surrounding the Sheffield Memorial Park on the Somme became increasingly frustrated with the steady flow of visitors, their tour buses and cars, and went so far as to periodically block off the road to the Park with his tractor and physically threaten people. The military historian and battlefield guide Paul Reed recalls the following incident:

> I was stopped by him with somebody last November and he made threats of physical violence. He attempted to kick this guy's car in … but we just accepted it and parked down the road and walked … but it's a public access road and he can't legally block it. (P. Reed, communication, April 1999)

The Commission has since erected a prominent red notice which requests that people walk rather than drive up to the Park.

Souvenir hunters, or 'battlefield stompers' as they are commonly known, are also a cause for concern to the locals. Like the tourist backpacker, stompers are often denigrated by their host community for their perceived inappropriate and unethical behaviour.[7] Some bring metal detectors with them, even though the practice of using them is illegal in Belgium and in some regions of France including the Somme area. For one owner of a bed-and-breakfast establishment on the Somme, they are her least favourite type of guest because they often return to the house with hand grenades and stoke mortars, oblivious to the risks they are taking both to themselves and their host. Many tourists are disturbingly unaware of the dangers of handling old, rusting ammunition, yet to all who handle it, the 'iron harvest' remains dangerously proactive (Saunders 2004: 18). Since 1918, French and Belgian ordnance teams have been clearing bullets, mortar bombs, hand grenades, rifles and even tanks from the landscape. In the deceptively peaceful countryside, the land doggedly remains soaked with the poisons of war, and the never-ending arsenal of trench warfare remains a constant legacy of the former battles. Shells lie in neat piles at the corners of fields, or clustered around the base of solitary memorials, awaiting collection by the bomb disposal units which tour the region, rather like, as Birkett observes, 'milkmen picking up empty bottles from the doorstep' (Birkett 1998: 14). The former curator of the museum at Delville Wood on the Somme remarked that children sometimes came in brandishing hand grenades or shells, saying 'I'm taking this home to Dad for a souvenir' (T. Fairgrieve, communication, April 2000). He continued:

Very often it's the coach drivers who come across the shells that the kids have picked up. One coach got stopped at Dover just for a normal check and they pulled everybody out and they found two grenades in the luggage compartment. I just hope I'm not on the same boat as some of them. Grenades can knock a hole in the bottom of a ferry. (T. Fairgrieve, communication, April 2000)

Although safe souvenirs can be purchased at many of the visitor centres and museum shops, according to Reed, most relics of warfare on the Front remain 'up for grabs' by visitors wanting to bring a memento back home: 'Farmers have stuff lying around and visitors go into their yards and I think they've had a bit of trouble occasionally with people trying to get things. ... I think that if the headstones weren't cemented into battens in the cemeteries, people would try to have those away.' (P. Reed, communication, April 1999). As he points out, 'tourists are thieves in their own right and have been right through the centuries'. In an attempt to curb pilfering by tourists visiting the battlefields around Ypres during the early years of the Armistice, notices were put on all the important ruins in the town which read: 'This is Holy Ground! No stone of this fabric to be taken away. It is a heritage for all civilised people' (Dendooven 2002: 30). Soldiers too often returned home with bits and pieces taken from the battlefields. According to Reed, the former Salient Museum in Ypres had an entire case devoted to 'bits of the town that had been lifted by soldiers during the war as souvenirs' which had eventually been returned by relatives or the soldiers themselves, who, 'in later life, felt guilty about keeping them' (P. Reed, communication, April 1999).

The Bulldozers of Progress

Despite the continuing success of the Western Front as a visitor attraction, an increasing number of sites are now at risk of disappearing 'beneath the concrete of economic progress' as new industrial parks, theme parks and urban expansions steadily encroach upon the old battlefields. Beyond the sanctified boundaries of the preserved tracts of the former Front lines, such as the memorial parks at Delville Wood, Beaumont Hamel and Vimy Ridge, the farming landscape contains whole 'underground cities' of trenches, dugouts, shelters and tunnels that lie hidden and undisturbed just below the depth of topsoil. The military historian Ted Smith observes that as more agricultural land is being cleared for development, an increasing number of old battlegrounds are being both rediscovered and then destroyed by excavators and concrete pourers (Smith 1999: 39). Yet, as Urry contends, for landscapes to be attractive and searched out by tourists, tourist discourse prefers that they be distinctive and authentic (Urry 1992: 20–21; see also Tucker 1997). Today, any alterations or developments which may impinge on the battlefields – visible or not – are likely to be met by often vociferous concern by visitors who prefer the landscape to reflect a state of permanence and stability.[8]

Disputes regarding the shape and ownership of the landscape, however, have been commonplace since the cessation of hostilities (Saunders 2001: 42). The town of Ypres, for instance, was rebuilt by the local population in the early 1920s despite Churchill's suggestion that it should remain in its ruined wartime state (Lloyd 1998: 121). According to a tour guide, since the end of the Second World War a combination of local ignorance about the conflict and the needs of commerce have been largely to blame for the loss of important sections of the battle zones. He observes that in the Ypres area: 'The Council destroyed Hellfire Corner which was one of the most significant places in the war. They did it in order to enable cars to travel fast to get to the [nearby] theme park. They did not know the significance of the corner.' (G. Parker, communication, June 1999).

Of more recent concern was the proposed construction in 2001 of an international airport near Chaulnes on the Somme which would have entailed not only the destruction of at least one village but also the removal of several military cemeteries. Although the French Government bowed to pressure from both local and international opposition and subsequently shelved the plan, for the first time the notion that soldiers' bodies were to lie undisturbed and 'in perpetuity' in the cemeteries was put into serious doubt. In 2005, the Belgian government, also under pressure from local and international opposition, announced its revision of a planned extension to the A19 motorway near Ypres which would have cut the Pilckem Ridge battlefield in half and left 'some of the tens of thousands of British troops still listed as missing in action under a carpet of concrete and tarmac' (Osborn 2001: 6). Meanwhile, north of Ypres, a new industrial complex, known as 'Language Valley', continues gradually to envelope a large sector of the old Front. Ted Smith laments that 'Language Valley and the like will not only be all that is left to represent the sites of many battlefields, but will also be the only markers of many of those fallen soldiers of the Great War with no known graves' (Smith, 1999: 39). Moreover, a continuing stream of further motorway schemes, as well as a proposal to construct a new canal to link the Seine and the Canal du Nord, and a plan to build a 25-kilometre circular test track in the Nord/Pas-de-Calais region for the next generation of high-speed trains, similarly threaten to cut through the heart of the battlefields (Malloch 2008: 31).

Inevitably the remains of thousands of dead soldiers, unsacralized and unburied, also lie beneath the surface of the battlefields. On average, about twenty or thirty bodies are recovered every year, but within the last decade the increased pace of urban expansion and development has led to far larger numbers being unearthed.[9] After examination, recovered corpses are buried with full military honours. Not all, however, are treated with such pomp and ceremony. As Cave asserts, it was widely alleged that when the Eurostar line was constructed through northern France, the building contractors, who were constrained by a tight schedule, ignored many remains from the war (Cave 2000: 13). Smith argues that the increasing amount of paperwork and bureaucracy required in order to report their discovery has resulted in farmers and construction workers routinely covering over them, 'having first pilfered the remains for cap-badges, collar-dogs and the like' (Smith 1999: 39). Whilst it is the case that scavenging for mementoes, either for personal gain or commercial profit, has routinely taken place since the Armistice and arguably during the war itself, with the growing interest in the First World War there has been a notable inflation in the value of artefacts from shell cases to soldiers' personal effects. This in turn has resulted in an increase in the pilfering of regimental insignia and other objects which could help to identify bodies. Once looked upon as just the detritus of war, this type of material is now seen as an important contribution to new insights and understanding of the conflict. Cave (2000) considers this type of souvenir hunting a form of grave robbing, recounting that:

> I have seen photographs of a complete German skeleton, plus a sniper's rifle and other accoutrements, laid out on someone's kitchen table. There have been incidents when some people in Delville Wood (the whole of which is designated as an Official War Grave) have been digging, presumably as a result of a response on a metal detector. (Cave 2000: 12–13)

The seriousness of the threat to the battlefield landscape has to some extent been highlighted by the recent development of a more professional archaeological approach to the First World War conflict (Saunders 2004: 18). As the Director of the In Flanders Fields Museum in Ypres, Piet Chielens notes, in former years military archaeology was 'never very high on the agenda' (P. Chielens, communication, April 2000). But whereas only buildings, monuments or objects were considered to be of prime importance, it is now becoming increasingly clear that it is the vanishing battlefields themselves that enable modern-day visitors to glance upon the real horrors of war. Indeed, as battlefield tourism is largely an outdoor activity, tourists expect to have the main focus of their trip directed towards the actual sites of warfare rather than on museum visiting. In the words of a guide, for the battlefield tourist 'the real museum is found on the ground' (G. Parker, communication, March 1999).

In particular, it was the work of a group of amateur Belgian archaeologists called The Diggers that first began to draw wider public attention to the historical importance of the battlefields. Before the construction of Language Valley began in the early 1990s, the group, working under a special licence from the Flemish Regional Authorities, unearthed an important trench system complete with duckboards and drainage ditches, and exhumed over a hundred bodies (Smith 1999: 38). Scores of personal items were found such as drinking bottles and shoes, along with gas shells, gas masks and boxes of hand grenades. Their work has subsequently been the subject of two British television documentaries. The first one, *Battlefield Scavengers* (ITV broadcast in 2000), brought The Diggers into prominence for all the wrong reasons because it accused them of plundering artefacts from the rediscovered trenches.[10] Nevertheless in the web pages of the In Flanders Fields Museum, Chielens credited the group with carrying out valuable work: 'The Diggers and their intentions were certainly portrayed in an inaccurate light. To us it is clear that without their painstaking exploration, scores of British, French and German soldiers, who died on this battlefield in 1915, would quite simply have been crushed by the bulldozers of progression' (Chielens 2001).

Two years later, however, a further documentary, *The Forgotten Battlefield* (BBC broadcast in 2002) gave The Diggers' archaeological excavations more sympathetic coverage.[11] The ensuing publicity prompted the local authorities at Ypres to preserve part of their excavations and in May 2003 the site was opened to the public (Reed 2006). In addition, following the excavation of the Ypres Salient battlefield at Pilckem Ridge by the Belgian Institute of Archaeology in 2002, which again unearthed trench systems, bunkers and human remains, the Belgian government recognized the need for a professional archaeological engagement with the battlefield sites. In 2003 it announced the opening of Belgium's Department of First World War Archaeology. In Britain, concern over the need for professional excavation and documentation led to the founding in 2002 of the All-Party Parliamentary War Graves and Battlefields Heritage Group (APWGBHG). The Group, which is made up of an assembly of peers and MPs, aims to support campaigners seeking to conserve and promote war heritage and battlefield sites and encourage best practice in archaeology (Barton 2003: 14–15).[12]

Following widespread consternation among tourists and various First World War battlefield interest groups, the APWGBHG has recently been involved in the halting of the construction of housing at a site called the Glory Hole near the village of La Boisselle on the Somme. The Glory Hole consists of a cratered, broken patch of land situated near to the Lochnagar Crater, a well-known tourist and memorial site.[13] During the war it was the scene of heavy fighting and was later described by Henry Williamson in his fictional account of his own wartime experiences, *The Golden Virgin* (1957), as 'a bone-yard without graves of British and German corpses'. Today it remains a dangerous place. It is not only peppered with numerous underground tunnels, there is also a strong likelihood that the area contains several unexploded mine charges. In 2005 one of the owners of the site – who was unaware of the plot's historical significance – sold a small section of it for urban housing development. When the APWGBHG was informed of the situation, a letter was sent on its behalf in January 2006 to the Conseil Général de la Somme which requested that the site be protected from development because of its historical importance (Lea 2006: 2). The French authorities, taking into account representations made against the development from several sources, withdrew the building permit on the grounds that the existence of the tunnels had made the land prone to subsidence, and work on the house was halted for almost a year. The new owner subsequently went to court and successfully applied for a new building certificate, after which the house was quickly completed. However, a temporary ban has since been put on any further construction work being carried out around the site. There are also efforts underway by the Somme Remembrance Association[14] to develop the location as a memorial and to have it officially classified as a 'site de memoire' (Bergez, communication, September 2008).[15] For Dunning, the owner of Lochnagar Crater, the Glory Hole has become a symbol of the clash between the needs and realities of modern-day living and the desire to preserve battlefield sites. Locally, the dispute became a very sensitive issue and, according to Dunning, many of the village residents were up in arms against the building ban because it threw into question whether any other land in their area would be able to be sold for development (Dunning, communication, September 2008).

Whilst British tourists may wish to safeguard certain parts of the former battle zones from building developments so that future generations can understand the events which took place there, for the modern inhabitants of the old Front lines, life goes on. People routinely live, farm and work on top of unmarked mass graves, mining tunnels, unexploded ammunition and leaking poison gas shells. For the locals who want to see their communities grow and thrive, new developments which may well encroach upon the battlefields are a necessity. A resident of Ypres commented: 'I really think that living people should be prioritised over and above the dead soldiers of World War One' (Discovery 2003). Furthermore, although there is customarily strong support and involvement from local communities in the commemorative practices of people touring the battlefields, in tandem with this there also exists a degree of puzzlement regarding the desire of increasing numbers of British visitors to remember events that occurred over ninety years ago. Some locals have surprisingly little knowledge about the significance of key sites of remembrance, as one guide who lives in the Somme area, revealed: 'Did I tell you about the time we passed the Thiepval memorial with our neighbour, and he had no idea what it was?' (V. Piuk, communication, September 2000).

Despite the area's deeply emotional significance for the visitors, it is not possible to preserve all of the sites and keep the old Front lines in a state of geographical purity – indeed, in the haste of reconstruction during the interwar years there was never the intention to preserve them. Although the Western Front's material markers of the past, such as the memorial parks, memorials to the missing and military cemeteries, may proclaim an air of enduring stability, this seeming constancy disguises the landscape's itinerant, unstable and changing nature (Bremer 2006: 27).

Conclusion

I would contend that the Western Front now occupies a more central place in the British imagination than at any other time since the Second World War. Although tourists travelling to the Front are eager to record pictures of its sights, by drawing on their emotions and imagination they also endeavour to build an empathic, intimate awareness of a place long emptied of its military occupancy (Gough 2001: 231). As the former manager of the Somme Tourist Board observed, 'the war had such an impact that one can feel it, even if we don't see it' (de Lotte, communication, April 2000). It is this sense of empathetic insideness that entices people to repeatedly return to the area and to appreciate its ambience. Even though vision is an important part of the tourist experience, a focus on the embodied, performative modes of tourism produces a less constrained representation of what tourists actually do (Franklin 2003: 279).

Yet despite its present-day significance for visitors as a sacred landscape of remembrance, the Western Front remains a deeply political, contested territory. Its former battlefields, as Morris observes, are multi-layered and contain 'different and intersecting ideas and meanings about identity, place and landscape production' (Morris 1997: 428). For both locals and tourists it is 'their' landscape from which they derive a sense of place and belonging (Tilley 1994: 15). For the locals, the omnipresent heritage of the First World War – unwanted and uninvited – stubbornly remains one of the defining historical and cultural elements of their locality, creating a tension between past and present. As Macintyre remarks, the war did not simply change the contours of the landscape, it became the landscape (Macintyre 1998: 22). For British tourists, many of whom have ancestral links to the area, its terrain has become soaked with the exclusive memory of their own social identities and losses. Their desire to imagine and examine past battles and to commemorate the dead, as well as their expectations that specific sites in the landscape should be recognized as being permanently and inherently sacred, may be frustrated by the sometimes conflicting wishes and ambitions of the indigenous population. The current fascination with the Great War, though, will eventually fade away and the conflict and the men who died in it will become an irrelevance in people's lives. Remembrance, as the military historian van Emden maintains, 'is always up for grabs – we will in the end not remember the Somme and not remember Passchendaele' (R. van Emden, communication, April 2000). However, for the time being, the memory of the men who took up arms and never returned home still casts long shadows over the Western Front landscape, and visitors continue to be drawn to explore its battlefields, hungry to celebrate both their individual origins and their collective place in the national past.

Notes

1. Books about the First World War that were published shortly before the fiftieth anniversary of the conflict include L. Wolff, *In Flanders Fields: The 1917 Campaign* (London, 1959); A. Clark, *The Donkeys* (New York, 1961); C. Barnett, *The Swordbearers: Supreme Command in the First World War* (London, 1963); J. Terraine, *Douglas Haig: The Educated Soldier* (London, 1963).
2. Wilfred Owen, 1918, Letter to Osbert Sitwell.
3. The Trench of Death is an area of preserved trenches near the town of Dixmuide, a few miles north of Ypres.
4. The CWGC was created in 1917 as the body responsible for the registration and burial of the Allied war dead. Prior to 1960 the organization was known as the Imperial War Graves Commission. The name of the cemetery referred to is Sanders Keep Military Cemetery.
5. This chapter is based on a continuing ethnographic study of battlefield tourism to the Western Front which began in 1997. It draws on my Ph.D. dissertation, 'Memorial Landscapes of the Western Front: Spaces of Commemoration, Tourism and Pilgrimage' (University of Surrey, Roehampton, 2003) and also represents a development of ideas initially set out in Iles (2006, 2008).
6. From the poem, 'Report on Experience'. The poem appears in his memoir, *Undertones of War* (1928; 1982).
7. See Ateljevic and Doorne (2001), Elsrud (2001) and Richards and Wilson (2004) for discussion on backpacker tourism.
8. Typically visitors will write to their MPs, newspaper editors, or various First World War interest groups, such as the Western Front Association which publishes a quarterly journal. They may also make representations directly to local authorities in France and Belgium.
9. In 2008 mass graves containing the remains of 250 British and Australian soldiers were discovered in Fromelles in France.
10. *Battlefield Scavengers* was broadcast by ITV on 12 November 2000. A complaint made by The Diggers to the Broadcasting Standards Commission about the documentary was upheld in part in 2001. The Diggers maintain some of their number may take items from the battlefields, but insist that any personal items that can be linked to bodies are kept with the body.
11. *The Forgotten Battlefield* was aired by the BBC on 6 March 2002.
12. The APWGBHG operates in conjunction with a variety of different organizations and groups, such as the CWGC, historians, academic groups and universities.
13. Lochnagar Crater was created by the detonation of a British mine as a precursor to the start of the Somme offensive on 1 July 1916.
14. The Somme Remembrance Association was formed in 2005 with the aim to further the remembrance of the soldiers who died in the Great War. The Association initiated the effort to stall the development of the site.
15. When an area is officially classified as a 'site de memoire' it is protected from further development.

Bibliography

Anderson, B. 1991. *Imagined Communities: Reflections on the Origin and Spread of Nationalism.* London: Verso.

Ateljevic, I. and S. Doorne. 2001. 'Nowhere to Run: A Study of Value Boundaries and Segmentation Within the Backpacker Market of New Zealand', in J.A. Mazanec, G.I. Crouch, J.R. Brent Richie and A.G. Woodside (eds), *Consumer Psychology of Tourism Hospitality and Leisure*, Vol 2. New York: CAB International, pp. 169–86.

Barton, P. 2003. 'The Corner of a "Foreign Field" that Will No Longer be Forever England', *Battlefields Review* 23: 13–15.

BBC. 2002. *The Forgotten Battlefield*, 6 March.

Bender, B. (ed.). 1993. *Landscape: Politics and Perspectives*. Oxford: Berg.

Birkett, P. 1998. 'Still Out There: 1 Million Shells: On the Battlefields of Flanders, Peter Birkett Meets the Team Clearing the Lethal Legacy of the First World War', *Weekend Telegraph*, 17 October, p. 14.

Blunden, E. 1982 [1928]. *Undertones of War*. London: Penguin.

Bowman, M. 2005. 'Looking for Stonewall's Arm: Tourist Performance as Research Method', in J. Hamera (ed.), *Opening Acts: Performance in/as Communication and Cultural Studies*. Thousand Oaks, CA: Sage, pp. 102–33.

Bremer, T.S. 2006. 'Sacred Spaces and Tourist Places', in D.J. Timothy and D.H. Olsen (eds), *Tourism, Religion and Spiritual Journeys*. London: Routledge, pp. 25–35.

Cave, N. 2000. 'Battlefield Scavenging', *Battlefields Review*, 1: 12–13.

Chielens, P. 2001. 'Diggers Dig for Remains of a War …', *In Flanders Fields Museum*. Retrieved 15 October 2001 from http://www.inflandersfields.be/.

Clifford, J. 1997. *Routes: Travel and Translation in the Late Twentieth Century*. Cambridge, MA: Harvard University Press.

Coleman, S. and M. Crang (eds). 2002. *Tourism: Between Place and Performance*. New York: Berghahn Books.

Crawshaw, C. and J. Urry. 1997. 'Tourism and the Photographic Eye', in C. Rojek and J. Urry (eds), *Touring Cultures: Transformations of Travel and Theory*. London: Routledge, pp. 176–95.

Crouch, D. 2002. 'Surrounded by Place', in S. Coleman and M. Crang (eds), *Tourism: Between Place and Performance*. Oxford: Berghahn Books, pp. 207–18.

Crouch, D. and N. Lübbren (eds). 2003. *Visual Culture and Tourism*. Oxford: Berg.

Dendooven, D. 2002. *Menin Gate and Last Post: Ypres as Holy Ground*. Koksidje, Belgium: De Klaproos.

Discovery Channel. 2003. *Mud, Blood and Tarmac*, 11 January.

Edensor, T. 1998. *Tourists at the Taj: Performance and Meaning at a Symbolic Site*. London: Routledge.

———. 2000. 'Staging Tourism: Tourists as Performers', *Annals of Tourism Research* 27: 322–44.

———. 2001. 'Performing Tourism, Staging Tourism', *Tourist Studies* 1(1): 59–81.

Elsrud, T. 2001. 'Risk Creation in Travelling – Backpacker Adventure Narration', *Annals of Tourism Research* 28: 597–617.

Ferguson, N. 1998. *The Pity of War*. London: Allen Lane/Penguin Press.

Franklin, A. 2003. *Tourism: An Introduction*. London: Sage.

Franklin, A. and M. Crang. 2001. 'The Trouble with Tourism and Travel Theory?', *Tourist Studies* 1(1): 5–22.

Gough, P. 2001. 'That Sacred Turf: War Memorial Gardens as Theatres of War (and Peace)', in J.M. Teutonico and J. Fidler (eds), *Monuments and the Millennium*. London: James and James, pp. 228–36.

———. 2007. '"Contested Memories: Contested Site": Newfoundland and its Unique Heritage on the Western Front', *The Round Table* 96(393): 693–705.

Heathorn, S. 2005. 'The Mnemonic Turn in the Cultural Historiography of Britain's Great War', *Historiographical Review* 48(4): 1103–24.

Iles, J. 2006. 'Recalling the Ghosts of War: Performing Tourism on the Battlefields of the Western Front', *Text and Performance Quarterly* 26(2): 162–80.

———. 2008. 'Encounters in the Fields – Tourism to the Battlefields of the Western Front', *Journal of Tourism and Cultural Change* 6(2): 138–54.

Kirshenblatt-Gimblett, B. 1998. *Destination Culture: Tourism, Museums and Heritage*. Berkeley, CA: University of California Press.

Illustrated Michelin Guides to the Battlefields. 1919. *Battlefields of the Marne 1914.* London: Michelin Tyre Co. Ltd.

ITV. 2000. *Battlefield Scavengers,* 12 November.

Laqueur, T. 1994. 'Memory and Naming in the Great War', in J.R. Gillis (ed.), *Commemorations: The Politics of National Identity.* Chichester: Princeton University Press, pp. 150–67.

Lea, D. 2006. 'Threat to the "Glory Hole", La Boisselle, Somme', *Soke Military Society Newsletter* 54, June. Retrieved 29 June 2008 from http://sokemilitarysociety.firstworldwarrelics.co.uk/June_2006.pdf.

Lloyd, D. 1998. *Battlefield Tourism: Pilgrimage and the Commemoration of the Great War in Britain, Australia and Canada, 1919–1939.* Oxford: Berg.

Longworth, P. 1985. *The Unending Vigil: A History of the Commonwealth War Graves Commission 1917–1984.* London: Leo Cooper/Secker and Warburg.

Lowenthal, D. 1985. *The Past is a Foreign Country.* Cambridge: Cambridge University Press.

MacCannell, D. 1976. *The Tourist: A New Theory of the Leisure Class.* London: MacMillan.

Macintyre, B. 1998. 'Where Earth Bears the Memories', *The Times,* 7 November, p. 22.

Macnaghten, P. and J. Urry. 1998. *Contested Natures.* London: Sage.

Malloch, H. 2008. 'Hedley Malloch writes … Re: Education Matters "Not another effing cemetery"', *Western Front Association: Bulletin* 80: 31.

McPhail, H. 1999. *The Long Silence: Civilian Life under the German Occupation of Northern France, 1914–18.* London: I.B. Tauris.

———. 2001. 'La Grande Guerre – ressentiment et ignorance britanniques', Unpublished report for L'Historial de la Grande Guerre, Peronne, France.

———. 2005. 'Thiepval and Battlefield Tourism', *Despatches,* January: 12–16.

Morris, M. 1997. 'Gardens "Forever England": Landscape, Identity and the First World War British Cemeteries on the Western Front', *Ecumene* 4(4): 411–34.

Mottram, R.H. 1936. *Journey to the Western Front: Twenty Years After.* London: G. Bell and Son.

Osborn, A. 2001. 'Motorway Threat to the Dead of Wipers', *The Guardian,* 19 December, p. 16.

Owen, H. and J. Bell. 1967. *Wilfred Owen: Collected Letters.* Oxford: Oxford University Press.

Oxenham, J. 1918. *High Altars: The Battlefields of France and Flanders as I Saw Them.* London: Methuen.

Potton, A. (n.d.), *Riding the Somme.* Unpublished.

Reed, P. 2006. 'Yorkshire Trench'. Retrieved 21 July 2008 from http://battlefields1418.50megs.com/Yorkshire_trench.htm.

Relph, E. 1976. *Place and Placelessness.* London: Pion.

Richards, G. and J. Wilson. 2004. 'Travel Writers and Writers Who Travel: Nomadic Icons for the Backpacker Subculture?', *Journal of Tourism and Cultural Change* 2(1): 46–68.

Rojek, C. 1995. *Decentering Leisure: Rethinking Leisure Theory.* London: Sage.

Samuel, R. 1994. *Theatres of Memory: Past and Present in Contemporary Culture.* London: Verso.

Saunders, N. 2001. 'Matter and Memory in the Landscapes of Conflict: The Western Front 1914–1999', in B. Bender and M. Winer (eds), *Contested Landscapes: Movement, Exile and Place.* Oxford: Berg, pp. 37–53.

———. 2004. 'Material Culture and Conflict: The Great War, 1914–2003', in N. Saunders (ed.), *Matters of Conflict: Material Culture, Memory and the First World War.* London: Routledge, pp. 5–25.

Shepheard, P. 1997. *The Cultivated Wilderness: Or, What Is Landscape?* Cambridge, MA: MIT Press.

Simkins, P. 1999. 'My Thirty-Five Years at the Imperial War Museum, Part 2', *The Western Front Association: Bulletin* 57: 30.

Smith, T. 1999. 'Of Ypres Battlefields – Disappearance and Discovery', *The Western Front Association: Bulletin* 53: 28–39.

Smith, V. 1996. 'War and its Tourist Attractions', in A. Pizam and Y. Mansfeld (eds), *Tourism Crime and International Security Issues.* London: Wiley, pp. 247–64.

Stedman, M. 1995. *Somme: Thiepval.* London: Leo Cooper.

Stedman, M. and E. Skelding. 1999. *Great Battles of the Great War.* Barnsley, South Yorkshire: Leo Cooper/Pen and Sword Books.

Tilley, C. 1994. *A Phenomenology of Landscape: Places, Paths and Monuments.* Oxford: Berg.

————. 2004. *The Materiality of Stone: Explorations in Landscape Phenomenology.* Oxford: Berg.

Tucker, H. 1997. 'The Ideal Village: Interactions through Tourism in Central Anatolia', in S. Abram, J. Waldren and D. Macleod (eds), *Tourists and Tourism: Identifying with People and Places.* Oxford: Berg, pp. 91–106.

Urry, J. 1990. *The Tourist Gaze: Leisure and Travel in Contemporary Societies.* London: Sage.

————. 1992. 'The Tourist Gaze and the "Environment"', *Theory, Culture and Society* 9(3): 1–26.

————. 2000. *Sociology Beyond Societies.* London: Routledge.

Williams, V. 1994. *Warworks: Women, Photography and the Iconography of War.* London: Virago Press.

Williamson, H. 1957. *The Golden Virgin.* Edinburgh: Macdonald and Co.

Chapter 10
TOURING THE DEAD:
IMAGINATION, EMBODIMENT AND
AFFECT IN GUNTHER VON HAGENS'
BODY WORLDS EXHIBITIONS

Jane C. Desmond

Introduction

The most popular touring exhibit of all time is Gunther von Hagens' *Body Worlds: The Anatomical Exhibit of Real Human Bodies*. Since it premiered in 1995 in Japan, this display of posed human corpses, preserved through a process called 'plastination', has garnered more than twenty-six million viewers worldwide, touring to several countries in Europe, Asia, and more recently in the United States and Canada.

This exhibition has generated a lot of publicity and not a little controversy, resulting in a substantial amount of public discourse in newspapers and magazines. It has also received scholarly scrutiny from a number of academics, but not as much as one might have anticipated given its massive popularity. A majority of the scholarly articles approach the exhibit from the perspective of bioethics debates, or, less commonly, analyse the power of the exhibit through a critical cultural studies lens focused on issues of representation, semiotics, and ideological implications (Kuppfers 2004; Stern 2006; and van Dijck 2005). None that I am aware of have given sustained consideration to the phenomenon by analysing it from a perspective based in tourist studies.[1]

In this chapter I suggest that employing such a stance can illuminate something of the actual experiences of the visitors and thus, in turn, help explain the extraordinary appeal of the *Body Worlds* exhibits. I argue that the exhibit actually functions not just as a museum experience but as a 'tourist' experience – touring the dead. While 'education' may be the overarching goal promoted by the exhibitors and sought by the visitors, it is a sense of 'awe' that ultimately results for many. To understand this effect we must focus not only on the show as a display of bodies but also on the understanding of the larger phenomena of tourism as a culturally grounded embodied practice.

I will draw upon recent discussions in tourism studies which emphasize the embodied nature of tourism practices, the active engagement of the imagination, and the importance of spatial experiences along with the experiences of physicality, cognition, and emotions in the experiences of tourists (Crouch and Desforges 2003; Crouch, Aronsson and Wahlstrom 2001; Perkins and Thorns 2001; Jansson 2006; Urry 1992). I will consider specifically the roles of imagination and embodiment in tourists' experience of *Body Worlds*.

In considering *Body Worlds* as a tourist experience, I posit the importance of several hallmarks of tourism. These include: an emphasis on vision; the physical co-presence of the tourist and the toured; a sense of expectation, exploration, and of the non-ordinary; and the notion of tourism as a temporary time apart from, yet intimately connected to, our daily lives. Our encounter and the meanings we make of it are shaped in part by our connection of a novel experience with our anticipation of it. This anticipation is based on pre-encounter images, public discourse, and life-experiences which form the basis for our anticipation. For *Body Worlds*, these frames include previous museum-going experience, real-life encounters with dead bodies, and mediated representations of forensic anatomy. In addition, the issue of 'authenticity' will loom large as part of the extraordinary appeal of the *Body Worlds* exhibit, as comments from tourists themselves will reveal.

I argue that the von Hagens' exhibit positions viewers as 'tourists of themselves', touring the dead which are presented in such a way as to universalize (i.e., de-historicize, de-racialize, de-sexualize and de-culturalize) dead human bodies as examples of our own living. This universalizing discourse – accomplished through the removal of the skin to reveal muscles and organs beneath – is a key to the exhibit's ability to travel widely and to draw huge audiences in so many countries. While culturally specific attitudes towards the body and towards the dead have, of course, a huge impact on how the exhibit might be perceived, for those tens of millions who choose to attend, the exhibit's message is clear: 'we are all the same under the skin'. Staring at the dead implicitly makes us confront the facticity of our own bodies and our own inevitable deaths.

Although the exhibit proffers scientific anatomical knowledge in the service of promoting a change of habits towards more 'healthy living', the key element in the power of the exhibit lies in the act of imagination which the exhibit triggers. Through looking at the dead, individuals are able to imagine the interiority of themselves, and to experience themselves as similar to the dead on display and to each other person sharing the tourist experience. Simultaneously, they can experience the coexisting sense of uniqueness or difference from each other person in the room, dead or alive, due to their singular subjectivity – 'themselves' – yoked to the quasi generic body. I argue that this combination of expectations exceeded, embodied experience, activated imagination, and unanticipated emotional response is a formula for transformative tourist experiences.

What is Plastination?

Before I describe the exhibit, I must summarize the technical process that makes it all possible: plastination. Developed by Gunther von Hagens, and embraced by medical schools as a teaching tool, plastination replaces bodily fluids (which comprise roughly 65 per cent of human body weight) with acetone. This is accomplished through diffusion via a forced vacuum impregnation of tissues at the cellular level in a pressure chamber. Human liquids are forced out and plastic is forced into the cells. Putrefaction ceases and the muscles become pliable before they harden for good.

This silicone infused body must then be brought into the pre-designed pose and, using fine needles and pieces of styrofoam, the dissector positions each organ, tendon and muscle for maximum visual access before the specimen hardens into its final shape. Muscles fan out from the bone, a brain emerges from its skull, a cavity in the torso swings open like a drawer to reveal its packed contents inside. This is a highly technical form of handicraft with each whole body specimen requiring up to one thousand five hundred hours to prepare, usually over eight to twelve months. The average cost is $35,000–$45,000 (U.S.) per body. Because the body fluids that cause decomposition are removed, von Hagens estimates that specimens could last a hundred years.

The exhibit consists both of body parts and twenty-five full body specimens. The visitor encounters the body parts first – organs, a skeleton, cross-sections of a lung – then (in the 2002 London version of the show) up a set of stairs to a second larger room where full body plastinates are presented. Each is directly exposed to the viewer: no plastic casement intervenes. Text is minimal, just the title of each piece: The Runner, The Chess Player, The Pole Vaulter, and so on, with bodies positioned accordingly and with occasional props like a chair, table or chessboard. Another section features more body parts showing the difference between cancerous and healthy tissue, a smoker's lung and a non-smoker's. The wall is decorated with blow-ups of Renaissance and medieval anatomical prints, quotes from philosophers like Kant and Goethe, and illustrations of dissections, all anchoring the present exhibit in the past and accruing the legitimacy that such an invocation of art, anatomy, and the search for knowledge can afford.

The final section, in another room so parents can divert their children if necessary, contains exhibits of fetuses at different months of development, and one of only two female bodies on display. It is the full body of a reclining pregnant woman, her torso split open from chest to belly revealing her unborn seven-month-old fetus.

One of the most interesting aspects of this exhibit is not the broader sense of a taboo being broken, but that of the ontological status of the 'exhibits' themselves. In the majority of cases the skin, all that is left in taxidermy, is totally missing. Along with it go markers of skin colour (and the potential for racialized interpretation by a lay audience). These bodies, their faces stripped away, are literally genericized at the same time they are explicitly unique (a real body, a real person who chose to donate her/his body, no mixing of body parts from one person to another to make a third, for example).

The plastination process itself also literally strips away distinctiveness by stripping away fleshiness, not just skin, but fat and soft tissue. No bulging paunches or sagging chins, wrinkled necks, or saddlebag hips here. Age becomes relatively indeterminate. The bodies are lean, muscular, although some are more muscular than others, clean, and nearly machine-like in their demonstration of the efficiency of the body's design – all that is necessary and nothing that is not.

The Social Context for Viewing Dead Bodies

The idea of tourism usually implies going somewhere to look at or more broadly experience something, someone, or some place. But in this chapter, I want to turn that definition around, considering the idea of tourism as applicable to blockbuster exhibitions that come to us. Our engagement with this possibility is still up to us, however, and requires planning, purchasing the right to look, travel, and preparation. *Body Worlds* was not an exhibition that one simply dropped in on, seeking a few hours of museum recreation. It was regarded and promoted as special and unique. Most people purchased tickets in advance, online. Tickets were sold for specific entry times, highlighting the achievement of access. For many viewers that I surveyed, a trip to see this exhibition thus entailed the building of anticipation through planning, discussing comments made by friends who had seen it, or the reading of reviews or website information. Several people I interviewed, for example, said they had 'heard it was great', or 'unique', or 'not to be missed', and that this influenced their desire to see the show. Counting the prices of the tickets (approximately $25 (U.S.) for adults and $16 for children over the age of two), food, transportation, and sometimes overnight accommodation, the preparations added up to a level of commitment to seeking the experience that cannot be ignored.[2] Many viewers travelled from far outside of the immediate exhibition area to see the show.[3] The tourists were bargaining that their commitment in time, money and energy would be paid off by seeing something 'great'. As I shall argue, most got more than they bargained for.

But to understand why they committed to see an exhibition of corpses, we must consider the wider context of their participation. In this case, I suggest that three elements are key: the general prohibitions in the United States against seeing the dead, the publicity of the show, and the two dimensional representations of real and fake bodily interiors available in best-selling mysteries and our most popular television shows.

Generalizing about looking at the dead is full of pitfalls because cultural conventions for and against seeing dead humans vary widely across time and space. It is safe to say, however, that purposeful looking at the bodies of the dead is tightly controlled socially, except perhaps in times of natural disaster or war when death occurs widely in the midst of chaos and strictures and rituals for seeing the dead may be widely disrupted. To anchor my discussion, I will address this issue from the position of one living in the contemporary United States, while acknowledging that to grasp fully the implications, motivations and meanings generated by millions of visitors to *Body Worlds* in many different countries across the globe, we must generalize with caution.

Although religious, familial, cultural, and community-based protocols for seeing the dead (which dead, under what circumstances, for what purposes) vary significantly within the contemporary U.S., it is reasonable to assert that in the course of our everyday lives, excluding participation in war, or work in the medical or police fields, few of us encounter the dead bodies of strangers. In fact, the only dead bodies we see regularly are those of animals. We zip past 'roadkill' on the highway, we dine in a restaurant under the taxidermied remnants of a moose head, and we stroll the aisles of the grocery store, past rows of animal remains packaged as tightly wrapped hamburger, or bags of the detached thighs of chickens, ready for that evening's meal around the dinner table. Human bodies are in another category.[4]

Dead Relatives/Funerals/Cemeteries

For most of us, our only encounters with the dead are likely to be at funerals of family or friends. While religious conventions differ, there is a formal intimacy in these ritualized encounters. When the memorial service is followed by interment, the body is shielded from view while being fully present, whether in the form of a full body or the ashes that remain after cremation. Cemeteries, as sites of ritualized encounter with the dead, usually provide three assurances – first that the dead are present in some physical form; second, that we will never have to see the physical remains; and third, that death can be compartmentalized from daily life, and the dead from the living, as the physical cemetery site is set off from other parts of civic and domestic space. These guarantees facilitate, and are crucial to, the mourning process – at least under the conditions considered here – in most communities in the contemporary U.S. and Western Europe.

It is possible to imagine other alternatives. Coffins could easily be sealed with heavy glass and mounted above ground in concrete cradles, enabling the viewer to witness, over time, the decomposition of the body. Something akin to this exists in some parts of Europe, for example, where the religious make pilgrimages to churches containing bodies of saints and reverently kiss the glass covering the shrouded body. But even in those cases, the dead are not anonymous, rather they are the opposite – famous and widely known among those in the community who visit them.

Most cemeteries facilitate the act of mourning and, in most of these situations, at least nominally, the viewers of the body are presumed to be united in grieving the loss of the dead. How very different then is the tourists' experience at *Body Worlds*:

- rather than shying away from or being protected from physical proximity to the dead body, tourists seek it out.
- rather than mourning, we are peering, celebrating, discussing and even self-educating.
- rather than having a familiarity with the dead, as at a funeral service, these dead are strangers to us, and most importantly, anonymous. Emotional distance acts to insulate the viewer from emotional connection with a specific cadaver.
- children are welcome and encouraged to view the bodies, even if some parts of the display (like reproduction) are presented as potentially troubling for them. At open-casket funerals, some parents may shield children from actually seeing or touching the dead body in the coffin, fearing emotional trauma.
- we pay for the privilege of seeing these dead.
- we experience the presence of the dead in the company of strangers, not the relatives or friends of the dead.
- the dead are not mass media fictions based on special effects but 'real', and they are not shielded from our view but rather are presented boldly, without a visual or physical barrier between them and ourselves. While touch is prohibited, it is not impossible.

The *Body Worlds* exhibits contravene all of the usual conventions for viewing dead bodies. They bring the dead to us for sustained viewing. Also, because of the limited duration of the events, we become part of a large but still limited cohort who has attended, partaken in, a specific and unique experience. This uniqueness is certainly a prime part of the attraction for those tourists deciding to visit *Body Worlds*.

Preparing Us to Look at the Dead:
Tourists' Experiences with Bodily Interiors

The uniqueness of the event is promoted by the organizers and presenters using words like 'unforgettable' and 'original'.[5] But not all original or unforgettable experiences are seen as desirable, especially so when dealing with the potentially anxiety-producing or even repulsive topic of human corpses. This type of promotion would have been much less effective, I suggest, if there were not other mass-mediated daily life contexts (in the U.S. at least) which have prepared the public to desire this type of experience: for example, the rapidly developing trend in murder mysteries and television shows which feature detailed encounters with the interiors of bodies through the function of the forensic scientist or the medical examiner.

While several scholars have effectively engaged with the von Hagens displays in terms of the history of anatomical displays, and some, like van Dijck (2005), have referenced the contemporary visual medical imaging techniques like MRIs of the inside of the body that form the current parallel to those earlier representations, I think that the current framework of mass-mediated visuals of death and of the interiors of bodies plays a larger role in establishing a context for non-squeamish viewing.

While most high school graduates in the United States will have seen something of an anatomical atlas in biology class, it is the televised forensics shows that continually expose so many of us now to the insides of the dead body, and proclaim that those insides are both meaningful after death and able to communicate a truth (through the medical examiner to the public prosecutor in a trial, for example). One publicity tagline for NBC's medical examiner drama *Crossing Jordan* assured us that 'The answers are always in the body.'

The immediate precedent of these shows in mass-mediated forms may be the explosive 1990s popularity of forensics mystery novels like the best-selling Kay Scarpetta novels by Patricia Cornwell, or the Kathy Reich novels featuring the lead character forensic anthropologist Temperance Brennan (Anderson 2002). The maxim 'the body doesn't lie' to science seems to ground the narratives of these novels as well as the recent television shows like *CSI* (Crime Scene Investigation) and its spin offs *CSI: Miami* and *CSI: New York*. The original *CSI* premiered in 2000, hitting the 'Top 10' spot in number of viewers, and since then through to 2008 (latest available figures) it has inhabited rankings 1–5 in U.S. Network shows ratings, indicating the sustained popularity of its formula. In the summer of 2004, *CSI* was the most-watched network programme in the United States. Viewership has averaged more than twenty million per season during those years.[6]

Such fixations on corpses may not have directly built desires to see a show like *Body Worlds* which is, after all, not a forensic show detailing causes of death or the mysteries of police work. However, they do offer a sort of 'practice' for the viewer of looking at (mediated fictions of) dead bodies in – depending on one's point-of-view – exquisite or excruciating detail. They create a cultural space which legitimizes, even glamorizes, such looking. In these shows we are offered viewing positions of coolly interested scientific detachment twinned with unique personalities of characters playing these scientists. The detached scientific gaze is not, therefore, channelled through a detached personality-less functionary. It is generated through a subject position we may inhabit. Watching these shows may have lowered the threshold of what was once regarded as inconceivable to view, and has simultaneously provided a publicness to the practice of such viewing, one that we re-enact in some ways in our own tours of *Body Worlds*. The mass media thus prepares the public to respond to the promotions for the exhibits in a potentially positive way, and shapes both our anticipation of the exhibit and our parameters for behaviour at it.

The '*CSI* effect' – what Cavender and Deutch have termed a 'new forensic realism' – infects public perception to such an extent that criminologists are now researching whether it is affecting the standards of evidence that juries deem necessary for conviction (Cavender and Deutch 2007: 68). For our concerns, here, the key point is that such a widespread public encounter with forensic science, as presented through the specific mediation of television police narratives, inculcates the idea of physical evidence as incontrovertible 'truth'. Further corollaries imply that vision is the road to such 'truth' (whether human vision or the techno-scientific vision of spectrometers), and that physical matter is not subject to interpretation, but simply, in itself, yields a truth beyond intellectual or moral interpretation. Corinna Kruse stresses this point about the legitimating discourse of scientism and its corollary social detachment. On *CSI*, she argues, characters assert that 'forensic scientists should disregard social distinctions' in a discourse about science as 'objective and disinterested' (Kruse 2010: 83).

The *CSI*-effect works especially well in science museums which themselves frame their exhibits in the ideological claim of objectivity as the route to knowledge. Therefore, for U.S. audiences steeped in *CSI* television and encountering *Body Worlds* in a science museum, the *CSI*-effect may be especially strong. To 'see' is to 'know'. In addition, the impulse to subtract social context in the service of an alleged scientific 'truth' perfectly matches the presentation ethos of *Body Worlds* which I will discuss in further detail later. The anonymity of the individual cadavers, and the erasure of markers of race/ethnicity/nationality/age and so on, helps activate the medico-scientific gaze and positions viewers as legitimate investigators, as *CSI* observers, not voyeurs or mourners. (However, as I will explore in my Conclusion, the differences between the live experiences of the embodied tourist walking through a room full of cadavers and the more passive encounter of the television viewer watching *CSI* is crucial to the exhibit's generation of affective response.)

While forensics shows may have made it 'cool' to look inside a body – indeed, so 'cool' that some high schools now even offer forensics classes[7] – the *Body*

Worlds exhibition lets us do so without the sticky mess of a real autopsy or the stink of a cadaver. In that way, we re-experience the sanitized experience of the television show where the image may be gruesome, but the television set emits no stink of seeping fluids, and the bodies are more often than not displayed on pristine stainless steel tables in spotless, non-contaminating environments. Just as in watching television, viewing these *Body World* corpses poses no danger of contamination, putrefaction or decay. We and they are in a sanitized, germ-free, safe co-habitory relationship in the exhibit.

This removal of the 'physical, messy death of living tissue' is, for scholar Petra Kuppers, a hallmark of a loss of a vital relationship between the exhibit and its viewers, and one that is promoted by the exhibitors and their 'desire not to make an affective display but to make a scientific, systematic statement about humanity' (2004: 137). The scientific gaze exposes muscles, not personal histories of lived events or medical histories (except for the diseased lung, etc.). Race, class, family background, name, exact cause and time of death, she notes, are all erased by the medical gaze. Our gaze, although practised through our television spectatorial positions in looking at the insides of dead bodies, is at the exhibit 'medicalized' but not precisely forensic in that we are not haunted by the sense of violence that attends forensic shows. In fact, the violence towards the body, the stripping of skin and the cutting away of extraneous fascia and fat that are precursors to the plastination process, is not invoked here. Instead it is masked.

I have argued elsewhere that this anti-taxidermic approach (no skin, instead of skin-only) is a crucial component to the acceptability of this display. But exactly how does this excising of history function in terms of viewers' experiences? We know that in terms of a structuring of the signifier, it references the medical gaze, and hence 'impartiality' and 'objectivity'. Yet the very structure of the exhibit (bodies like our own ... all alike under the skin) simultaneously undermines this and allows for the co-existence of multiple perceptions and affective experiences by the 'tourists' to the exhibition.

Destination Image

In addition to the frameworks for approaching dead bodies that I have mentioned above (funerals, *CSI* television programmes), the visitor, like a tourist elsewhere, comes to the exhibit with a 'destination image' in mind. This complex of associations tied to a particular site is a melding of images, ideas and values drawn from popular discourse, personal experience, and the explicitly manufactured advertising for a destination. In the case of a tourist destination like Hawai'i for example, a visitor from the continental United States might associate the islands with images of a 'tropical paradise', warm breezes, sun, sex and sand, and the so called 'exoticism' of Native Hawaiian culture developed from depictions of Hawai'i by outsiders in books, magazines and films over the last century.

If we think about the 'destination image' for the *Body Worlds* show in the United States, we must consider the importance of the venues as well as the popular press reports and the specific advertising mounted for the shows. In the United States, *Body Worlds* has been hosted exclusively by major science museums. This is a particular 'Americanization' strategy as noted by Linda Schulte-Sasse (2006). In previous incarnations, the exhibit had hovered more consciously between 'art' and 'science'. In London, where I first saw the show in 2002, the exhibit was housed in an old brewery, the Atlantis Gallery. This old warehouse, stripped to its now hip bare brick walls, painted white, and enhanced with strategically placed potted plants, had the look of a downtown art gallery. Moreover, earlier exhibits had been shown in 'in between' public spaces, not art galleries per se, and not science museums, but public exposition spaces like Mannheim's Museum of Technology and Work (1997), a venue choice which, in the German context, did not prevent vociferous religious criticism and invocations of the Nazi past of experimenting on humans, including the alleged labelling by one writer of von Hagens as a modern day Joseph Mengele (Schulte-Sasse 2006: 371). Other venues similarly emphasized spectacle and included a former erotic art museum in Hamburg, Germany's red-light district, touted by press as the 'ultra-naked, uncensored' exhibit in a converted slaughterhouse and a meat market in Brussels (371). These locations certainly did not provide the legitimizing mantle of 'science' which has framed the discourse about the exhibition and viewer's expectations in the U.S.

Indeed, like Schulte-Sasse, after seeing the exhibit in London, I never thought it would be mounted in the U.S. because of the potential for religious objections of disrespect for the dead, but the publicity strategy in the U.S. has resulted in almost uniformly positive press.[8] Publicity strategies were different from in Europe where more sensationalistic approaches featuring pictures of 'aliens, Halloween posters and costume parties' drew the eye of the consumer. In the U.S. the educational value, not the visual spectacle, has been foregrounded in promoting the exhibits (Moore and Brown 2007: 234). That strategy is twofold: first, exhibiting only in highly respected 'science' museums, no art venues and no public exhibit halls and, secondly, the public vetting of the exhibit by specially appointed ethics advisory committees at several of these sites such as the opening venue in the U.S., the California Science Center in Los Angeles. These committees have assessed the exhibition as appropriate for their publics and have explicitly reviewed the provenance of the bodies, sustaining von Hagens' claim that all corpses are the result of informed consent, an emphasis on individual volition that carries a lot of weight in the U.S. context (Schulte-Sasse 2006: 370). Such assurances overcame rumours that some corpses had been obtained without consent from prisoners in China or mental patients in Russia.[9] All of these strategies tailored the exhibit to the U.S. public which has a strong, recent history of religious controversy over bodily/ethical issues such as abortion rights. This is a form of matching the promotion of the destination (exhibition) image to the expectations and desires of the potential tourists. In the U.S. context, this scientism provides permission to look but does not circumscribe the entire tourist experience as we will later see.

In the U.S. publicity, three things were promised: authenticity, uniqueness and moral/ethical safety. The press release for the American premiere of *Body Worlds* (from 2 July 2004 – 23 January 2005 at the California Science Center) calls the exhibition a:

> first-of-its-kind exhibit in which visitors learn about anatomy, physiology and health by viewing real human bodies, preserved through an extraordinary method called 'plastination' ... the use of authentic specimens gives vivid insight into anatomy ... that could not be possible with constructed models, photos or textbooks. (California Science Center Press Release 2005)

The display of real human remains is thus justified on the basis of public health education, and the uniqueness of the opportunity, along with the necessity for using real human corpses, is highlighted. Moral safety is guaranteed in the press release statement that 'The consensus of the [California Science Center's] Bio-Ethics Advisory Committee was that the exhibit has considerable educational value and is appropriate for the Science Center as long as the donation of all bodies for public education display is verified' (Rudolf, Perlov and Sass 2005: 1). The tourist is thus guaranteed a safe experience of a unique encounter, just as he or she might be when contemplating a cruise down the Amazon or a visit to Tahiti. The difference here is that 'education' is foregrounded as the primary pleasure from this encounter rather than sensual indulgence or exotica. However, I argue here that, given the contexts for encountering the dead that I have sketched out earlier in this chapter, few experiences are more 'exotic' to most consumers than an encounter with 'authentic' human remains in a public setting supplying the 'right to look'.

Once arriving at the exhibit, the tourist's expectations are further guided by the brochure handed out with the timed-entry tickets. For the 2007 *Body Worlds 2* Exhibit at the Museum of Science and Industry in Chicago (a different set of plastinates from that featured in the first *Body Worlds*), the brochure I was handed features a picture of the 'Ballerina' posed balancing on one foot (encased in a real toe shoe). Three highlighted words encapsulate the desired experience we are about to encounter: 'Original'. 'Authentic'. 'Inspiring'.

Responses from tourists indicate that they embrace this proposed framework, finding the exhibit not creepy, in bad taste, disgusting or frightening but solemn, inspiring and illuminating. Their experiences largely match the produced destination image, and at times exceed it, guaranteeing a positive tourist experience.[10] This experience in turn leads to positive word-of-mouth descriptions of the exhibit which result in raised visitor counts.

Embodying the Visitor: What is the Experience?

Beyond the bona fides provided by respected scientific public institutions, and beyond the positive word-of-mouth advertising and the exhibition framing manufactured by the presenters, what exactly did visitors experience as they went through the exhibition, and did it live up to their expectations? Let me consider this issue in light of recent developments in tourist studies emphasizing the importance of embodied experiences for tourists, along with reports on *Body Worlds* visitors' experiences. These latter have been obtained both by other scholars and through my own observations and surveys.

Recent work in tourism studies has urged a more substantial engagement with the embodied aspects of the tourist experience. In the last decade, especially in the U.K. context, several scholars have argued persuasively for the necessity of moving beyond our previous emphasis on the power of the tourist gaze(s), most powerfully laid out by John Urry (1992), to carefully consider other embodied aspects of the tourist experience. These have included not only an emphasis on a multi-sensorial body – taste, touch, smell and hearing – but also on the navigation of bodies across space and in relation to others, to topographies, and to buildings and objects of material culture. Technologies as they interface with this embodied practice, from hiking boots to audio-guides and multi-media shows, have also come in for scrutiny.[11] These approaches conceive of tourists as active, embodied agents.[12]

Among the theoretical influences in this discussion is 'performance studies', with its emphasis on the choreography of events, encounters and interactions in space, and more broadly a notion of performativity, that is, the ways that subjects enact life events.[13] Recent tourism scholarship has argued for an integration of these multiple approaches and for putting them in concert with previous theories that emphasized the visual construction of the destination image and the ways in which tourist infrastructures guided tourist activities and meaning-makings. And, finally, we can look more closely at the relationships among tourist experiences and those subjects' other life experiences, including how individuals create social identities and social meanings.

Ultimately, all of this work urges us to look closely at what tourists actually 'do': in space, in time, imaginatively, cognitively, affectively, and interpretively (Jansson 2006). It is what tourists do, the effects of those actions on places and populations, and what meanings the tourists make of what they do that are important here. For example, ecotourism adventures may overburden fragile ecosystems and at the same time the tourist zooming across the sand in a dune buggy may feel a sense of physical freedom, risk-taking, exhilaration, stimulating adrenalin, and empowerment that carries over into her or his life 'after tourism'.

In terms of touring the *Body Worlds* shows, the exhibitors, especially in the U.S., have carefully designed a path of travel through the exhibition that gradually immerses the visitor into the experience. The viewer first encounters a presumably more familiar 'real' artefact of the dead, a skeleton, not a plastinated person's remains. Then, segments of the exhibit unfold featuring body parts and body systems first, along with philosophical statements and images of the history of anatomy. The perhaps surprising lack of smell is important and reassuring. One of my informants specifically mentioned this, stating that it was different from his expectations which included the possibility that the bodies might smell bad. Once the visitor reaches the full body plastinate exhibits, he or she realizes that these corpses give off none of the formaldehyde smell that permeates embalming or human anatomy dissection rooms. Oddly, the dead bodies seem to radiate health – a sort of blood flushed sense of life as opposed to the grey, pallid, inertness of the medical school cadaver, or the burnt husk of a *CSI* shot of remains. A hushed atmosphere, guards, and the inculcation of awe help generate a nearly reverent medical gaze.[14]

In my observations of crowds in London in 2002, and in Chicago in 2007, I saw the following: a constant flow of hushed discussion among groups of family or friends as they pointed and stared at specific exhibits – some even commented to strangers who were investigating the same plastinate; a referential pointing at one's own body to find or explain correspondences with what they were seeing; a genuine attentiveness, not a glancing tour around the exhibit, but rather a sense of seeing and thinking about what is being seen – the exhibits are spread out in such a way as to allow this, and people often stopped for a long time in front of

'The Runner', a human plastinate by Gunther von Hagens included in the 2004–2005 *Body Worlds* show in Los Angeles. (Source: Photo copyright © Gunther von Hagens, Institute for Plastination, Heidelberg, Germany [http://www.bodyworlds.com].)

each plastinate, peering closely. Beyond these soft-spoken conversations, there was a sense of hushed quiet which even included the children. I became aware in that space not only of my own body but of everyone else's similarly constructed bodies around me. Perhaps they did too? A visitor's arm reaching forward, for example, became visible to me as the rotation of a ball-and-socket joint and the contraction of the upper arm muscles. This specificity of the experience was never mentioned in any of the promotional material I encountered, but emerged instead as an unexpected and enriching part of the experience of the exhibit through the act of participating physically in it. In fact, this emergent embodied knowledge breaches the act of visual perception – looking 'at' the exhibition – and transforms it into a kinaesthetic one through the understanding of the body's interiority and capacity for motion that the exhibit facilitates.

Examples of discussions I overheard are telling:

- 'I'll tell you where I get very sore – it's these three tendons [points to top of a plastinate's arch] here,' says a middle-aged man to his female companion.
- A mother carefully explains to her two inquiring sons, aged between about seven and ten years, which of the foetuses, at various stages of development, might have lived outside the womb and which could not.
- 'Look at those lungs; it's just disgusting!' states a twenty-year-old woman to her two peers as they look at the dissected lung of a smoker.
- Grabbing his child's leg and squeezing it, a parent says: 'This is your femur, and this is your hip' (pokes the child's hip), making the correspondence between the living and dead bodies clear and using the exhibit as an educational tool.
- A couple of twenty-year-olds, male and female, search for the unlabelled anterior cruciate ligament on one of the plastinates while discussing a friend's knee operation. They are applying what they see to their own life experience.
- Two teenage girls, about sixteen, discuss the plastinates saying: 'I don't think those are real eyes.' 'Yes, they are.' 'No, they'd be dripping with eye juice if they were!' These teens are assessing the degree of 'realness' of the exhibit and implicitly noting its potential limits. As such, they enact what Maxine Feifer and others have called 'post-tourist' behaviour, a postmodern sense of ironic positioning that navigates a knowing encounter with structures of inauthentic authenticities (Feifer 1985).
- Three teenage males of African descent look at the 'Muscleman' plastinate and comment: 'That one's Chinese! Look at his eyes.' This type of commentary or speculation on the ethnic origin of the plastinates was extremely rare.
- A four-year-old girl, looking at the foetuses at various stages of development in the reproduction section asks, 'Is that a *real* baby?' Even small children were fascinated, not frightened or repulsed, and struggled to grasp the degree of 'realness' of the exhibition.[15]

I argue then, that, in effect, we are touring ourselves through the distanciation and production of otherness that death brings. We enter a realm of the exotic – publicly scrutinizable dead human bodies – a 'cultural' nexus unique in this mode of display in which we can calculate our own similarity and difference to those people, bodies and body parts on display, thus gaining further knowledge about ourselves and those around us at the exhibit. But, the presumed distanciation of the medical gaze here boomerangs back to the viewer because in effect we are not viewing an 'other' with pathologies but are seeing a rendition of ourselves.

As these overheard discussions reveal, viewers are activating their powers of imagination to transfer an understanding of the heretofore unviewable interior of 'the' human body to a mental map of their own specific self-experienced body. I believe this imaginative act of translation and understanding is a key part of the awe inspired. It is not just that we are in the meta-living display of the animated dead but, rather, that what they signify is less themselves, as individual dead beings, than our interior physical selves, that which we can never see while living. We only see the interior of our bodies through the mediation of CAT scan representations or X-rays, or when gravely injured we might see a bone poking though our own bleeding flesh, never in three dimensional forms. This makes the experience a unique one for each visitor, and yields an emotional, not just cognitive, response.

One of my informants, a 37-year-old male writing anonymously in answer to my survey, put it eloquently:

> Seeing *human* bodies created the emotionally troubling experience of having to be both the subject and object at once. You're looking at a thing, but you are also looking at yourself. ... In time, you too will be dead and could conceivably be on display just like the person in front of you. It is a somewhat unbalancing and thought-provoking experience.

Thus, unlike most tourist experiences where we seek out contact with difference, here we encounter sameness. And where we might elsewhere tour the past, through visiting its historical remnants or reproductions, here we are actually looking at our own inescapable futures, as we too will all be dead someday.

Sociologist Tony Walter (2004) examined seven hundred comments from the London exhibition comment books and an additional one thousand five hundred English language web comments from Summer 2002. Based on his analysis, he argues that unlike the distancing clinical detachment that anatomy students must produce to separate themselves from the life of the dead person whose body they are dissecting, *Body Worlds* visitors can exhibit a scientific gaze but imbue it with emotion, especially awe. 'I AM AMAZING AFTER ALL' in exuberant capital letters writes one of the viewers of the London exhibition that Walter quotes. And even for the majority that do not record awe, most, he says, experience a milder form of wonder – 'fascination' (479–80). For some, this awe is directed at the idea of a God who could create these bodies, while others find a more secular sense of amazement at the complexity of the human body. For example, Moore and Brown (2007), after examining over two thousand five hundred comments from comment books for the exhibitions in London, Toronto, Singapore, Cleveland,

Houston and Denver, offer two contrasting quotes: 'It is hard to imagine anyone not believing in God after seeing this' (Denver); and, 'This is an awesome display of the power of natural selection' (Houston).

As this pairing of quotes makes clear and, as Moore and Brown argue, the exhibition itself serves as a microcosm for debating many of the urgent ethical issues of the day. Some took the exhibition as proof of 'Intelligent Design', others as an example of evolution. Some visitors wondered at the relation of the body to a 'soul', while others noted that there were too many penises and not enough clitorises. Or, that the exhibit merely repeated gender stereotypes with active sports-oriented males and 'pretty' ballerina females or pregnant women. The male seemed normative and the female reduced to representing beauty or reproductive specificity. This perception of the exhibition as palimpsest of current issues is not surprising if, as I argue, the viewers tour the exhibit as a tour of themselves. Despite all the efforts to strip away the social histories of each anonymous donor, the social reality comes into the exhibition with the first foot set in by a viewer.

I conducted extended surveys/interviews with several members of the Champaign-Urbana community who had travelled to the Chicago Museum of Science and Industry to see the exhibition sometime during its 2007 run. In their comments, I found support for some of the previous assertions and was able to uncover further issues as well. While these surveys are not randomized, and I make no claim that they are representative, they offer the opportunity to uncover additional issues due to specific questions not covered by other surveys or by scanning comment books.

Most of my respondents, all of whom had at least some college education, reported that they made a special trip (a two-and-a-half-hour drive to Chicago) solely to see the exhibition, and some incurred the additional cost of staying overnight.[16] Although some noted the gendered stereotypes identified above, some had not thought about it actively while viewing the exhibition, and some felt that, on the whole, this was not inappropriate given the predominance of those stereotypes in our world outside of the exhibit. For almost all, the 'realness' and 'authenticity' were very important in their decision to attend the exhibition. Only one couple said they would have been as interested if the exhibits were just models of plastic or if the exhibited plastinates were all of animals and not humans. One 35-year-old Euro-American woman in the education field put it this way: 'We've all seen the pictures and life-size models of the human body, but having this *be actual people, whose bodies looked like mine or my family's*, made a big difference for me' (emphasis added). In all cases the event met their expectations for uniqueness and in some cases exceeded it, resulting in a pleasurable tourist experience. They all thought it was worth the expenditure in time, money and effort. As one middle-aged woman respondent stated: 'It was even more incredible than I thought it would be.'

This notion of the experience exceeding the tourist's expectations ran through the responses of my informants. One middle-aged woman attending with her chiropractor husband said: 'the detail and the precision [of the plastinates] defies words'. Another woman in her thirties wrote: 'it was beyond my expectations. I figured I'd see posed bodies, but some of the detailed dissections were amazing'. Another respondent said: 'It was sort of what I expected, but on a much grander scale. I never expected full bodies, posed!' And a 60-year-old summed up the experience this way, focusing on the emotional effect: 'The experience was much deeper than I had anticipated. I had the sense that other visitors there had a similar feeling given the tone [they] exhibited while viewing the exhibits.'

The superlatives are telling: 'defies words', 'amazing', 'grand scale', a 'deep experience'. The experience seems to go beyond enchantment and fascination to a more powerful feeling of connecting oneself to others in a most profound way. The promotion of the educational and scientific value of the exhibition drew people to it, and guaranteed their sense of safety in approaching a unique, even taboo, experience of seeing the dead. But, ultimately, the scientism of the display was exceeded by the emotional connections people made during their physical inhabitation of the exhibition space, and their travel through it. Through their encounter with the exhibition they not only learned about human anatomy but also experienced themselves as part of a larger connectivity and process. This combination of knowledge-sought spectacle, activation of the imagination, and emotional impact yielded a transformative, even transcendent, tourist experience that was not only pleasurable but highly memorable. My informants were eager to write about their experiences, to 'process' the complexity of their responses by sharing them with an interested stranger, even months after their visit to the exhibition.

The anonymity of the donors and the protection of that anonymity through how they were physically displayed was crucial in facilitating this sense of connectivity, an issue I tried to probe in my survey of attendees. As extensive as some other scholars' surveys were, they did not ask what I think is a key question about the limits of the acceptable. In my survey, I asked people to imagine the exhibit differently – namely, how they would feel if the donors were pictured in a photograph or identified by age, occupation, life history, race or ethnicity. Most did not want to know, saying it would detract from the anatomy, or that they would only want to know those facts (like cause of death) that might have shaped what we saw in the body on display or the reasons why the person chose to donate her/his body.

The 'universalizing' function of the anonymity, not just a lack of name but a lack of life story, was a key element enabling the imagination of the other as self which I am positing as one of the main interpretive acts by visitors. I suggest that this anonymity simultaneously activates the *CSI*-effect of detached 'scientific' looking in a room full of corpses, and facilitates the imaginative act of identification between the viewer and the dead. As one 45-year-old male high school graduate working in the public safety field put it, the lack of information 'puts the plastinates on a level playing field'.

I also asked visitors to imagine the limits of the acceptable. Von Hagens has created posed plastinates that run, play chess, dance ballet, practise yoga, ice skate with a partner, bounce a basketball and pole-vault through the sky. Sports and leisure dominate these images, yet they hardly exhaust the repertoire of ways in which humans use their bodies or activate their muscles. When asked specifically about the limits of representation of sex and violence, almost all my respondents stated they did not want to see violence, and only a few said that demonstrating sex would be acceptable (penile penetration in heterosexual sex was suggested by one as something illuminating to understand), and then only if framed from an anatomical point of view (i.e., what happens and how).[17]

It is possible to rethink the role of the exhibition as one to prevent violence, perhaps, by demonstrating the effect on muscles and organs of a gunshot wound or knife injury. But these options clearly pulled too far away from the 'neutral' to be imagined as appropriate representations of anatomical bodies in action. We can imagine also that scenarios, like those depicted in museum dioramas, could possibly be showing a group of people in a social relationship engaged in shared activities. To repeat gender stereotypes, this could, for example, show a woman cooking dinner, a man reading a newspaper on a couch, a boy playing with a dog, and a girl playing with a doll in the living room of their home. This type of Norman Rockwell scene, while offensive to some for its 1950s idealization of gender roles, would also be offensive to others because it stays too close to daily life – it brings the social into the scientific and creates social relationships whereas almost all of the plastinates are posed alone and in solitary actions.[18]

Similarly, the display of plastinated children, while regarded by my respondents as possibly educational, was too emotionally unsettling for most, even knowing that the parents or guardians would have to have given permission. Here, too, the scientific gaze and its potential pleasures would be interrupted by the eruption of social acknowledgement of sadness at the early death of a child.

Conclusions

As my extended surveys reveal, most visitors made a special trip to see this exhibition, regarded it as important and educational, approached it with positive anticipation and fascination, and saw in it a reflection of their own social beliefs about religion, abortion rights and gender stereotypes. Most regarded the display as a way of understanding themselves and their loved ones (the achy rotator cuff, the operation on the spine), and felt that the fact that the bodies were 'real' was crucial to the appeal and power of the exhibit. In this sense, the promised 'authenticity' of the tourist experience was paramount both to the tourists' anticipation of the destination and to their on-site response to the exhibit. That the realness lay in the raw material was all that mattered. For some, their favourite figures, like the 'exploded figures' with a brain popping out of a skull, or a section of entrails held out to the side to reveal the pelvic cavity, were no less 'real' than whole body plastinates with greater muscular integration.

Touring ourselves 'beneath the skin' where all social categories of difference seem to fall away – except the sexual difference of reproduction – was seen as a unique opportunity worth paying for, travelling for, anticipating, researching, planning and discussing as a touristic opportunity. Parents, especially, prepared for the trip and used web resources to prepare their children in the same way one might read a travel guidebook prior to touring a foreign country (California Science Center Family Visitors Report 2004–2005).

The attentive or contemplative looking of the 'tourist gaze' is rearticulated here as a medical/scientific gaze, but one that is experienced through physical proximity to 'real' models or copies of ourselves experienced with a public enveloped in an atmosphere of fascination and a privileged 'right to look', elsewhere unavailable. Our physical co-presence with these re-animated remains of once living individuals is the most profound experience of this visit, this touring of the dead where we come to see ourselves alive, and experience our own bodies kinaesthetically while simultaneously confronting our own inescapable mortality.

By approaching the *Body Worlds* exhibition phenomenon as an embodied tourist experience, we can see the importance of the choreography of experience, encounters in space, the cohabitation of a cohort sharing that experience (the 'visitors'), and the act of imagination that is the hallmark of interpretation. In addition, this analysis suggests that we can fruitfully conceive of tourist practices as a continuum of encounters, activities and interpretations that are anticipated as unique and that call forth a special type of attentiveness attuned to the new or unknown.

Our preparation for these experiences consists not only of special reading or planning, but also in the experiences of 'knowing' proffered in everyday life and underwritten by powerful ideologies of knowledge. In this case, the *CSI*-effect and its media-driven presentation of forensic looking as valorized access to truth is a powerful contributor to our expectations. But it is the 'liveness' of the exhibition, here ironically only possible due to death, that contrasts with our previous media experience, elicits an active not passive viewing response, and generates emotions. It calls us into the role of active tourist ready to seek out a unique experience. Opportunities for these experiences may travel to us or we may travel to them, resulting in anticipation and, ultimately, a choice to engage them. In these cases, our physical co-presence with something or someone regarded as 'other' (people, places, artefacts) is key, so that all of our bodily senses, along with cognitive and emotional work, yield interpretive, experiential, even transformative, pleasures.

My analysis of *Body Worlds* suggests that this union of anticipation with a resulting embodied experience that exceeds our expectations in its capacity to activate our imaginations and affective responses marks out touristic experiences that are so memorable that we need to process them cognitively and emotionally after they are over. This lingering effect marks these experiences as potentially transformative, and provides urgency to our investigations of the linkages between anticipation, embodiment and affect in the realm of tourism research.

Notes

1. The only article to mention it in a tourist studies discussion places it in the category of a continuum of 'dark tourism', but does not investigate the phenomenon of the exhibit in detail. See Stone (2006). I would argue that *Body Worlds* is not an example of 'dark tourism' or the tourism of sites associated with death, because it is fundamentally about life, not about the death of the individuals on display.

2. Discounted group rates were offered for student groups, and teachers' materials were also provided to prepare the students, so that cost was not necessarily a deterrent for the non-adult population.

3. For example, a report on the visitors to the show at the California Science Museum shows that visitorship from counties surrounding Los Angeles increased significantly for the *Body Worlds* show, while local attendance among families in the L.A. county proportionately decreased as a part of the total. From 'Body Worlds' Family Visitors: A Demographic Study of the North American debut of Body Worlds: The Anatomical Exhibition of Real Human Bodies', *California Science Center*. Retrieved 3 May 2009 from http://www.bodyworlds.com/Downloads/Family%20Visitors.pdf

4. Obviously vegetarians, vegans, some pet-lovers, and some animal welfare activists experience this daily oblivion to, and sanctioned display of, animal death dramatically differently than I have described it here, but they remain in the minority.

5. Words taken from publicity brochures handed out at the Chicago Museum of Science and Industry *Body Worlds* exhibit, Spring 2007 (anon).

6. For details on viewership ratings, see Wikipedia's article at http://en.wikipedia.org/wiki/Crime_Scene_Investigation. Retrieved on 6 June 2009.

7. For one example, Berrios (2006). See also Hinchcliffe (2006), about Tammy Chance, who teaches a forensics class at Jordan High School in Durham, NC.

8. For an example of press that was not positive, see Susser (2007). See also Arts and Faith Discussion List in 2004–2005 at http://artsandfaith.com/index.php?showtopic=2979, which features an extended thread devoted to positions pro and con on the *Body Worlds* exhibits.

9. See Leiboff (2005) for an interesting consideration of the legal status of remains, the issue of consent, and the possibility of an artist 'owning' them.

10. For an example of this, see Chon (1990).

11. Crouch, Aronsson and Wahlstrom (2001).

12. Perkins and Thorns (2001).

13. Crouch and Desforges (2003).

14. See Walter (2004).

15. This is based not only on my own observations, but also on the report on family attendees and their expectations at the California Science Center exhibit.

16. This level of education and the social class it may imply among visitors is not necessarily normative, especially given that urban schools made fieldtrips to the exhibits, including to the Chicago venue I visited, and educational materials for schools were available online. Public school attendees presumably represent a wider range of social class background and associated financial assets. For a discussion of the youth demographic attending the *Body Worlds* exhibits in the U.S., see the study 'Body Worlds' Family Visitors: A Demographic Study of the North American debut of Body Worlds: The Anatomical Exhibition of Real Human Bodies' (2004).

See Leiberich et al. (2006) for an additional article discussing the specific case of German visitors' perceptions, attitudes and emotions. (National and community histories play a crucial role in reception, and a comparative examination of responses in Germany, Singapore, Japan and the U.S. would potentially be illuminating.)

17. As I complete this piece, von Hagens has just put on display his first plastinate pose of heterosexual sex. As recent newspapers report, one of the two hundred pieces in his latest show, 'The Cycle of Life' which opened in Berlin on 7 May 2009, shows a male and female plastinate posed in a sexual act, with the male on his back and the female astride him. The donors of these bodies gave permission for their bodies to be displayed in a sexual way. Not surprisingly this piece is attracting a lot of controversy, including some calls for its removal from the show. See 'Controversial Doctor unveils Corpse Sex Exhibition', and 'Gunther von Hagens exhibition criticized over Corpse Sex Display'.

18. In addition, some grappled with this idea of identities re-created in the posing of the plastinates. Did the back bending 'Yoga Lady' actually practise yoga while alive?

References

Anderson, D. 2002. 'Physicians as Detectives in Detective Fiction of the 20th Century', *Southern Medical Journal* 95(10): 1134–40.

Anon. 2005. 'More Than 665,000 Visitors to Body Worlds'. *California Science Center.* Retrieved 4 May 2009 from http://www.californiasciencecenter.org/GenInfo/MediaRoom/PressReleases/BodyWorlds/BW2.php

Anon. 2009a. 'Arts and Faith Discussion List 2004–2005'. Retrieved 4 May 2009 from http://artsandfaith.com/index.php?showtopic=2979.

Anon. 2009b. 'Body Worlds' Family Visitors: A Demographic Study of the North American debut of Body Worlds: The Anatomical Exhibition of Real Human Bodies', *California Science Center.* Retrieved 3 May 2009 from http://www.bodyworlds.com/Downloads/Family%20Visitors.pdf.

Anon. 2009c. 'Controversial Doctor Unveils Corpse Sex Exhibition'. Retrieved 11 August 2009 from http://www.cnncom/2009/WORLD/europe/05/07germany.vonhagens.dead.bodies/index.html.

Anon. 2009d. 'Gunther von Hagens Exhibition Criticized over Corpse Sex Display'. Retrieved 11 August 2009 from: http://www.telegraph.co.uk/news/newst...ther-von-Hagens-exhibition-criticised-over-corpse-sex-display.html.

Berrios, J. 2006. 'Real CSI Drama: Class Finds Corpse', *The Miami Herald,* 6 June 2006. Retrieved 4 December 2006 from http://web.lexis-nexis.com/universe/printdoc.

Cavender, G. and S. Deutsch. 2007. 'CSI and Moral Authority: The Police and Science', *Crime Media Culture* 3(1): 67–81.

Chon, K.S. 1990. 'The Role of Destination Image in Tourism: A Review and Discussion', *Tourist Review* 45(2): 2–9.

Crouch, D., L. Aronsson and L. Wahlstrom. 2001. 'Tourist Encounters', *Tourist Studies* 1(3): 253–70.

Crouch, D. and L. Desforges. 2003. 'The Sensuous in the Tourist Encounter: Introduction: The Power of the Body in Tourist Studies', *Tourist Studies* 3(5): 5–22.

Desmond, J. 1999. *Staging Tourism: Bodies on Display from Waikiki to Sea World.* Chicago: University of Chicago Press.

Feifer, M. 1985. *Going Places: The Ways of the Tourist from Imperial Rome to the Present Day.* London: MacMillan Publishers.

Hinchcliffe, K. 2006. 'Jordan High: Students Step into the Shoes of Crime Solvers', *Durham Herald-Sun,* 15 November, C1.

Jansson, A. 2006. 'Book Review: The Media and the Tourist Imagination: Converging Cultures', *European Journal of Communication* 21(3): 247–50.

Kruse, C. 2010. 'Producing Absolute Truth: CSI Science as Wishful Thinking', *American Anthropologist* 112(1): 79–91.

Kuppers, P. 2004. 'Visions of Anatomy: Exhibitions and Dense Bodies', *Differences: A Journal of Feminist Cultural Studies* 15(3): 123–54.

Leiberich, P., et al. 2006. See Peter Leiberich, Thomas Loew, Karin Tritt, Claas Lahmann, and Marius Nickel, 'Body Worlds exhibition – Visitor Attitudes and Emotions', *Annals of Anatomy* 188(6): 567–73.

Leiboff, M. 2005. 'A Beautiful Corpse', *Continuum: Journal of Media and Cultural Studies* 19(2): 221–37.

Moore, C.M. and C.M. Brown. 2007. 'Experiencing Body Worlds: Voyeurism, Education, or Enlightenment?', *Journal of Medical Humanities* 28(4): 231–54.

Perkins, H.C. and D.C. Thorns. 2001. 'Gazing or Performing?: Reflections on Urry's Tourist Gaze in the Context of Contemporary Experience in the Antipodes', *International Sociology* 16(2): 185–204.

Rudolph, J.N., D. Perlov and H.M. Sass. 2005. 'Body Worlds: An Anatomical Exhibition of Real Human Bodies – Summary of Ethical Review, 2004/2005'. Retrieved 18 June 2009 from http://www.bodyworlds.com/Downloads/english/Media/Press%20Kit/BW_LA_SummaryofEthicalReview.pdf

Schulte-Sasse, L. 2006. 'Advise and Consent: On the Americanization of Body Worlds', *BioSocieties* 1(4): 369–84.

Stern, M. 2006. 'Dystopian Anxieties Versus Utopian Ideals: Medicine from Frankenstein to the Visible Human Project and Body Worlds', *Science as Culture* 15(1): 61–84.

Stone, P.R. 2006. 'A Dark Tourism Spectrum: Towards a Typology of Death and Macabre Related Tourist Sites, Attractions and Exhibitions', *Tourism* 54(2): 145–60.

Susser, D.S. 2007. 'Body Worlds Comes to Phoenix: Some Say Artfully Displayed Corpses Not Kosher', *Jewish News of Greater Phoenix*, 9 February, 59(21). Retrieved 29 March 2009 http://www.jewishaz.com/issues/printstory.mv?070209+body

Urry, J. 1992. 'The Tourist Gaze "Revisited"', *American Behavioral Scientist* 36(2): 172–86.

van Dijck, J. 2005. 'Bodyworlds: The Art of Plastinated Cadavers', *The Transparent Body: A Cultural Analysis of Medical Imaging*, Seattle: University of Washington Press, pp. 41–63.

Walter, T. 2004. 'Body Worlds: Clinical Detachment and Anatomical Awe', *Sociology of Health and Illness* 26(4): 464–88.

Chapter 11
AFTERWORD: THE TOUR AS IMAGINED, LIVED, EXPERIENCED AND TOLD

Edward M. Bruner

The thrust of this volume is on how the host community learns about tourist expectations and devises a performance that satisfies tourist desires. The guest–host relationship is one of unequal power, so that if the tourists are dissatisfied they can just walk away but the hosts have no alternative but to adapt if they want a share of the tourist dollars. Some host communities are embedded in the tourism industry and under the control of large-scale tourist agencies, as in Bali, while others are more local, indigenous enterprises.

Rather than comment on the individual papers, which would only duplicate what was done in the Introduction, I choose to reflect upon the relationship between expectations and experience. This is not only a key theme of the book and fundamental to tourism studies, but is also, I claim, at the heart of the ethnographic method, and extends to the practices of everyday life. Obviously, my exuberant statement requires an explanation. I begin with ethnography.

When an anthropologist studies another culture there is work to be done before the trip begins, such as reading the relevant literature, learning about the destination, formulating an initial conception of the culture of the people, and preparing a research proposal. The scholar probably has taken courses on the culture area and talked to other anthropologists about the project and the people. This information constitutes the pre-understandings, or expectations – what is in the mind of the scholar before the journey begins. In this globalized world there are no naïve anthropologists or tourists: everyone begins with expectations. Once on site the anthropologist settles in, gathers data by observation, participation, interviewing, and just 'hanging out'.

In the field there are invariably moments when a discrepancy emerges between the ethnographer's pre-understandings, and what s/he finds while engaged in the study. This is the tension between expectations and experience. The discrepancy may be very subtle, just a slight variation, when an informant says or does something unexpected, or not entirely clear, or it may be that a behaviour occurs that is completely baffling. The inexperienced ethnographer may pass this off, dismiss it, or explain it away. But to the best ethnographers the discrepancy presents a research opportunity to explore the difference between the expectation and the finding, because this is the only way to learn something new about the culture. If the researcher found in the field exactly what s/he had expected before the trip then nothing new would have been learned as a result of the research process. The end result may be that the anthropologist not only rethinks his/her own pre-understandings but writes about the contradiction and thereby revises the literature and makes a contribution to ethnographic scholarship. The same process occurs in linguistics as the meaning of a word is established by the context in which it is used. Especially when learning a new language, the hearing of a word used in a new way in a new context provides an opportunity to expand one's understanding of the meanings of that word.

It is similar in everyday life. Who among us has not formed an expectation of someone only to realize through interaction that the other person was not behaving as anticipated? A person previously defined as gentle unexpectedly behaves in cruel ways; a thesis advisor who had been solicitous suddenly becomes indifferent. In some instances this experience leads to a rapid realization that one's expectations need to be revised or abandoned. It may on the other hand take some time to work through the discrepancy, as one might stubbornly or unknowingly hold on to the expectation for years, or deny that it exists, or regard it as a temporary aberration, or blame oneself, or seek different explanations, or rationalize so as not to acknowledge that the other was not the person that one had anticipated. It is pathological when someone does not learn from experience, indicating a person so narcissistic and self-absorbed that external events have little influence. This is a dynamic process as experience disrupts expectations, but then revised expectations shape anticipations of forthcoming experiences. It is essential hermeneutics.

The process is a two-way street. On my first fieldtrip to study a hill tribe in Sumatra, the village elders called an evening meeting of the entire community to meet my wife and me. I explained in my rudimentary Indonesian that I was an anthropologist who had come from America to study their culture and way of life. After I had finished, the village chief took the floor and told the assembled villagers that as we were going to live in their community it was an opportunity to observe us closely and to learn how Americans behaved. The villagers and I were objects to each other; I was studying them as they were studying me. As I experienced their culture I revised my expectations about Southeast Asian hill tribes, and they in turn revised their understanding of Americans. I am not sure to this day who the keenest observers were.

What then about the relationship between expectations and experience in tourism? It is complicated. On the one hand the tourists have expectations based on travel brochures; tourism industry advertising; exposure to general conceptions and images which circulate about the destination culture; conversations with travel agents and friends; television, newspapers, books and increasingly the internet; and a host of other sources. On the tour there are congruencies and discrepancies between expectations and the experience.

Congruence may lead to a sense of authenticity. For example on a tour in Thailand one tourist brought with him old copies of *National Geographic* magazine. When he saw women working in terraced rice fields or saffron clad monks emerging from a temple, he recognized them as similar to the images in *National Geographic*, and thus they met his pre-tour expectations, and thereafter he expressed satisfaction that he was seeing the 'real' or authentic Thailand, the one pictured in *National Geographic*. On another occasion a tour group went to see a performance of classical Thai dancing held in a large restaurant in Bangkok. The dancers were excellent but the tourists were dissatisfied because the restaurant was too modern and too crowded, the waiters too harried, and everyone in the audience was a foreign tourist. It all seemed too commercial and somehow not really Thai. The setting had trumped the performance. If the dancers had performed in a more humble, village, rural, or less commercial setting the tourists may well have been very satisfied indeed. What the tourists did not know was that these days Thai classical dancing is performed mostly for tourists.

The pre-understandings serve as a filter influencing what the tourist 'sees'. In Cairo on a crowded downtown street, with automobiles and busy pedestrians in modern Western dress going in every direction, there appeared a donkey cart driven by an old man wearing peasant clothes. A group of tourists rushed over to photograph the cart and its colourful driver as it appeared quaint, possibly authentic, and somehow more 'Egyptian'. It met the tourists' preconceptions of what they expected to find in Egypt, but it was the tourist expectations that constructed their experience by selective perception. The tourists themselves made their experience congruent with their expectations.

The tourism agencies and professionals have a huge stake in this process. Their organized tours must correspond to tourist expectations to some degree otherwise there would be a tourist revolt. Tourists feel cheated if they do not visit all the sites mentioned in the tourism brochure, which serves as a kind of tourist contract. But the most sophisticated tour operators often build in some unadvertised and unexpected events for the tourist to add a sense of excitement and drama to the tour. It is the unforeseen that most frequently forms the basis of tourist stories about their travel. Yes, a visit to the pyramids of Giza, but while there an unadvertised camel ride in the desert, certainly an adventure but one not mentioned in the brochure.

In many ways, however, it is impossible for the experience to be totally consistent with expectations. The pre-tour expectations are conveyed through words and images, yet the tour experience is embodied and involves smells, sounds and bodily reactions that can only be had while physically moving through the destination culture. Tourists may react emotionally to the destination in ways not anticipated by the pre-understandings. Further, tourists are individuals who differ in life experiences, age, gender, education, sophistication, interests and other variables, and they may well interpret both the pre-understandings and what they find on tour very differently. Neither expectations nor experiences are monolithic. In my studies, I have found that tourists' experiences on tour are often inchoate and not well articulated. Tourists also viewed what was presented to them on tour with what I have called a questioning gaze, especially in foreign areas where they had no independent way of accessing the accuracy, authenticity or validity of what was being presented to them. They differ in other ways too — for example, some tourists demand an obsessive correspondence to their vision of authenticity while others are more concerned with a good show, authentic or not.

To explore the problematic more deeply, the tour (or a life) may be viewed from a fourfold perspective:

> The tour as imagined, consisting of expectations and pre-understandings: what is in the mind of the tourist before embarking on the trip.
>
> The tour as lived, the actual objective living-out of the tour in the destination country. It is very difficult to describe what really happens on tour, in part because so much is happening at once and descriptions are not bias-free neutral accounts. The tourist account is really the tour as told, not as actually lived. Becoming a tour guide, as I have done, embeds the scholar in the tour, a good methodological move but the scholar does not live the tour as the tourist does.
>
> The tour as experienced: what emerges to the consciousness of the tourist, the inner reactions to the tour as lived.
>
> The tour as told: the recounting of a tour and the telling of a narrative about the travel.

To summarize the fourfold scheme: first, the tourist imagines what the trip will be like; second, what the tour is actually like; third, how the tourist experiences the journey; and fourth, what the tourist tells himself and others about the tour. An importance of the fourfold distinction is that there are always, inevitably, discrepancies between each of the four perspectives. It is not just a distinction between expectation and experience, which is the way it is often mistakenly portrayed in the tourism literature. The tourist may envision the tour as an exciting adventure, experience it as confusing, intimidating and exhausting, write to his family that it was wonderfully educational but then tell his friends that it was disappointing. The telling is always dependent on the context and the audience. In the end, the only data we really have are the pre-tour expectations and the tour as told, as the scholar has little access to the tour as objectively lived and no access to the tour as experienced as we can never know another's experience, although we can make inferences.

These are dynamic processes that extend over time. The tour as narrated may begin while on tour visiting some early sites and extend to post-tour tellings after returning home as the tourist describes the tour to family and friends and prepares his/her digital images for a showing. The tourist may experience the tour as fragmented, as consisting of brief visits to multiple sites and attractions that somehow do not seem connected. Only after the tour is over, and in a context where the tourist is called upon to talk about the tour, is a coherent story constructed. Freud calls this process 'secondary elaboration' based upon his analysis of dreams where the dream itself consists of disconnected fleeting images that only come together into a consistent story after the dreamer describes the dream to the analyst. The story of the dream does not correspond completely to the dream itself, so the dream narrative is a construction. In this sense a tour is like a dream. After the post-tour narrative is formed, the tourists may retrospectively reexamine and reevaluate the tour as well as their experiences on tour so as to make them more consistent with the constructed narrative.

My reflections and thoughts, presented abstractly, do not match the richness and complexity of the case studies presented in this volume. It is not just the tourists who have expectations and experiences but also the local actors, the tour organizers, the industry professionals, the host community, the state tourism bureau and other stakeholders. What we have is a multifaceted interactional system. It is complicated, and the beauty is in the complexity.

NOTES ON CONTRIBUTORS

Edward Bruner is Professor Emeritus in the Department of Anthropology at the University of Illinois at Urbana-Champaign. He has particular interests in cultural anthropology, tourism, interpretive anthropology, narratology, performance, processes of change, urbanization, ethnicity, Indonesia, and American culture. He has developed the anthropology of tourism field of study and is author of numerous publications including: *Culture on Tour: Ethnographies of Travel*, Chicago: University of Chicago Press (2005); and the co-edited *International Tourism: Identity and Change*, London: Sage (1995).

Alexis Celeste Bunten is the ethnographer for the Intellectual Property in Cultural Heritage (IP in CH) initiative housed at Simon Fraser University, and a Senior Fellow at the FrameWorks Institute in Washington D.C. Her research interests include self-representation, cultural production, Native American Arts, cultural commodification, tourism and indigenous media. Before attending graduate school, she worked in the heritage industry in Alaska. Representative publication: 'Sharing Culture or Selling Out? A Case Study of Self-Commodification in the Native-Owned Cultural Tourism Industry along the Northwest Coast of North America' (*American Ethnologist*, 2008).

Jane Desmond is Professor in Anthropology and affiliated faculty in Gender and Women's Studies at the University of Illinois at Urbana-Champaign, and co-founder and current Director of the International Forum for U.S. Studies: a Center for the Transnational Study of the U.S. Her primary areas of interest focus on issues of embodiment, display, and social identity, as well as the transnational dimensions of U.S. Studies. Her areas of expertise include performance studies, critical theory, visual culture (including museum studies and tourism studies), the critical analysis of the U.S. in global perspectives, and, most recently, the political economy of human/animal relations. She has previously worked as a modern dancer and choreographer, and in film, video and the academy. She is author of: *Staging Tourism: Bodies on Display from Waikiki to Sea World* (University of Chicago Press, 1999), and editor of *Dancing Desires: Choreographing Sexuality on and off the Stage* (University of Wisconsin Press, 2001).

Jennifer Iles is Senior Lecturer in Sociology at Roehampton University. Jennifer has research interests in battlefield tourism, the heritage industry, death studies and experiential learning. Amongst other publications, she is author of: 'Encounters in the Fields – Tourism to the Battlefields of the Western Front' (*Journal of Tourism and Cultural Change*, 2008) and 'Recalling the Ghosts of War: Performing Tourism on the Battlefields of the Western Front' (*Text and Performance Quarterly*, 2006).

Kelli Ann Malone was Professor of Anthropology at Franklin Pierce College in New Hampshire for ten years before taking a Fulbright Fellowship at the Dublin Institute of Technology in 2006. Now residing in Ireland, Kelli is a lecturer in Irish History at Champlain College and is involved in the Irish tourism and heritage industry. She conducts accredited college tours of Ireland's archaeological heritage sites, is busy with research, and lives in the Midlands surrounded by the people and places she loves. She is author of *Coach Fellas: Heritage and Tourism in Ireland* (Left Coast Press, 2009) and *Discovering Ancient Ireland* (The History Press, 2010).

George Paul Meiu is a Ph.D. candidate in the Department of Anthropology at the University of Chicago. He carries out research among the Samburu of northern Kenya, examining how gender, generation and kinship are reconfigured in relation to cultural tourism and the commodification of ethnic identity. His publications on the topic include 'Riefenstahl on Safari: Embodied Contemplation in East Africa' (*Anthropology Today*, 2008), and 'Mombasa Morans: Embodiment, Sexual Morality, and Samburu Men in Kenya' (*Canadian Journal of African Studies*, 2009).

Jonathan Skinner is Senior Lecturer in Social Anthropology at Queen's University Belfast. His research interests oscillate between tourism, risk and post-colonial literature on the British colony Montserrat in the Caribbean, and a long-term participatory assessment of jive and salsa dancing communities in the U.K. and the U.S.. Recent publications include *Before the Volcano: Reverberations of Identity on Montserrat* (Arawak, 2004) and the co-edited volume *Managing Island Life* (University of Abertay Dundee, 2006).

Dimitrios Theodossopoulos is Senior Lecturer in Social Anthropology at the University of Kent. His earlier work examined people–wildlife conflicts and indigenous perceptions of the environment. He is currently working on ethnic stereotypes, indigeneity, authenticity and the politics of cultural representation in Panama and South East Europe. He is the author of *Troubles with Turtles: Cultural Understandings of the Environment on a Greek Island* (Berghahn Books, 2003), and editor of *When Greeks Think about Turks: The View from Anthropology* (Routledge, 2006) and *United in Discontent: Local Responses to Cosmopolitanism and Globalization* (Berghahn Books, 2009).

Hazel Tucker is Associate Professor in Tourism at the University of Otago, New Zealand. Her main area of research interest is tourism's influence on socio-cultural relationships and representations. She is author of *Living with Tourism* (Routledge, 2003) and co-editor of *Tourism and Postcolonialism* (Routledge, 2004) and *Commercial Homes in Tourism* (Routledge, 2009). Other areas of research interest include gender and tour guiding and interpretation.

Jacqueline Waldren is Research Associate at the Institute for Social and Cultural Anthropology, Oxford University, and Director of the Deia Archaeological Museum and Research Centre, Majorca. Her research among locals and foreigners on a Mediterranean Island advanced tourism studies in anthropology. She is author of *Insiders and Outsiders: Paradise and Reality in Mallorca* (Berghahn Books, 1996), and co-editor of *Tourists and Tourism* (Berg, 1997) and *Anthropological Perspectives on Local Development* (Routledge, 1998).

Index